Arata
THE LEGEND
7

WE ARE MAN, BORN OF HEAVEN AND EARTH,
MOON AND SUN AND EVERYTHING UNDER THEM.

EYES, EARS, NOSE, TONGUE, BODY, MIND...

PURITY WILL PIERCE EVIL AND
OPEN UP THE WORLD OF DARKNESS.

ALL LIFE WILL BE REBORN AND INVIGORATED.

APPEAR NOW.

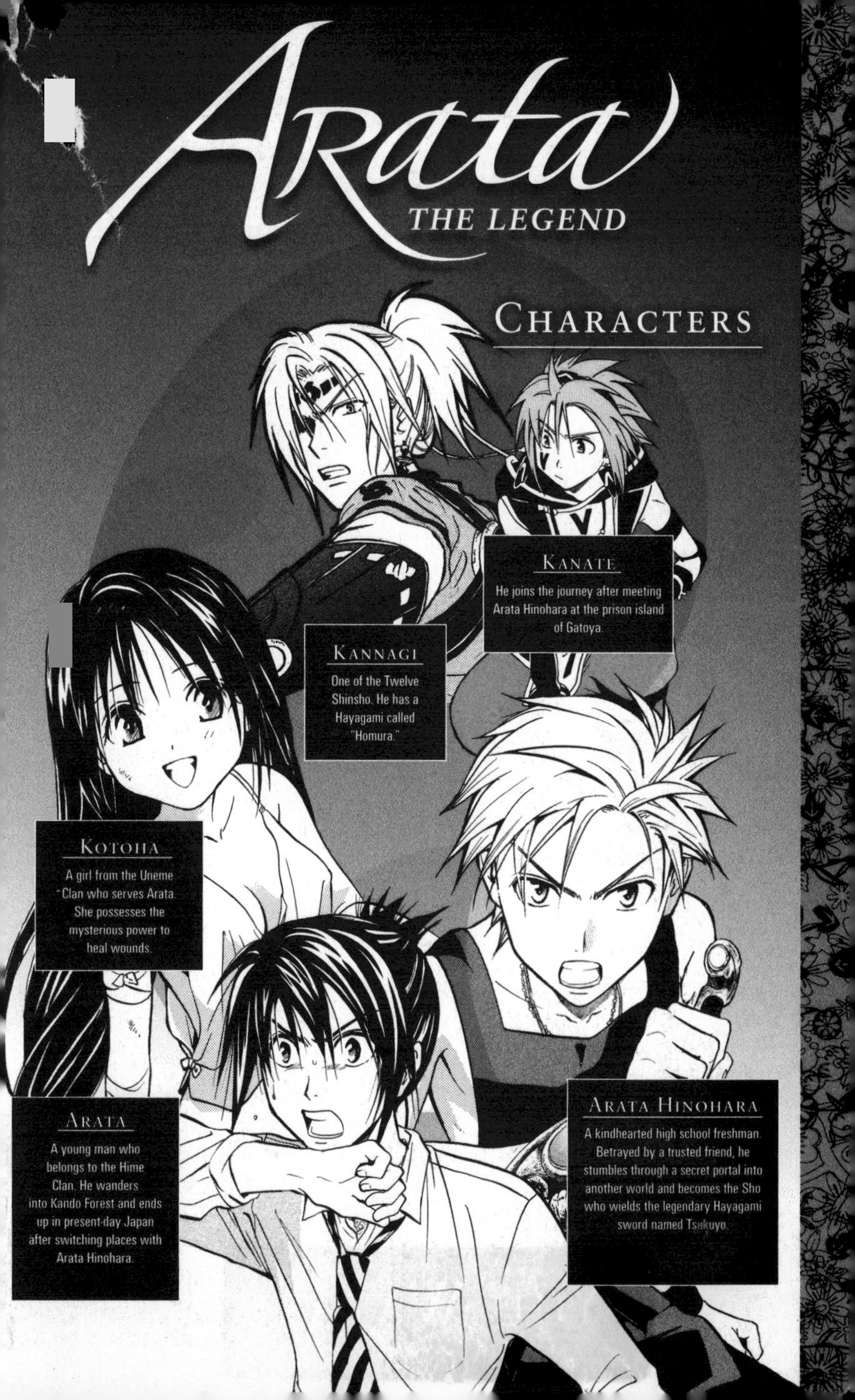
Arata
THE LEGEND
CHARACTERS
KANATE
He joins the journey after meeting Arata Hinohara at the prison island of Gatoya.
KANNAGI
One of the Twelve Shinsho. He has a Hayagami called "Homura."
KOTOHA
A girl from the Uneme Clan who serves Arata. She possesses the mysterious power to heal wounds.
ARATA HINOHARA
A kindhearted high school freshman. Betrayed by a trusted friend, he stumbles through a secret portal into another world and becomes the Sho who wields the legendary Hayagami sword named Tsukuyo.
ARATA
A young man who belongs to the Hime Clan. He wanders into Kando Forest and ends up in present-day Japan after switching places with Arata Hinohara.

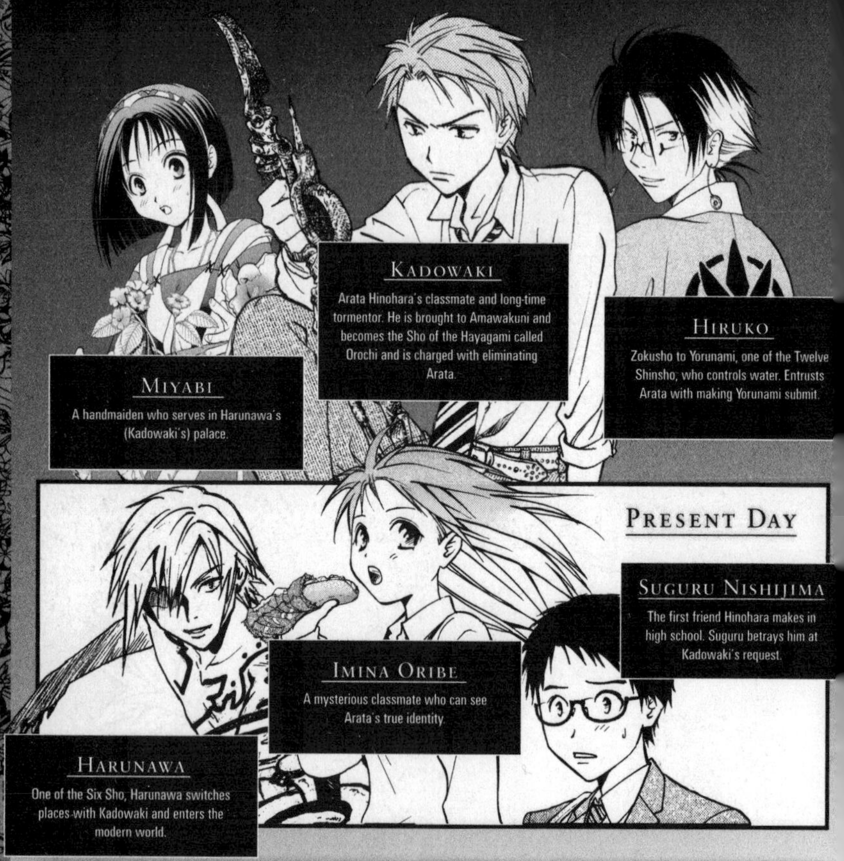
KADOWAKI
Arata Hinohara's classmate and long-time tormentor. He is brought to Amawakuni and becomes the Sho of the Hayagami called Orochi and is charged with eliminating Arata.
HIRUKO
Zokusho to Yorunami, one of the Twelve Shinsho, who controls water. Entrusts Arata with making Yorunami submit.
MIYABI
A handmaiden who serves in Harunawa's (Kadowaki's) palace.
PRESENT DAY
SUGURU NISHIJIMA
The first friend Hinohara makes in high school. Suguru betrays him at Kadowaki's request.
IMINA ORIBE
A mysterious classmate who can see Arata's true identity.
HARUNAWA
One of the Six Sho, Harunawa switches places with Kadowaki and enters the modern world.

THE STORY THUS FAR

Betrayed by his best friend, Arata Hinohara—a high school student in present-day Japan—wanders through a portal into another world where he and his companions journey onward to deliver his Hayagami sword "Tsukuyo" to Princess Kikuri.

Kadowaki is summoned to Amawakuni and proclaimed the Sho of the Hayagami "Orochi." He engages in battle with Arata Hinohara, but the showdown is halted when Arata "demonizes"... Later, Arata and his friends enter the commercial town of Suzukura to find out more about the Shinsho Yorunami. Suzukura is governed by Hiruko, Yorunami's Zokusho, and money is everything here. Arata makes a good impression on Hiruko, so Hiruko decides to entrust Arata with making Yorunami submit...

Arata 7
THE LEGEND

CONTENTS

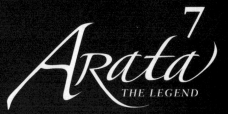

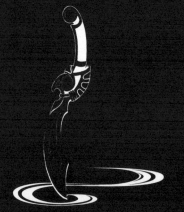

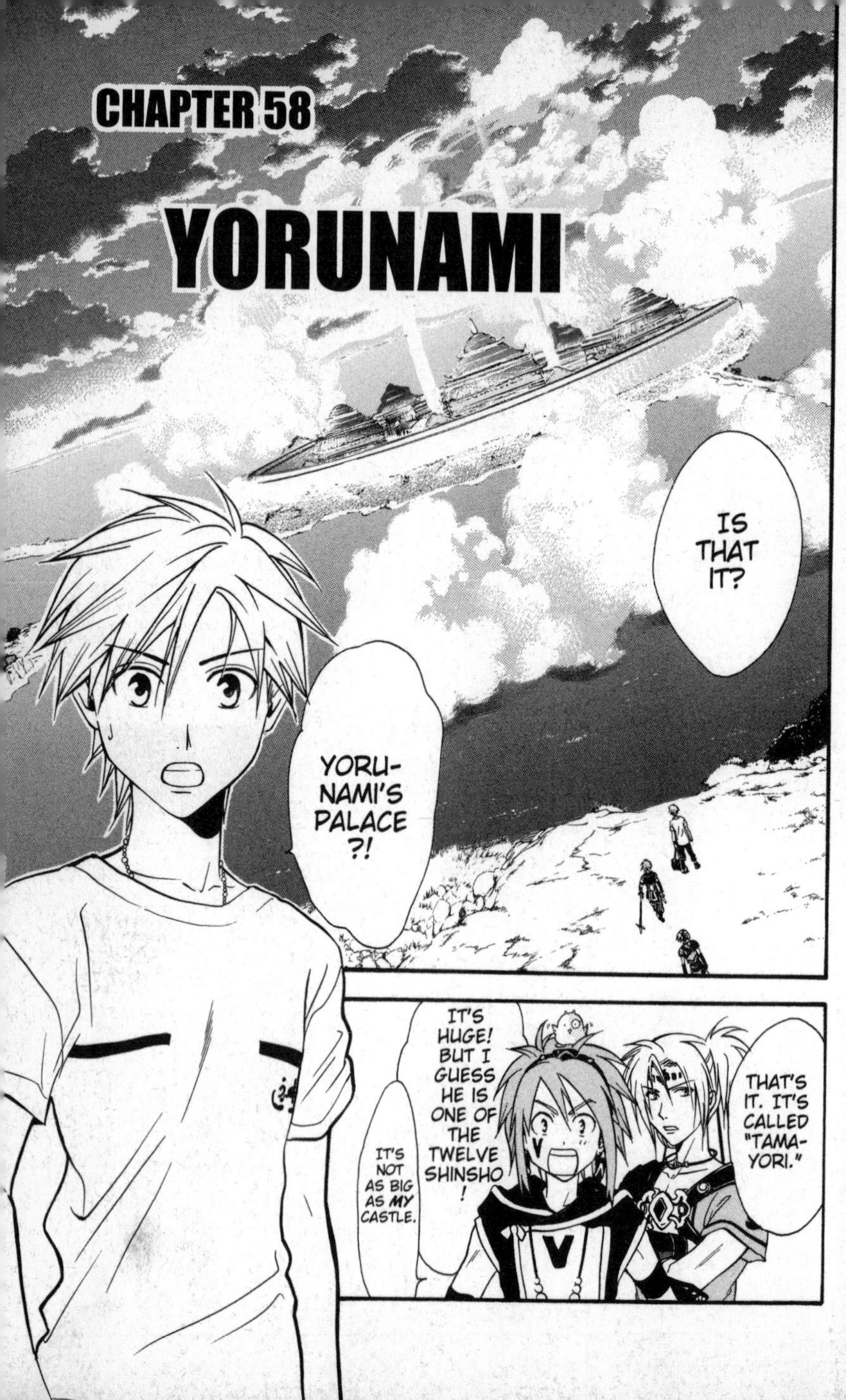
CHAPTER 58
YORUNAMI
IS THAT IT?
YORU-NAMI'S PALACE ?!
THAT'S IT. IT'S CALLED "TAMA-YORI."
IT'S HUGE! BUT I GUESS HE IS ONE OF THE TWELVE SHINSHO!
IT'S NOT AS BIG AS *MY* CASTLE.

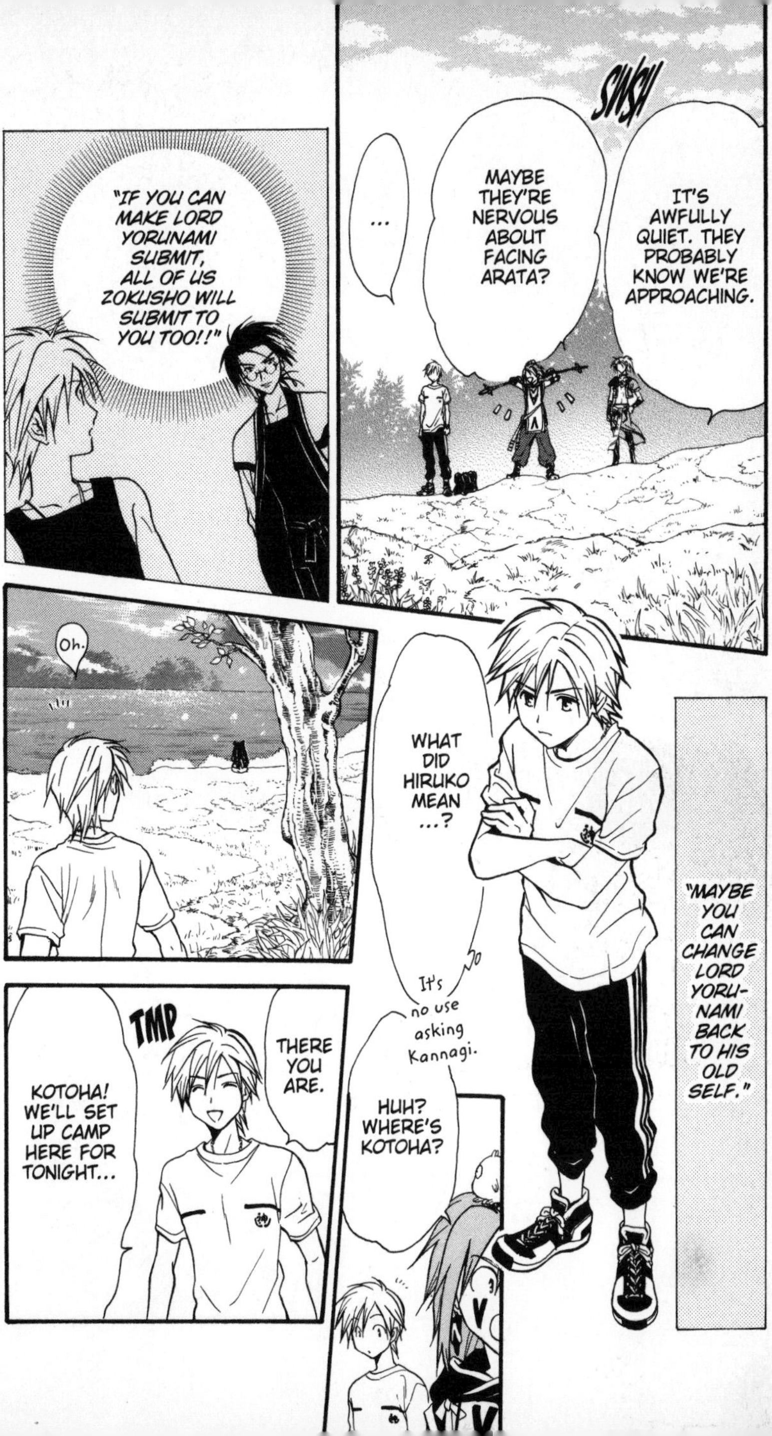
SWSH
IT'S AWFULLY QUIET. THEY PROBABLY KNOW WE'RE APPROACHING.
MAYBE THEY'RE NERVOUS ABOUT FACING ARATA?
...
"IF YOU CAN MAKE LORD YORUNAMI SUBMIT, ALL OF US ZOKUSHO WILL SUBMIT TO YOU TOO!!"
"MAYBE YOU CAN CHANGE LORD YORUNAMI BACK TO HIS OLD SELF."
WHAT DID HIRUKO MEAN ...?
It's no use asking Kannagi.
HUH? WHERE'S KOTOHA?
Oh.
TMP
THERE YOU ARE.
KOTOHA! WE'LL SET UP CAMP HERE FOR TONIGHT...

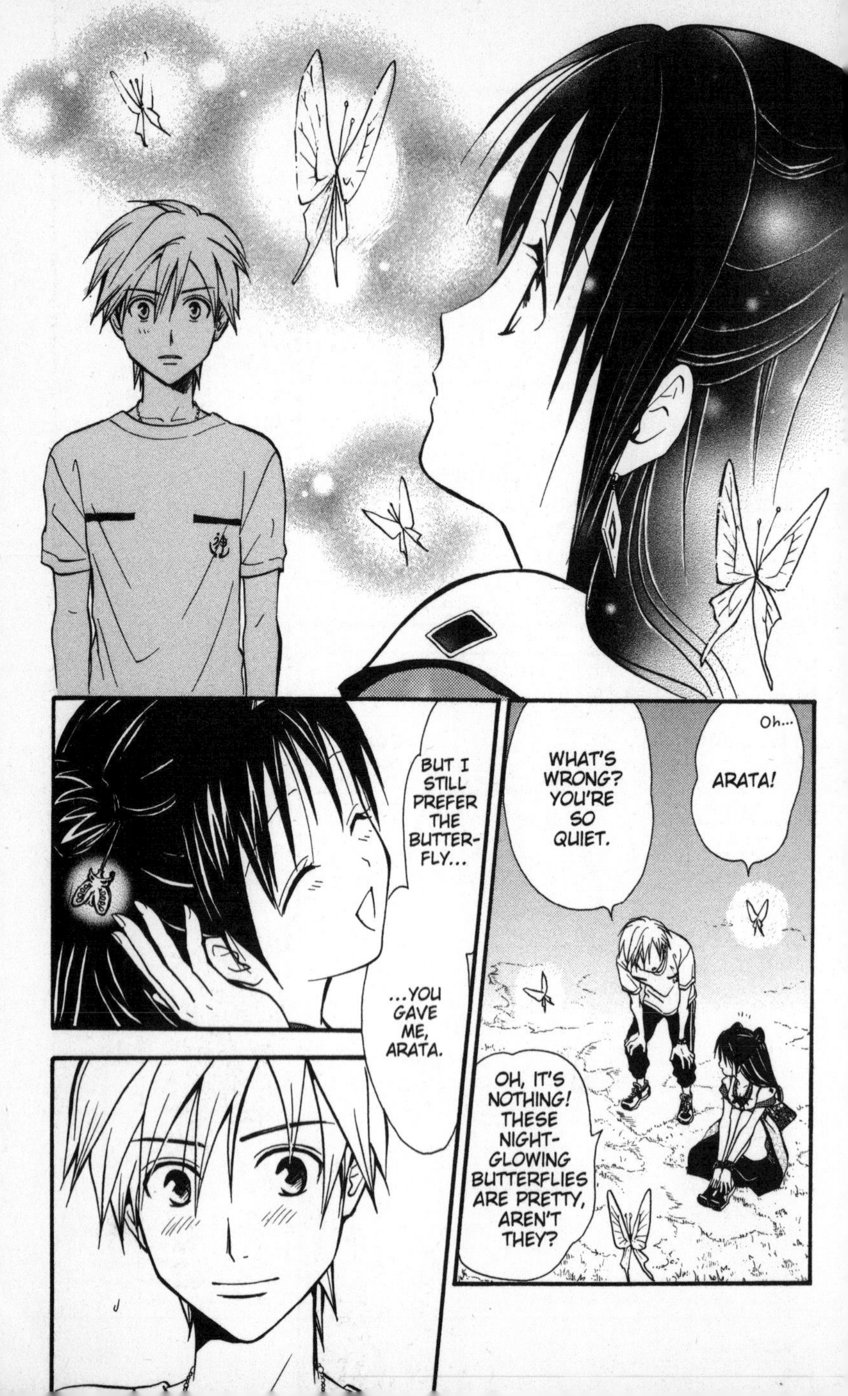
Oh...
ARATA!
WHAT'S WRONG? YOU'RE SO QUIET.
OH, IT'S NOTHING! THESE NIGHT-GLOWING BUTTERFLIES ARE PRETTY, AREN'T THEY?
BUT I STILL PREFER THE BUTTERFLY...
...YOU GAVE ME, ARATA.

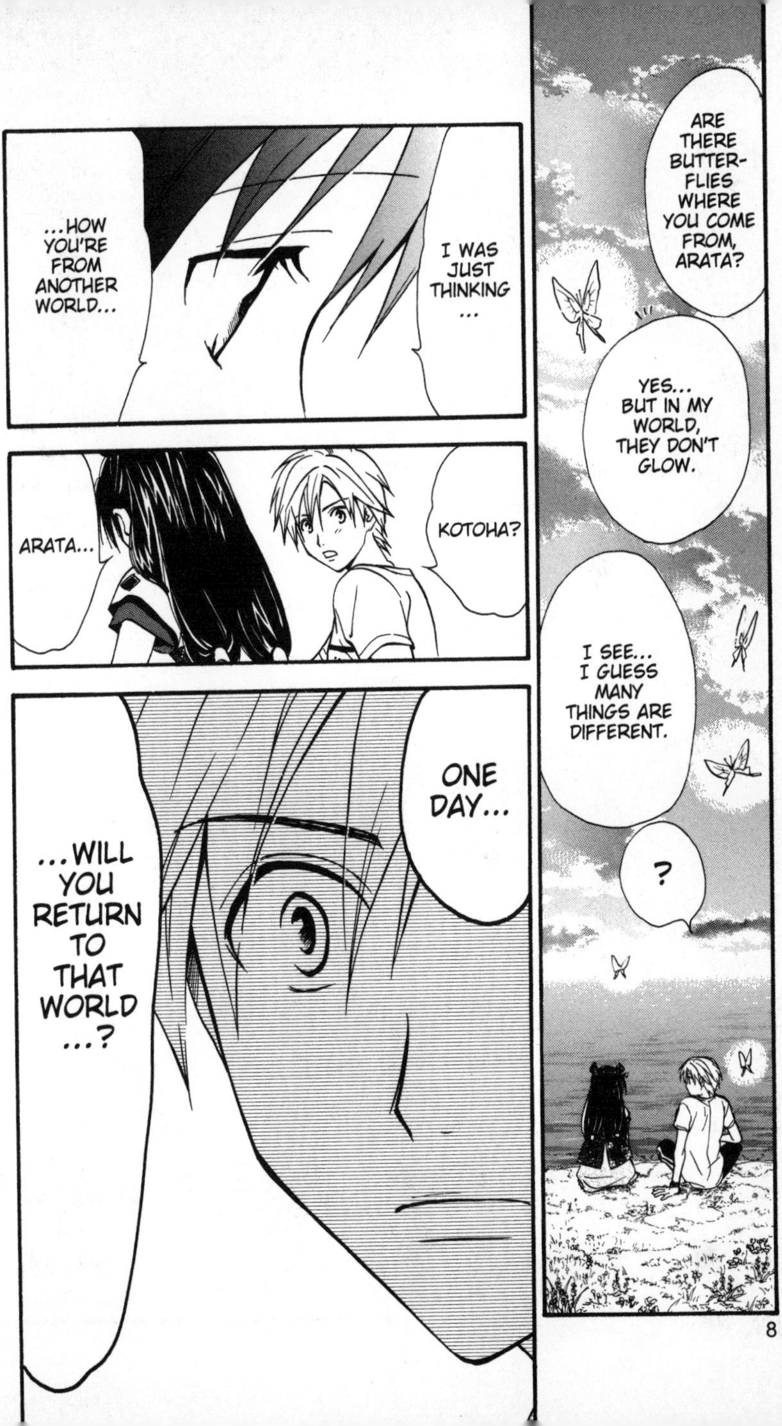
ARE THERE BUTTER-FLIES WHERE YOU COME FROM, ARATA?
YES... BUT IN MY WORLD, THEY DON'T GLOW.
I SEE... I GUESS MANY THINGS ARE DIFFERENT.
?
I WAS JUST THINKING ...
...HOW YOU'RE FROM ANOTHER WORLD...
KOTOHA?
ARATA...
ONE DAY...
...WILL YOU RETURN TO THAT WORLD ...?

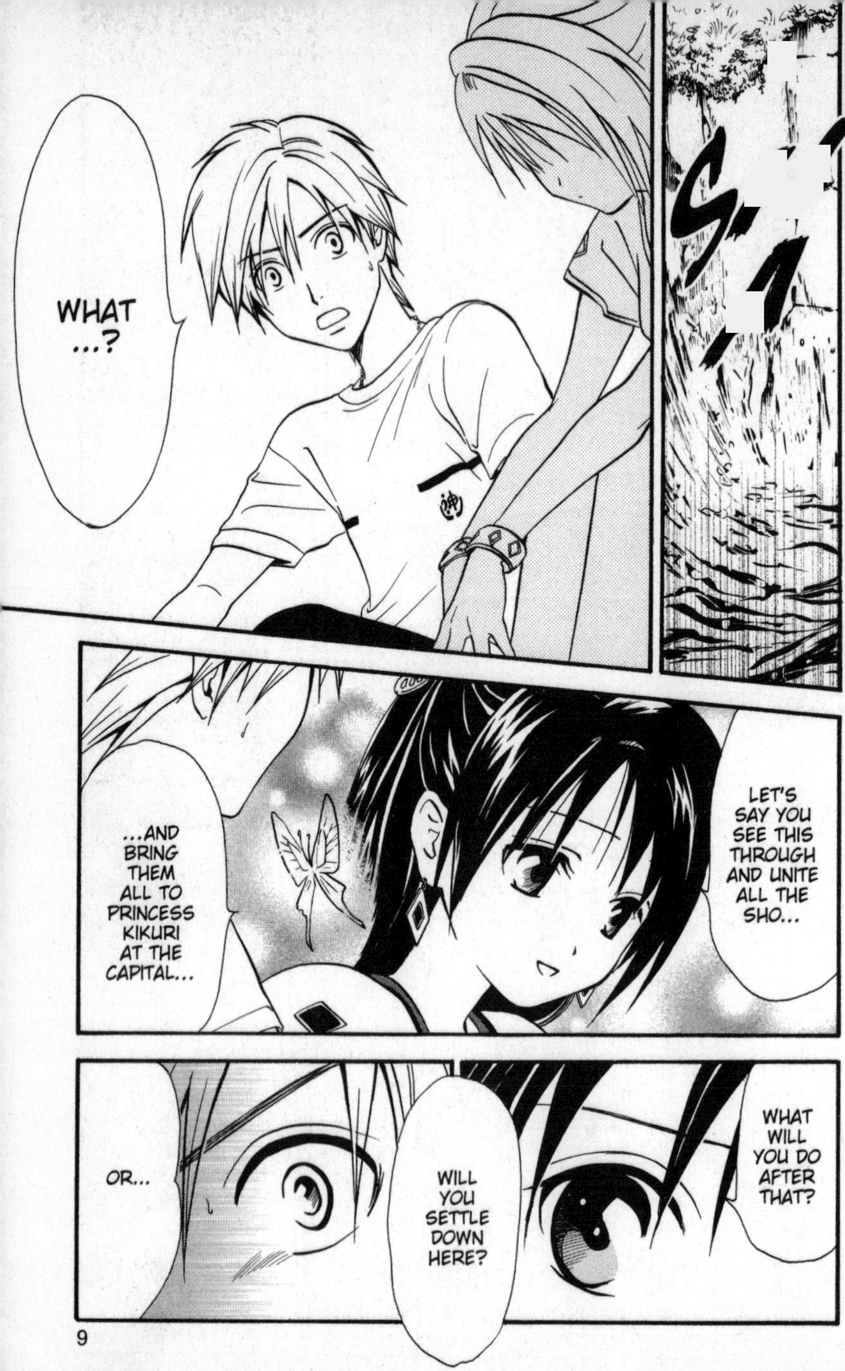
WHAT ...?
LET'S SAY YOU SEE THIS THROUGH AND UNITE ALL THE SHO...
...AND BRING THEM ALL TO PRINCESS KIKURI AT THE CAPITAL...
WHAT WILL YOU DO AFTER THAT?
WILL YOU SETTLE DOWN HERE?
OR...

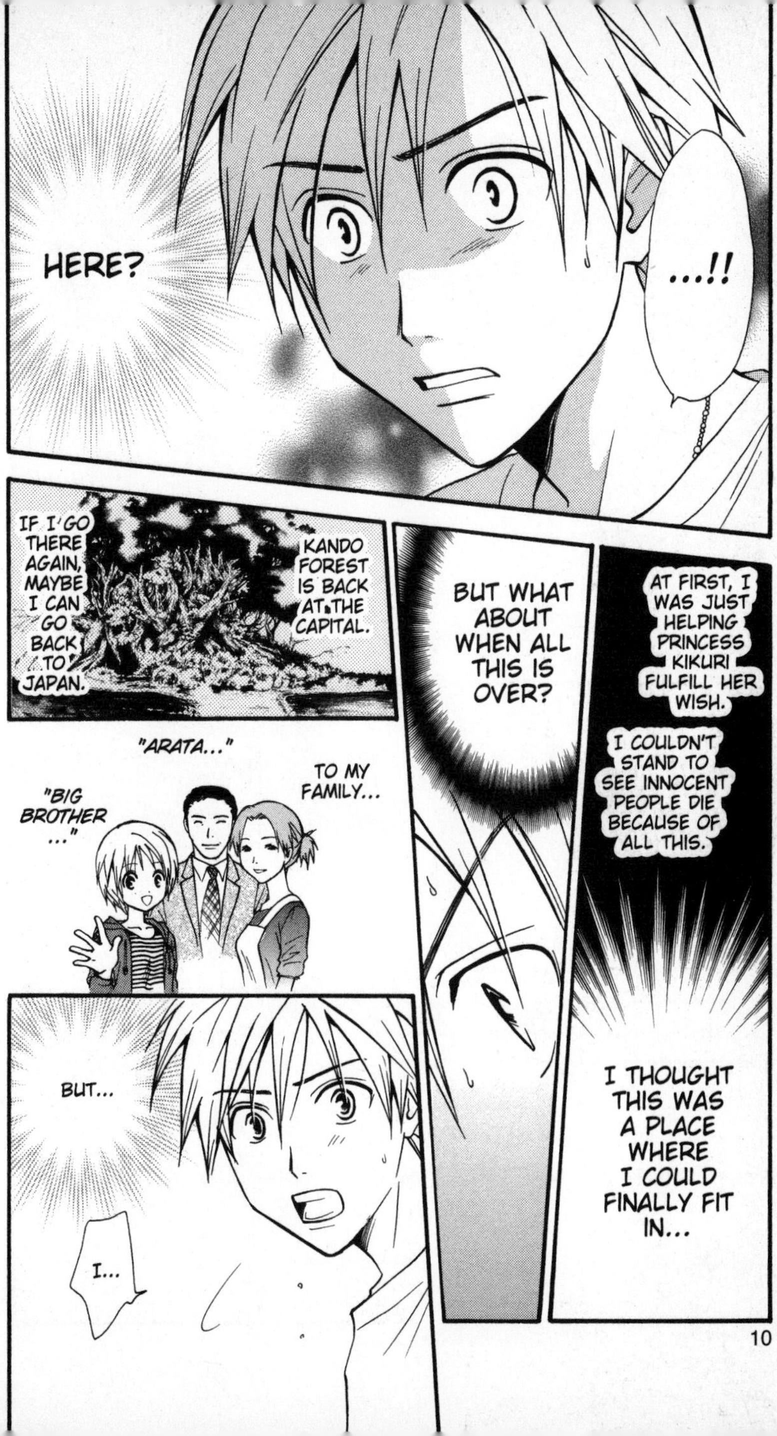
...!!
HERE?
AT FIRST, I WAS JUST HELPING PRINCESS KIKURI FULFILL HER WISH.
I COULDN'T STAND TO SEE INNOCENT PEOPLE DIE BECAUSE OF ALL THIS.
I THOUGHT THIS WAS A PLACE WHERE I COULD FINALLY FIT IN...
BUT WHAT ABOUT WHEN ALL THIS IS OVER?
KANDO FOREST IS BACK AT THE CAPITAL.
IF I GO THERE AGAIN, MAYBE I CAN GO BACK TO JAPAN.
TO MY FAMILY...
"ARATA..."
"BIG BROTHER..."
BUT...
I...

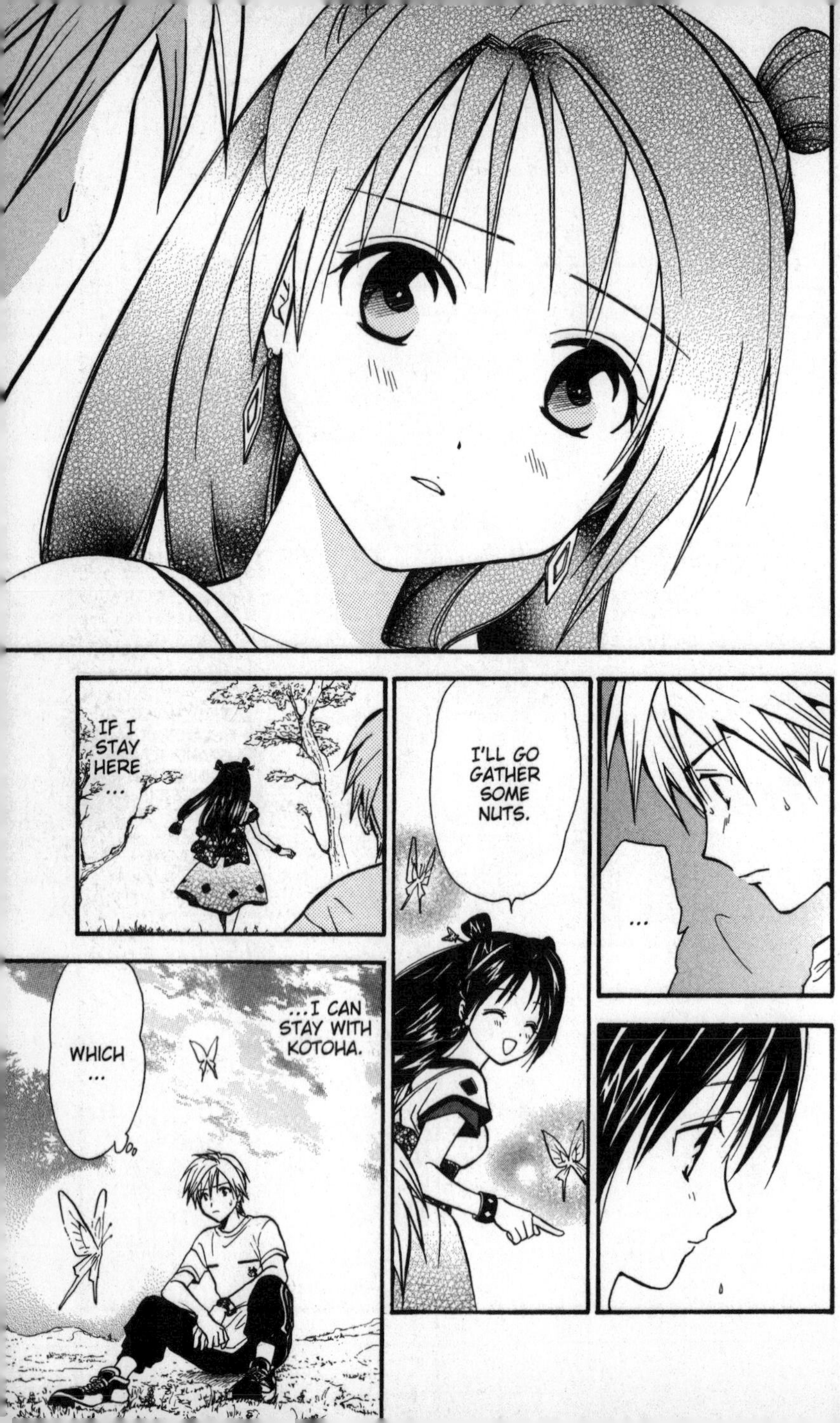
...
I'LL GO GATHER SOME NUTS.
IF I STAY HERE ...
...I CAN STAY WITH KOTOHA.
WHICH ...

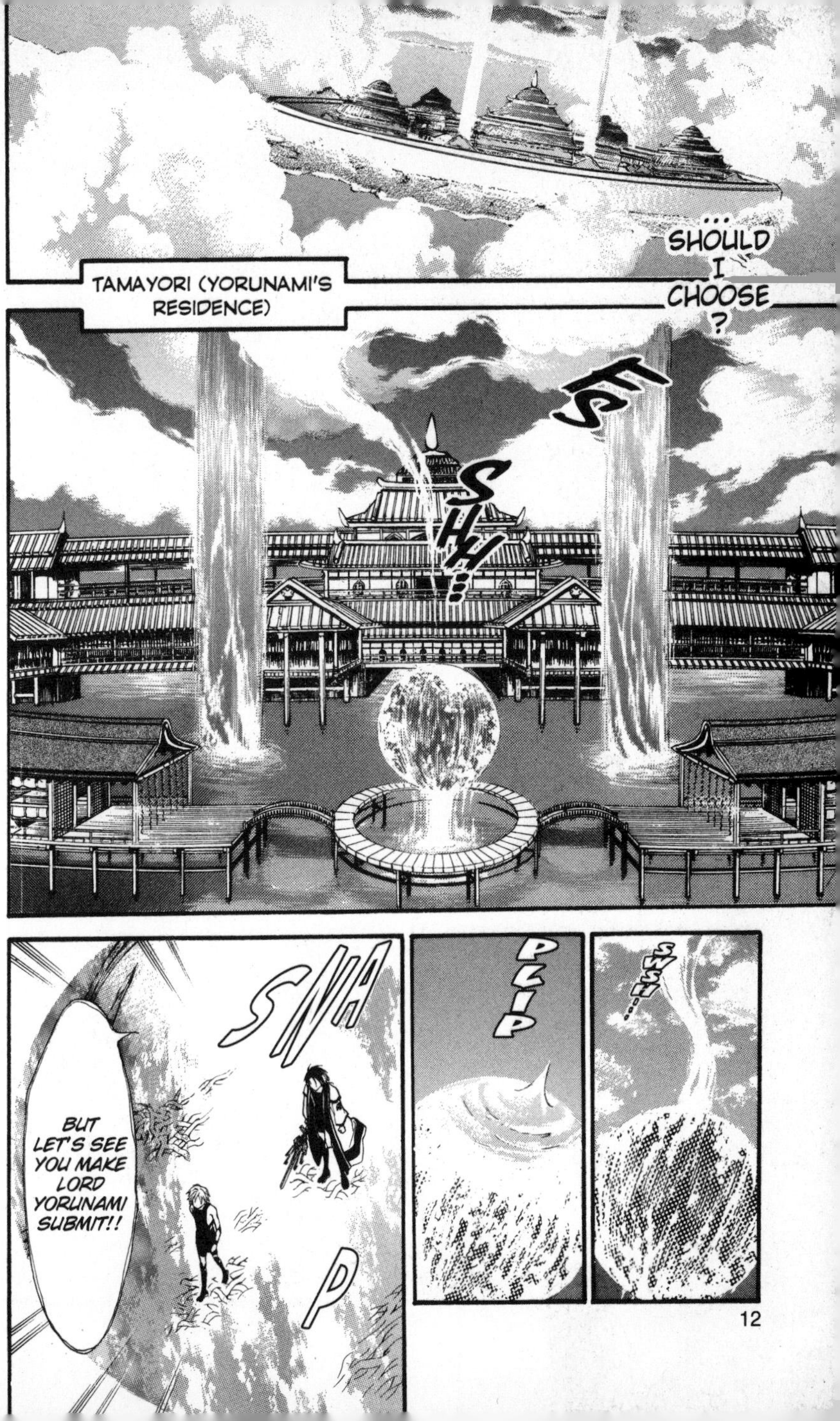
...SHOULD I CHOOSE?
TAMAYORI (YORUNAMI'S RESIDENCE)
FSSHH...
SWSH...
PLIP
SNAP
BUT LET'S SEE YOU MAKE LORD YORUNAMI SUBMIT!!

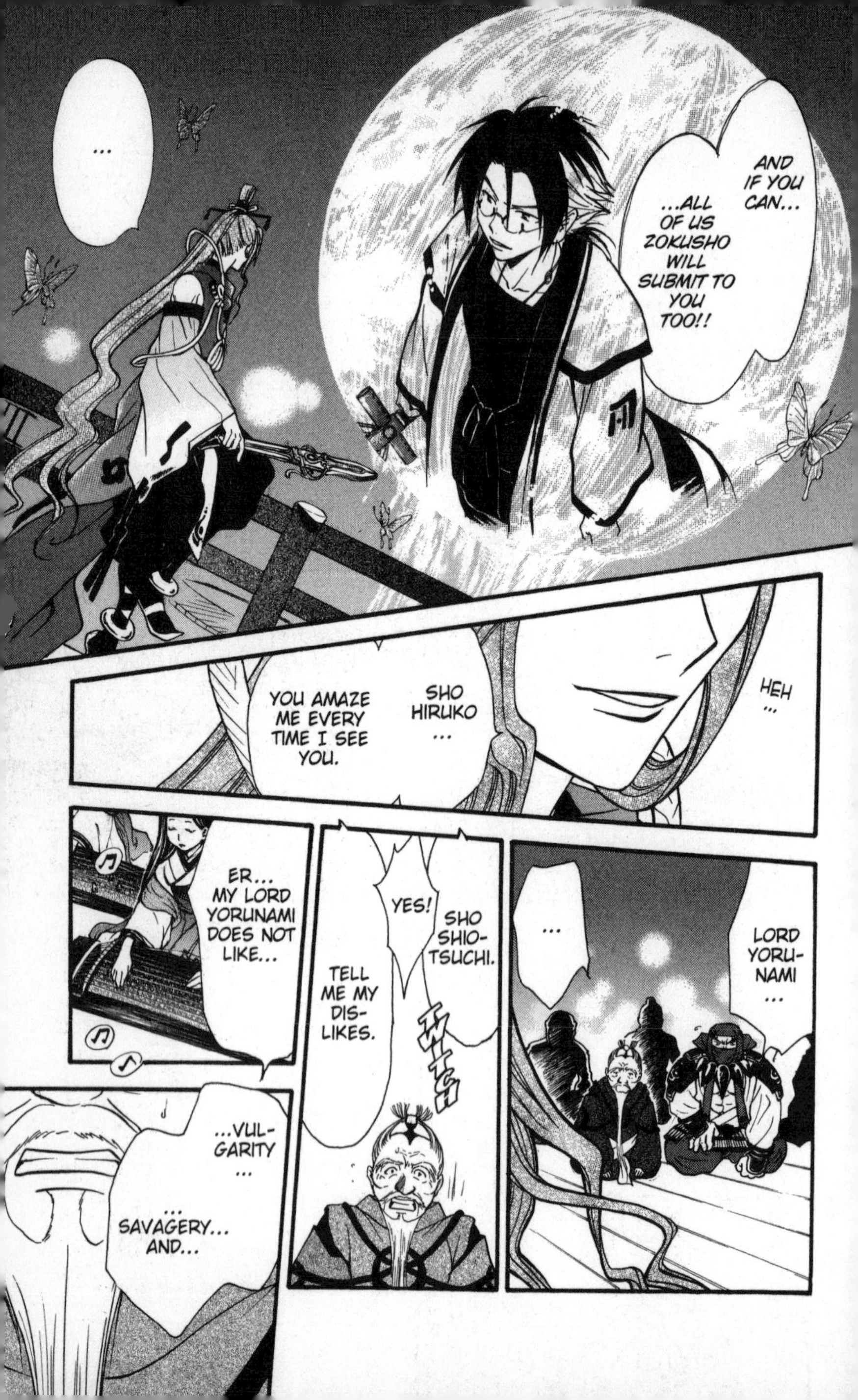
AND IF YOU CAN...
...ALL OF US ZOKUSHO WILL SUBMIT TO YOU TOO!!
...
HEH...
SHO HIRUKO...
YOU AMAZE ME EVERY TIME I SEE YOU.
LORD YORU-NAMI...
...
SHO SHIO-TSUCHI.
YES!
TWITCH
TELL ME MY DIS-LIKES.
ER... MY LORD YORUNAMI DOES NOT LIKE...
...VUL-GARITY...
...SAVAGERY... AND...

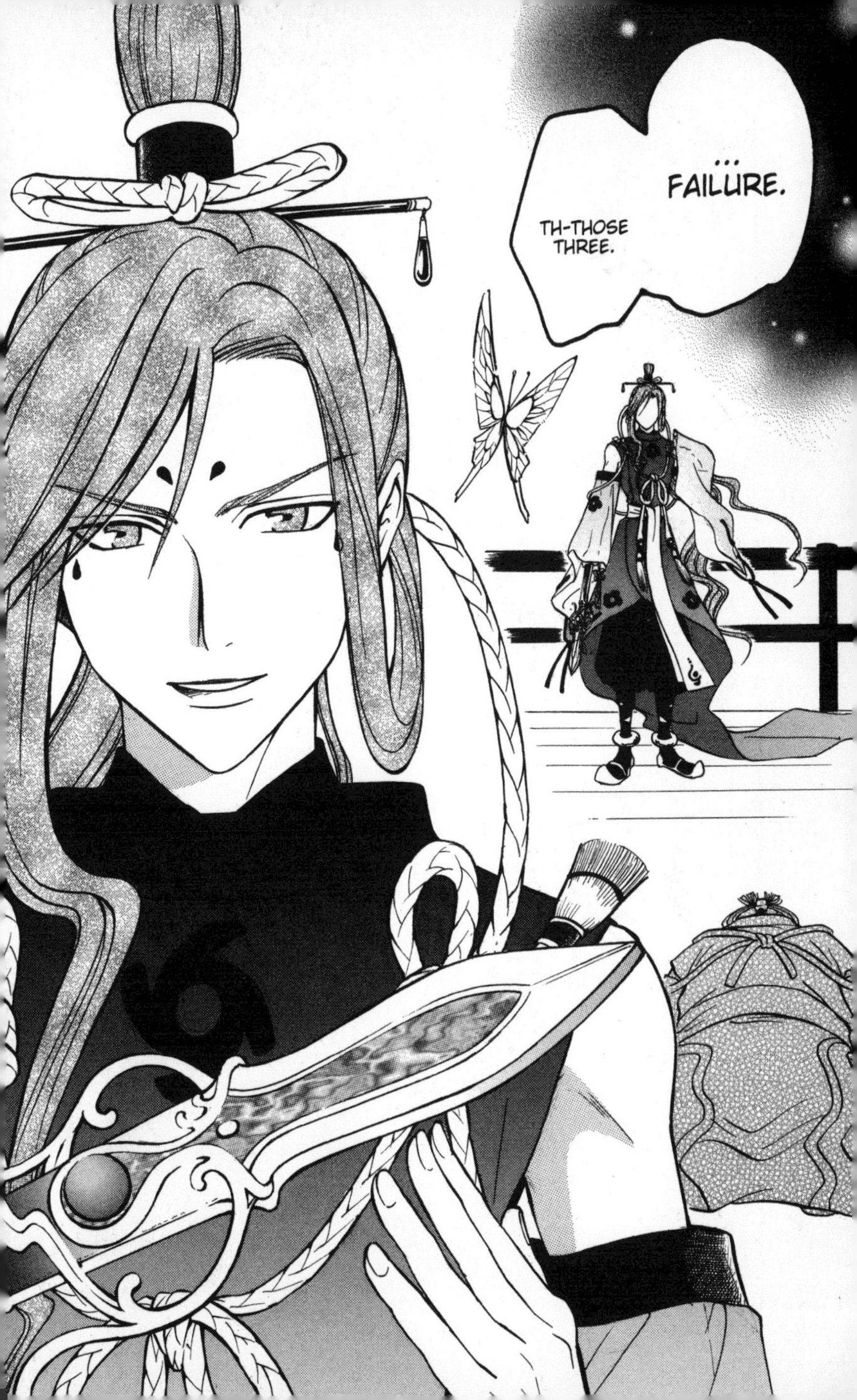
...FAILURE.
TH-THOSE THREE.

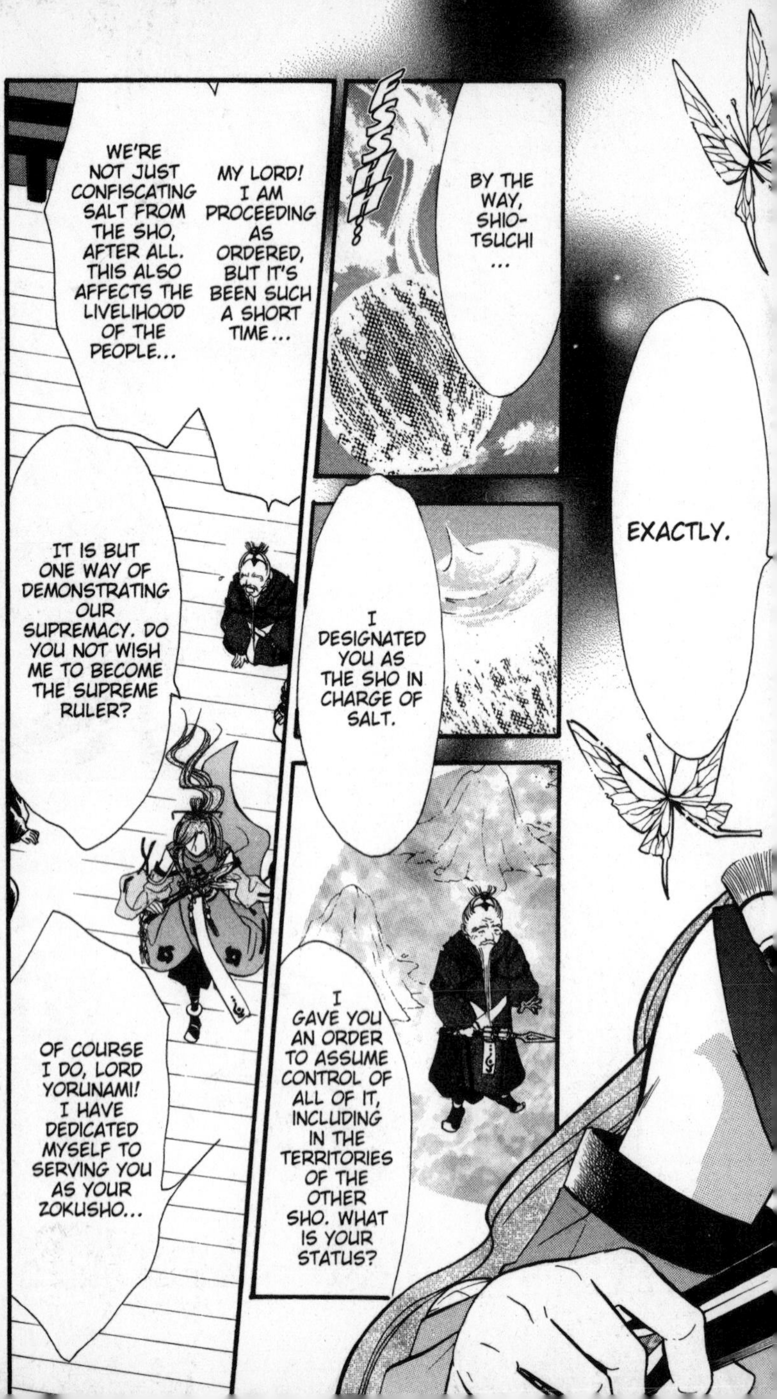
EXACTLY.
FSSHH...
BY THE WAY, SHIO-TSUCHI...
I DESIGNATED YOU AS THE SHO IN CHARGE OF SALT.
I GAVE YOU AN ORDER TO ASSUME CONTROL OF ALL OF IT, INCLUDING IN THE TERRITORIES OF THE OTHER SHO. WHAT IS YOUR STATUS?
MY LORD! I AM PROCEEDING AS ORDERED, BUT IT'S BEEN SUCH A SHORT TIME...
WE'RE NOT JUST CONFISCATING SALT FROM THE SHO, AFTER ALL. THIS ALSO AFFECTS THE LIVELIHOOD OF THE PEOPLE...
IT IS BUT ONE WAY OF DEMONSTRATING OUR SUPREMACY. DO YOU NOT WISH ME TO BECOME THE SUPREME RULER?
OF COURSE I DO, LORD YORUNAMI! I HAVE DEDICATED MYSELF TO SERVING YOU AS YOUR ZOKUSHO...

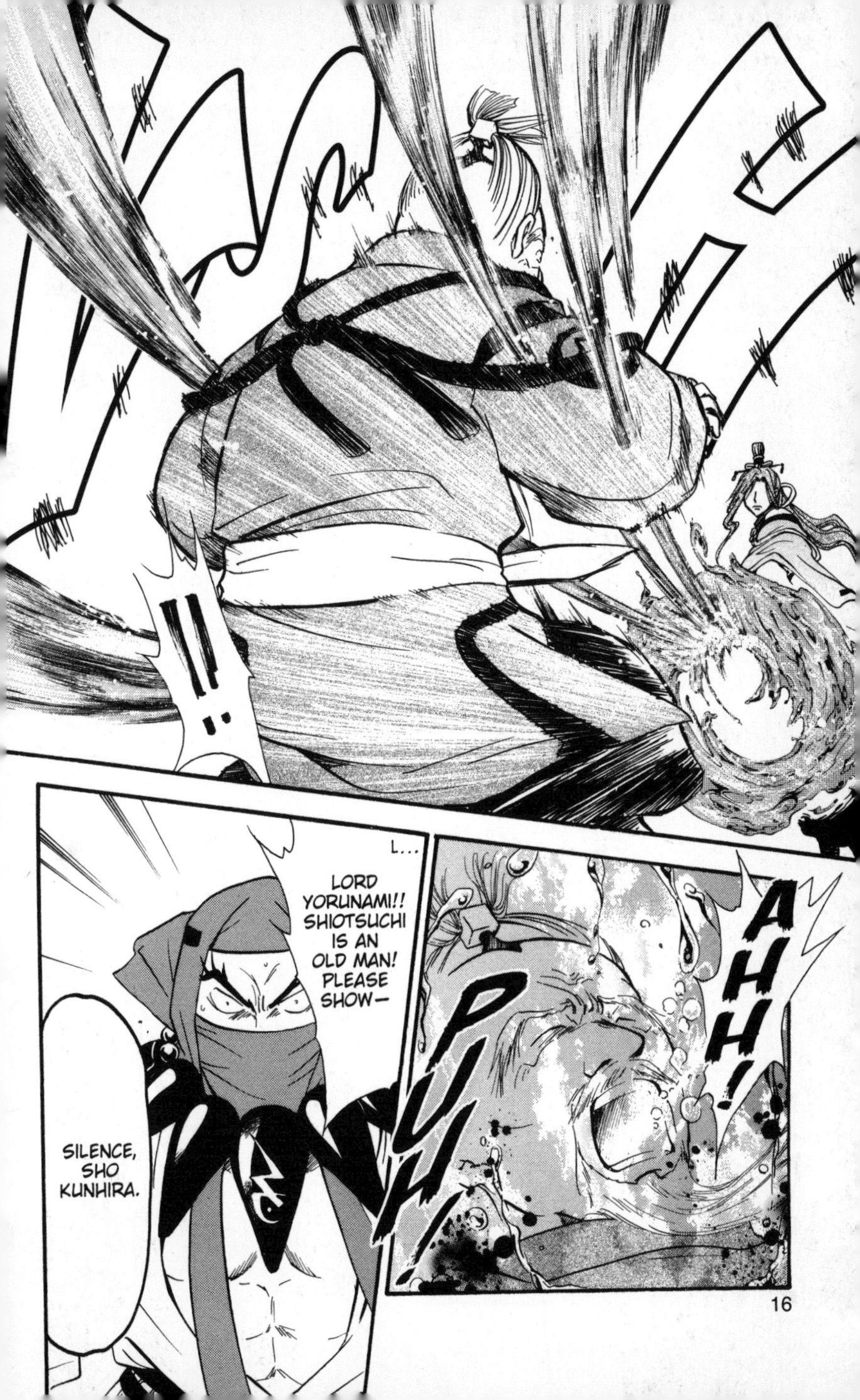
AHH!
L...
LORD YORUNAMI!! SHIOTSUCHI IS AN OLD MAN! PLEASE SHOW—
SILENCE, SHO KUNHIRA.

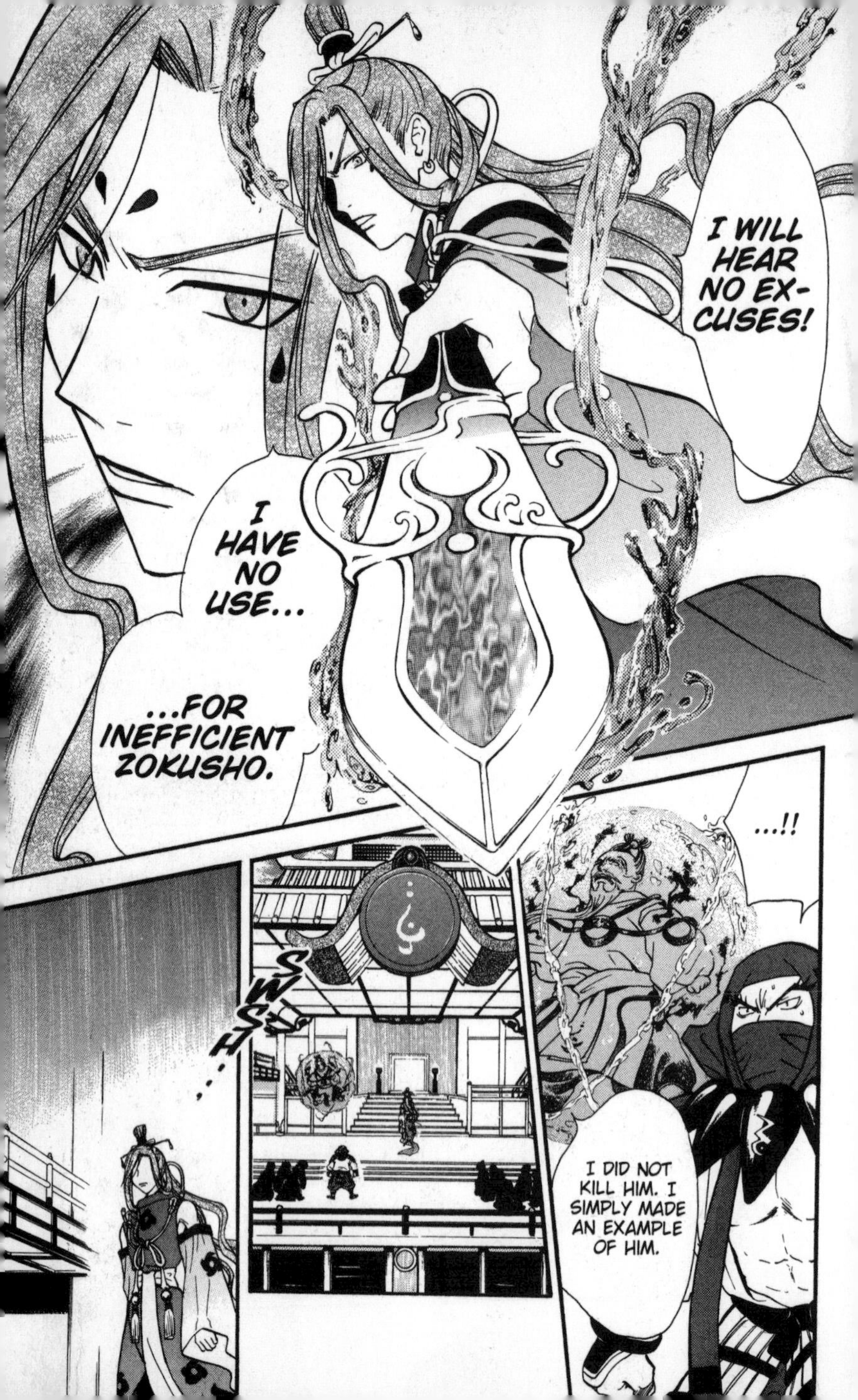
I WILL HEAR NO EX-CUSES!
I HAVE NO USE...
...FOR INEFFICIENT ZOKUSHO.
...!!
I DID NOT KILL HIM. I SIMPLY MADE AN EXAMPLE OF HIM.
SWSH...

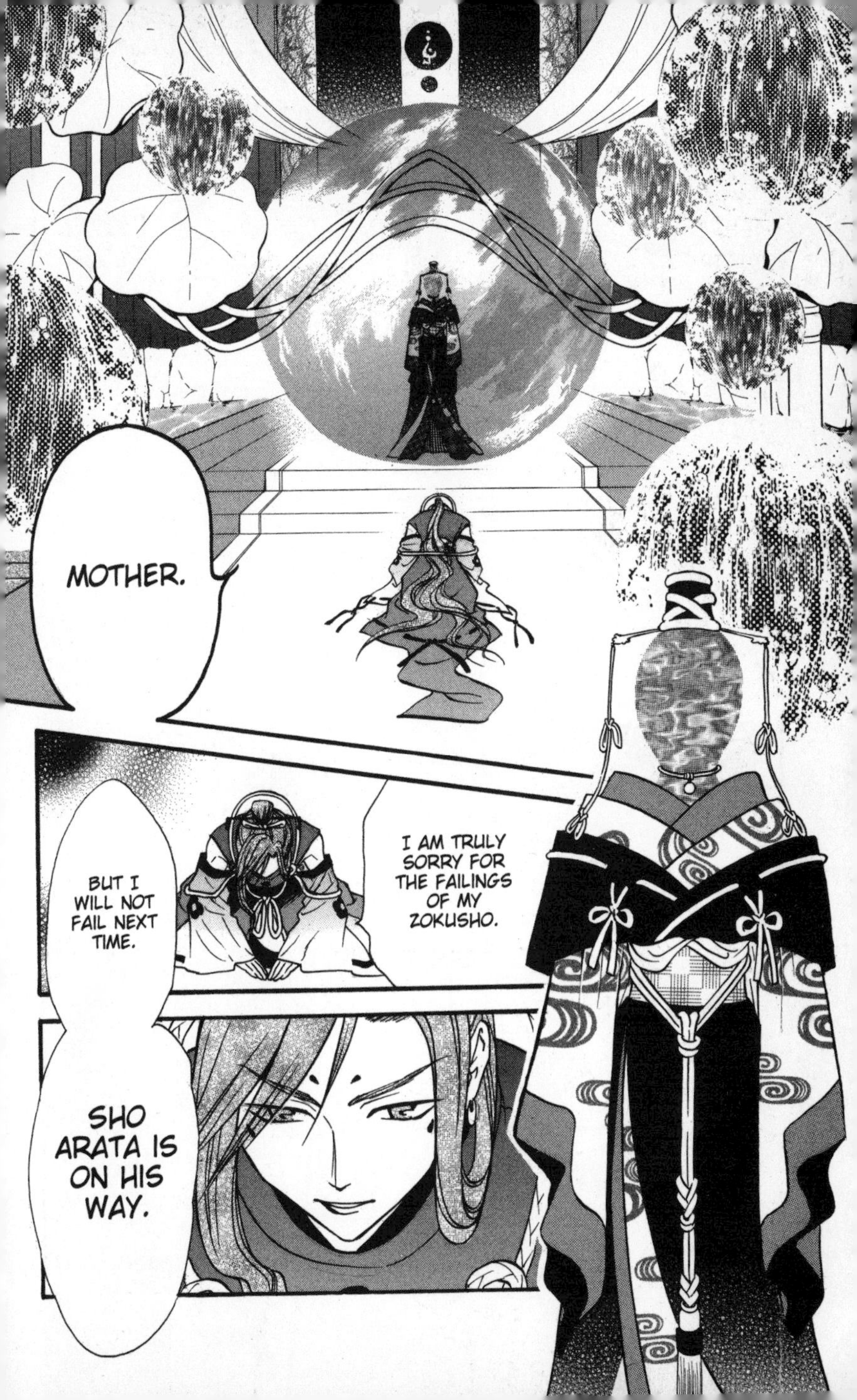
MOTHER.
I AM TRULY SORRY FOR THE FAILINGS OF MY ZOKUSHO.
BUT I WILL NOT FAIL NEXT TIME.
SHO ARATA IS ON HIS WAY.

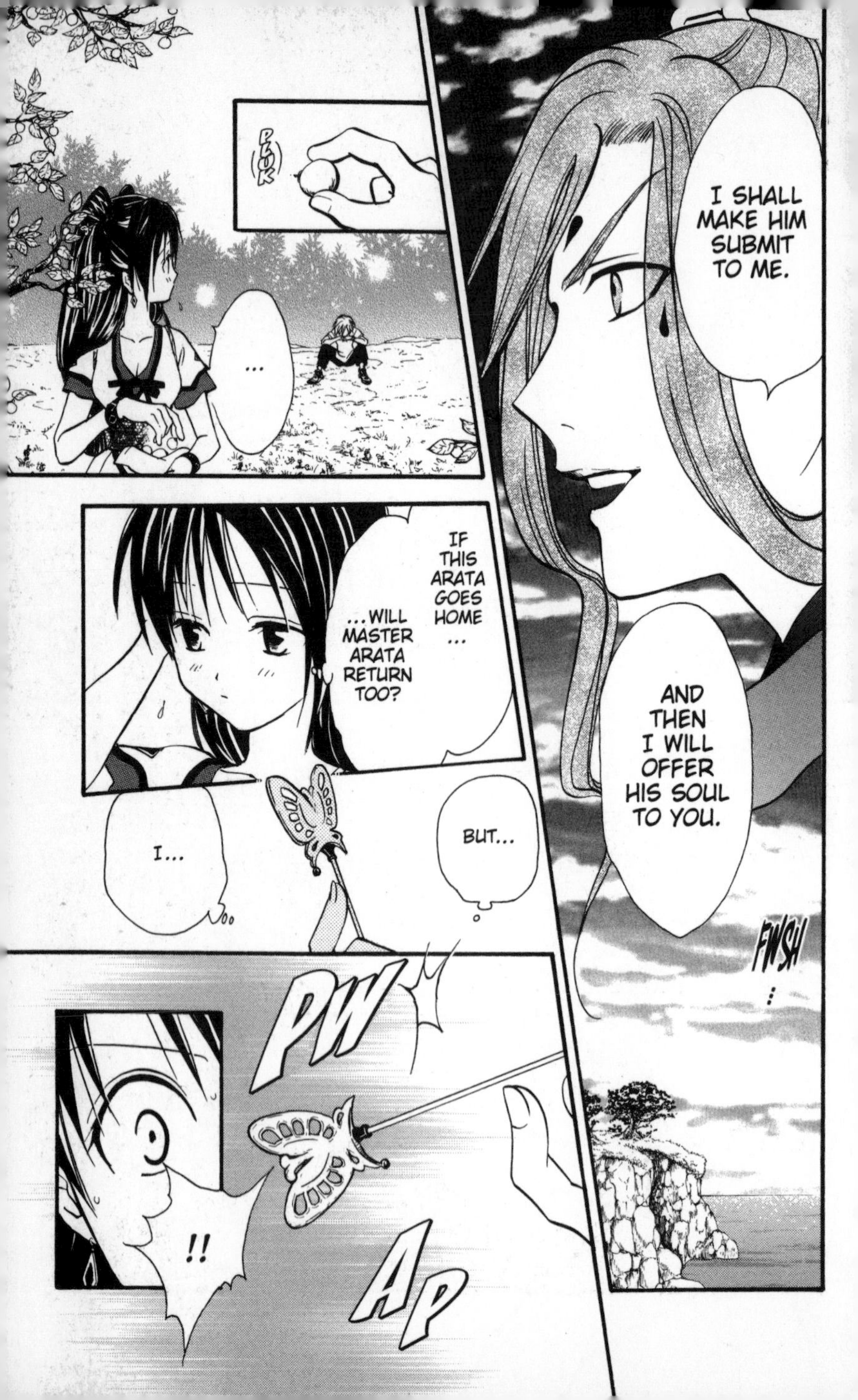
I SHALL MAKE HIM SUBMIT TO ME.
AND THEN I WILL OFFER HIS SOUL TO YOU.
FWSH
PLUK
...
IF THIS ARATA GOES HOME...
...WILL MASTER ARATA RETURN TOO?
BUT...
I...
PWAP
!!

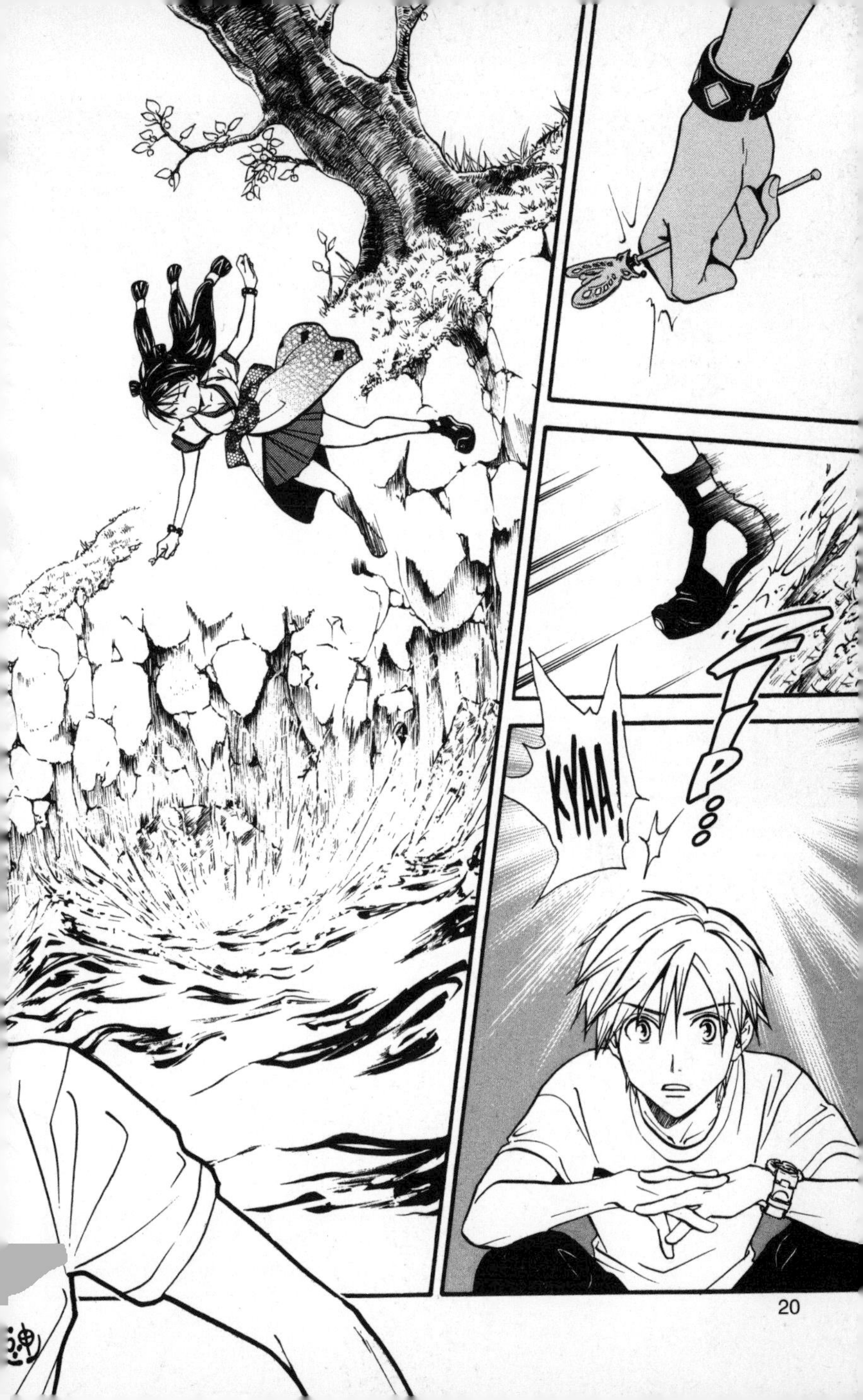
ZIPooo
KYAA!

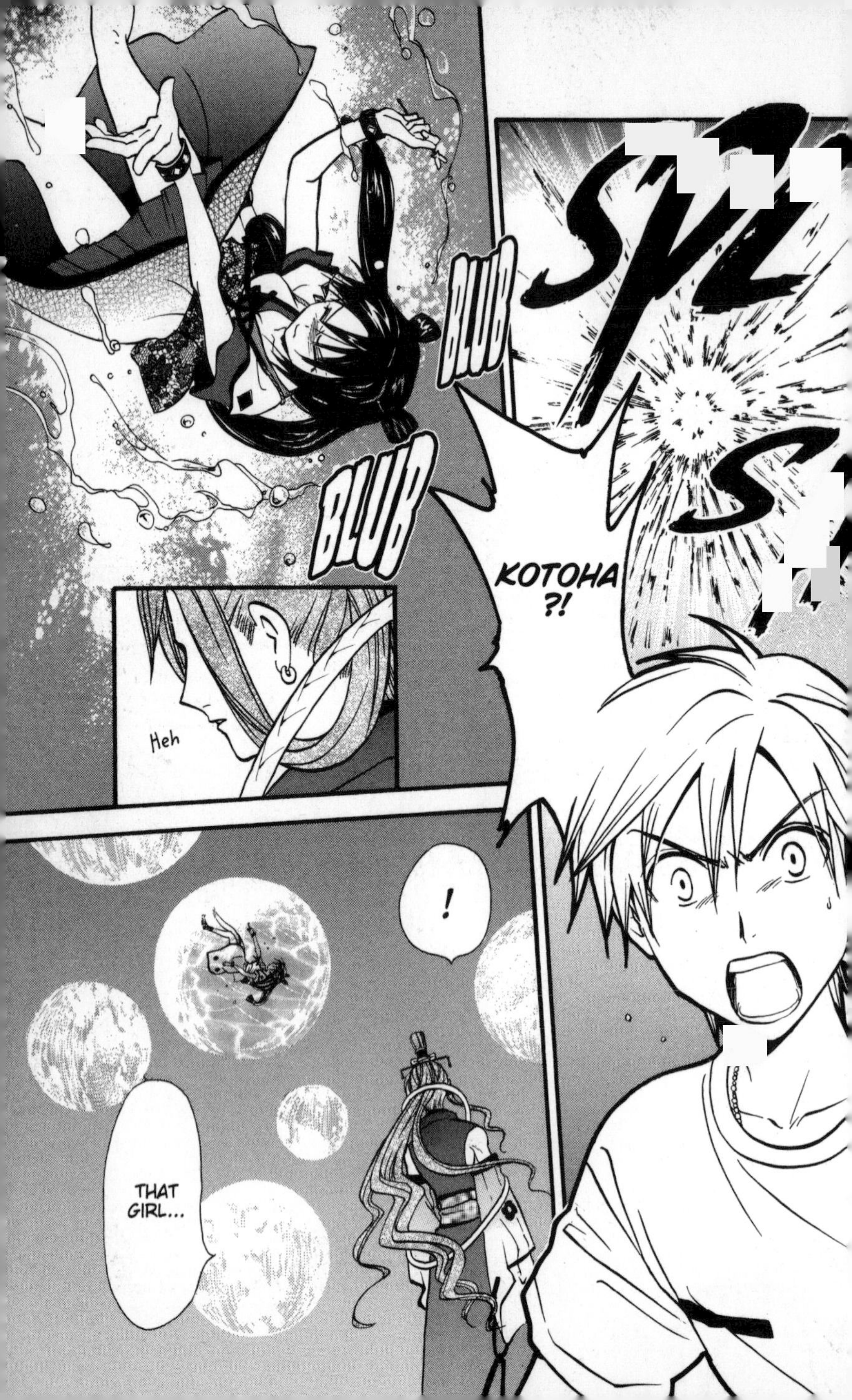
KOTOHA ?!
BLUB
BLUB
Heh
!
THAT GIRL...

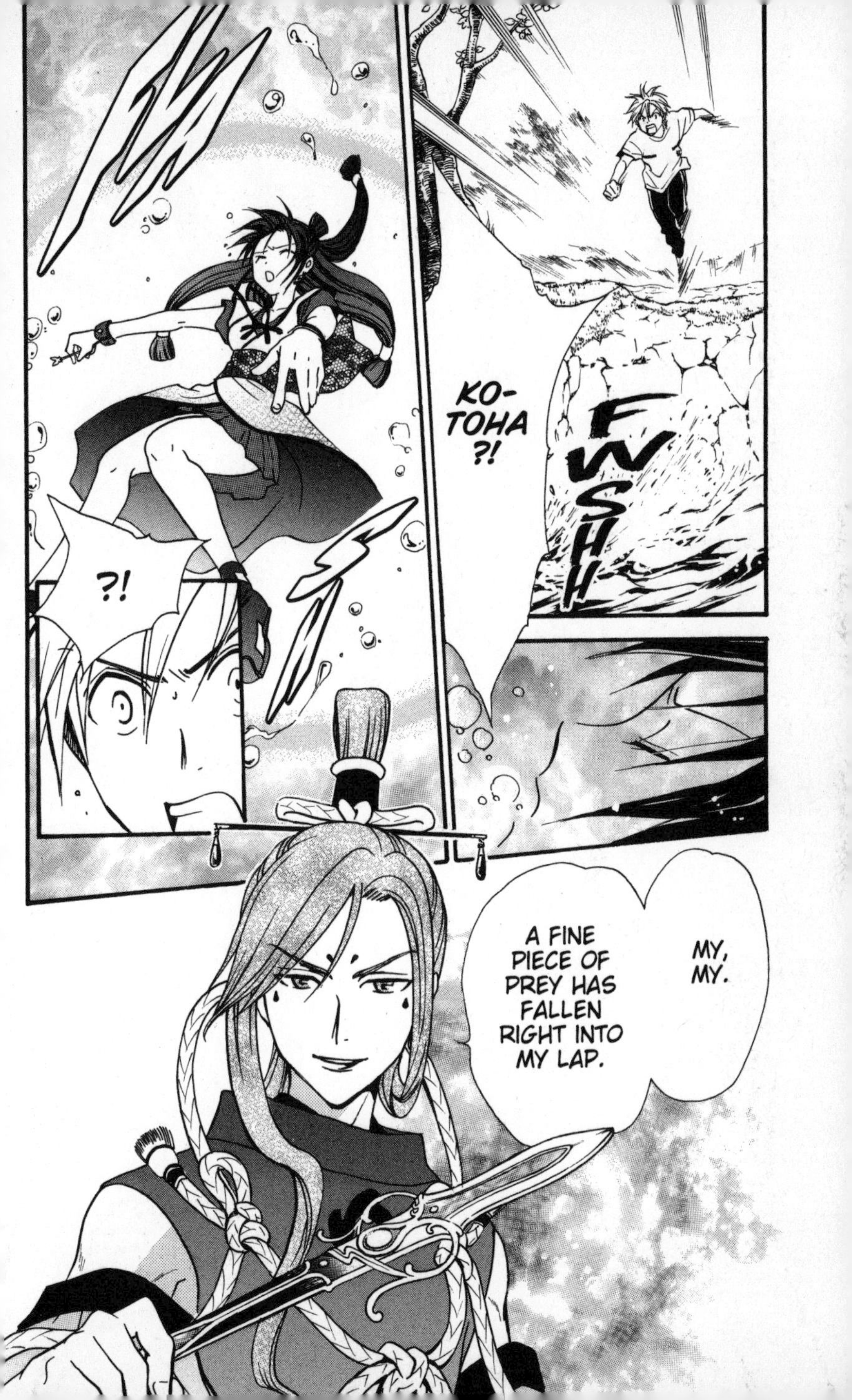
KO-TOHA?!
FWSHH
?!
MY, MY.
A FINE PIECE OF PREY HAS FALLEN RIGHT INTO MY LAP.

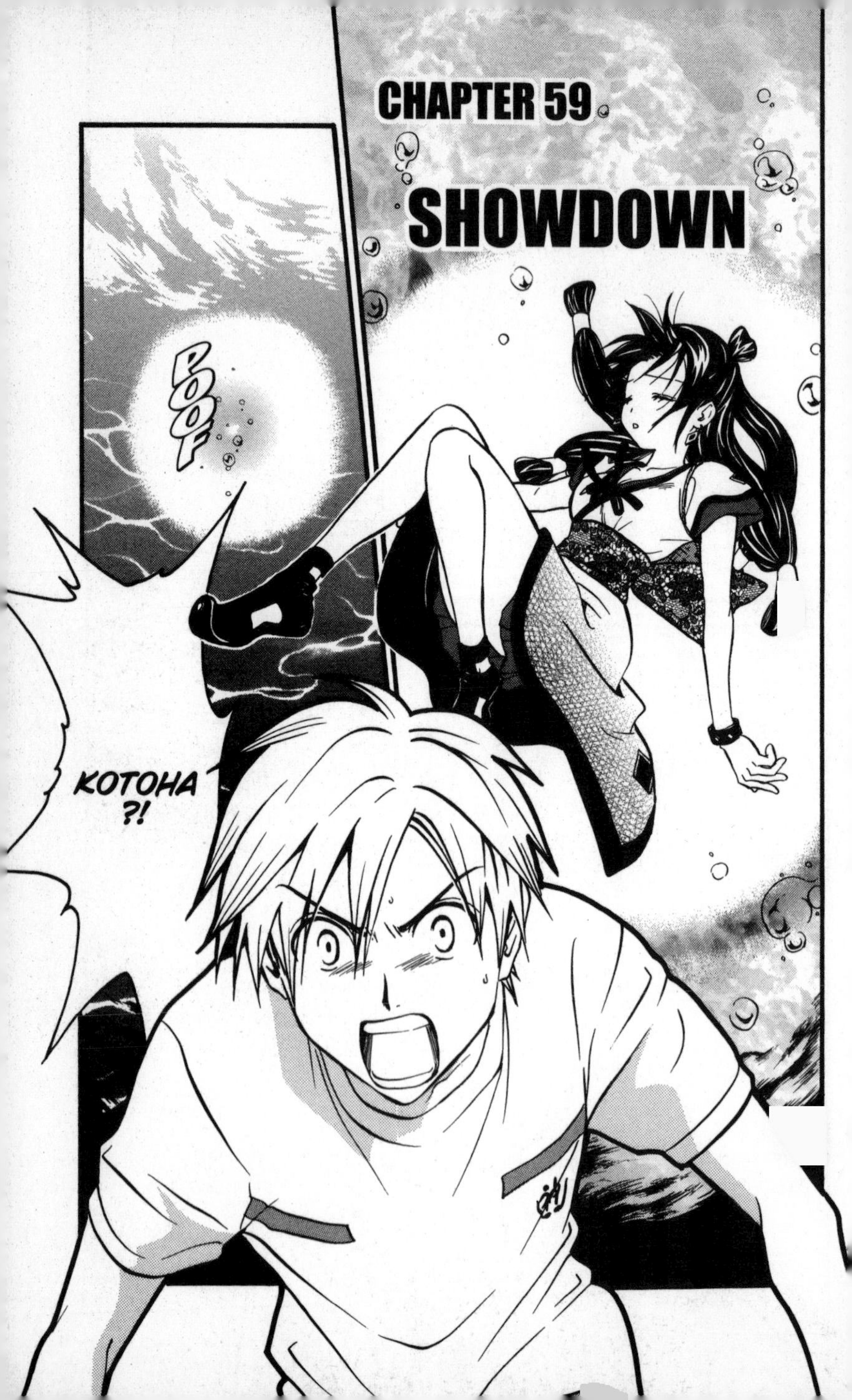
CHAPTER 59
SHOWDOWN
POOF
KOTOHA ?!

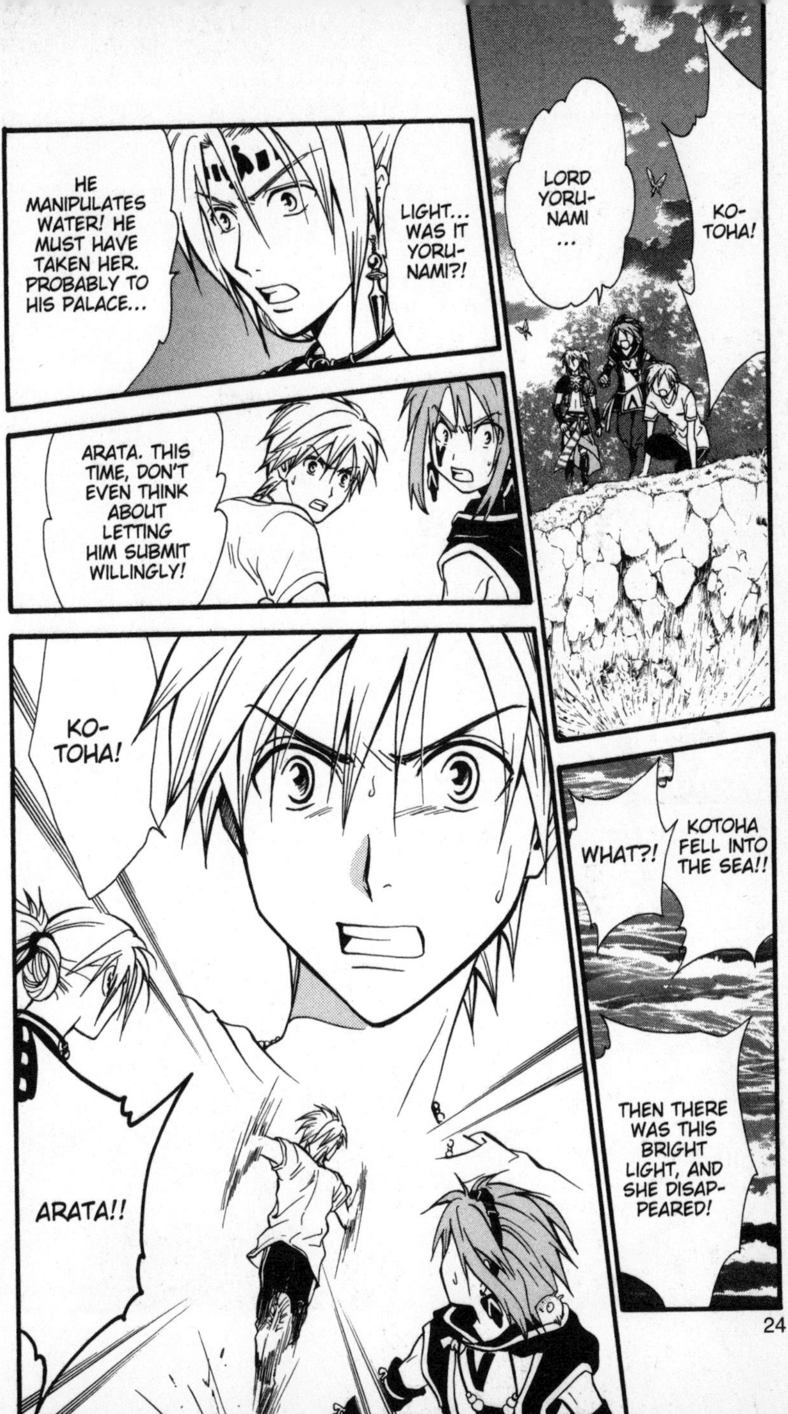

KO-TOHA!
LORD YORU-NAMI ...
KOTOHA FELL INTO THE SEA!!
WHAT?!
THEN THERE WAS THIS BRIGHT LIGHT, AND SHE DISAP-PEARED!
LIGHT... WAS IT YORU-NAMI?!
HE MANIPULATES WATER! HE MUST HAVE TAKEN HER. PROBABLY TO HIS PALACE...
ARATA. THIS TIME, DON'T EVEN THINK ABOUT LETTING HIM SUBMIT WILLINGLY!
KO-TOHA!
ARATA!!

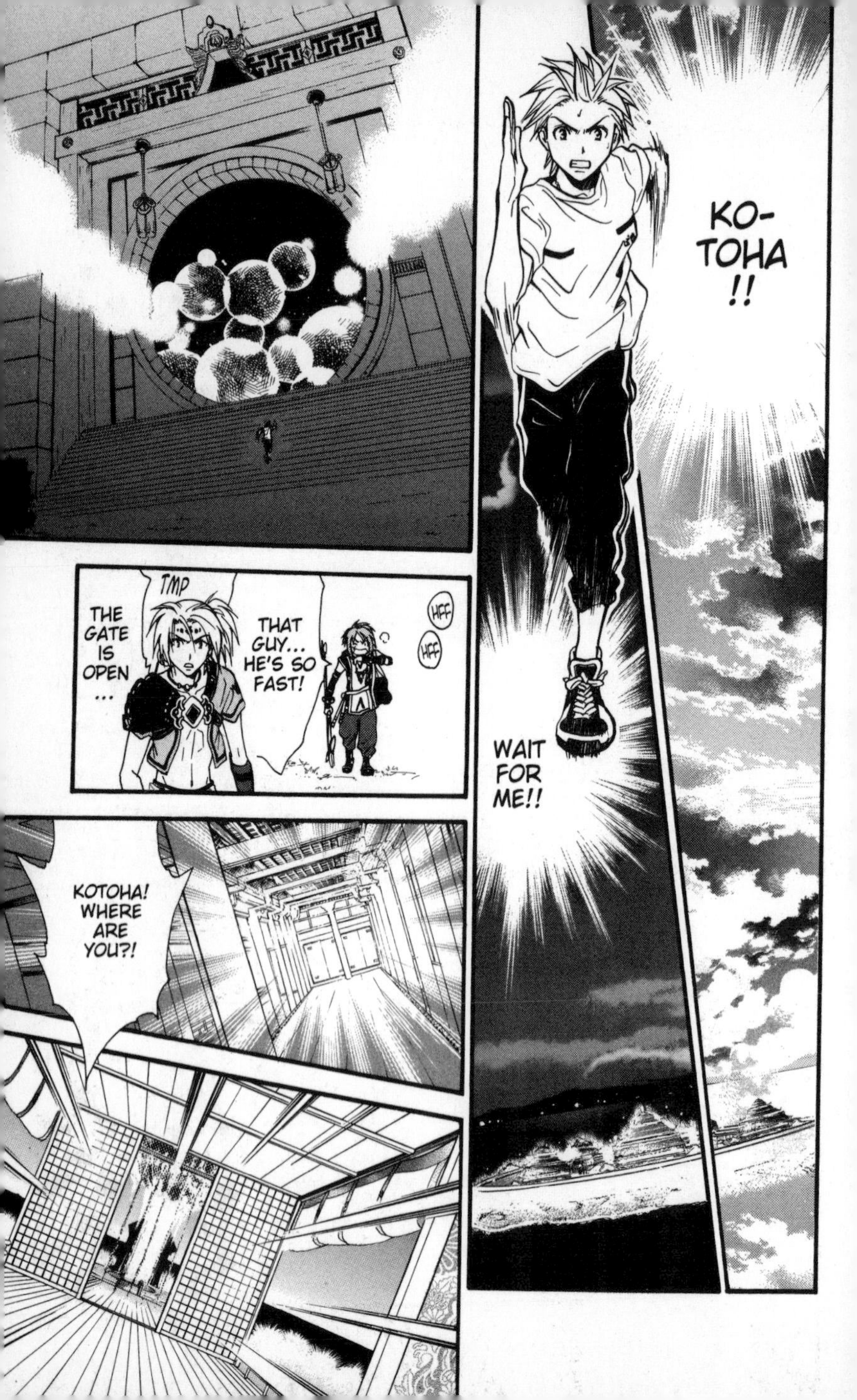
KO-TOHA!!
WAIT FOR ME!!
HFF
HFF
TMP
THAT GUY... HE'S SO FAST!
THE GATE IS OPEN...
KOTOHA! WHERE ARE YOU?!

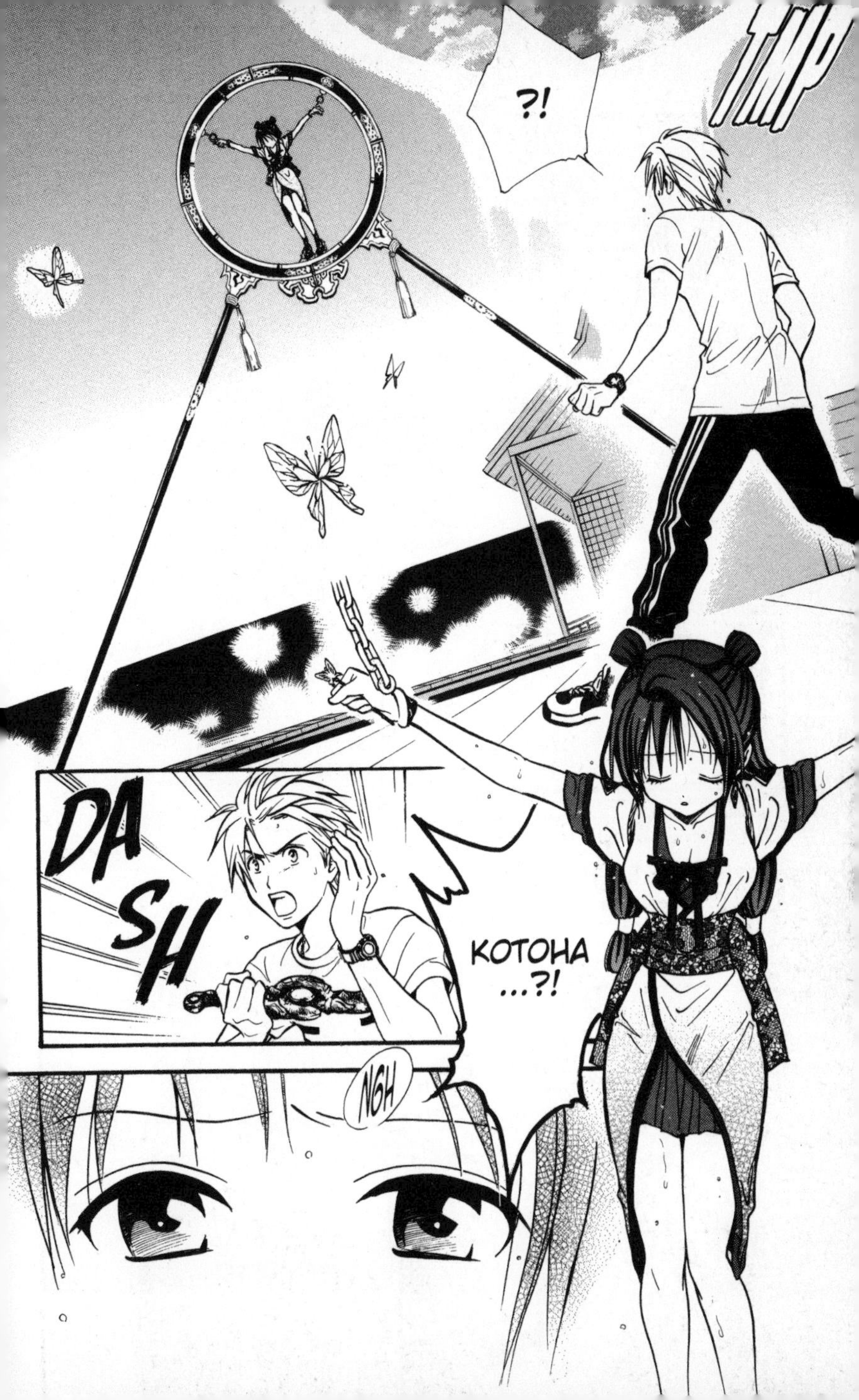
TMP
?!
KOTOHA ...?!
DASH
NGH

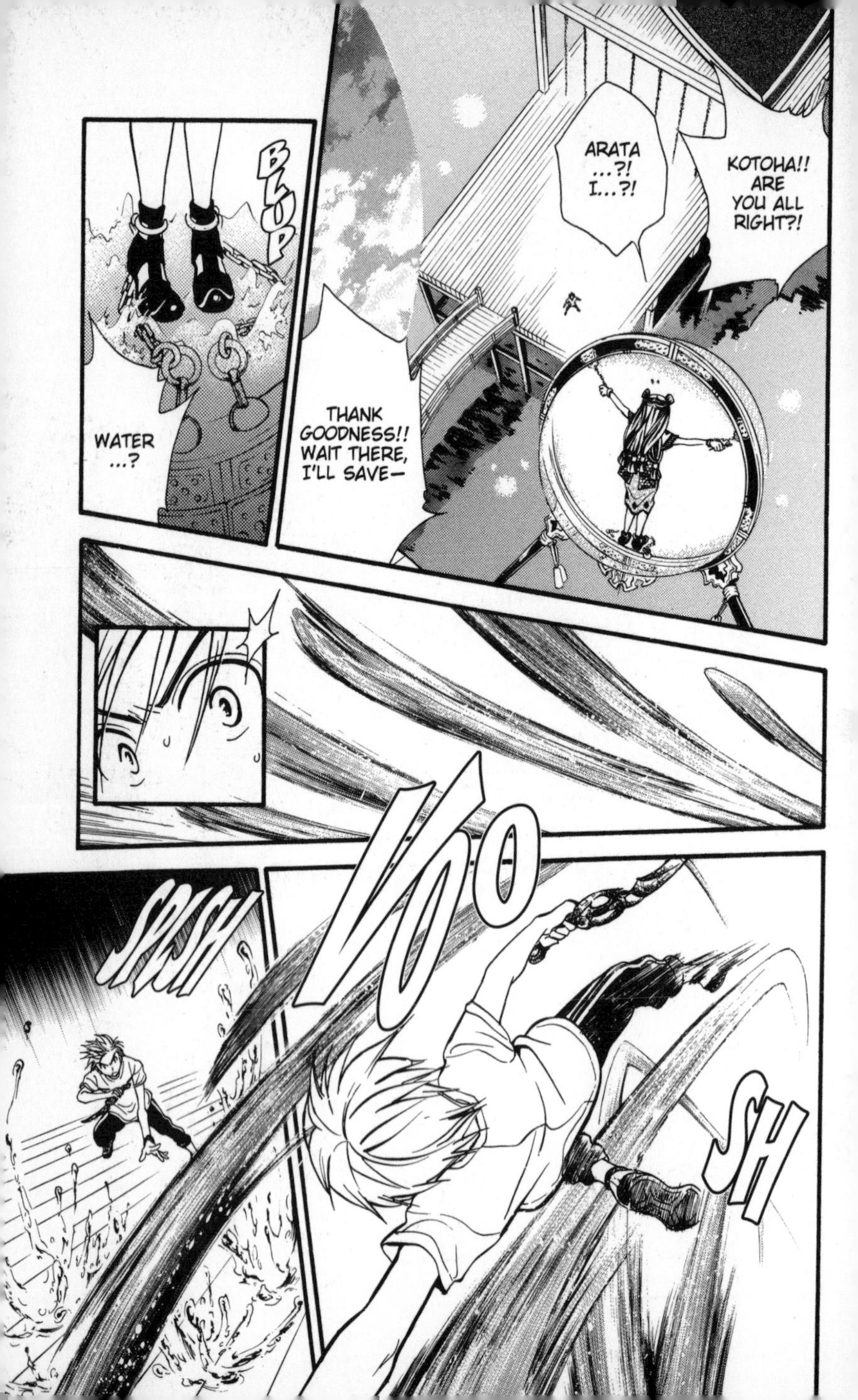
KOTOHA!! ARE YOU ALL RIGHT?!
ARATA ...?! I...?!
THANK GOODNESS!! WAIT THERE, I'LL SAVE—
BLUP
WATER ...?
VOO
SH
SPLSH

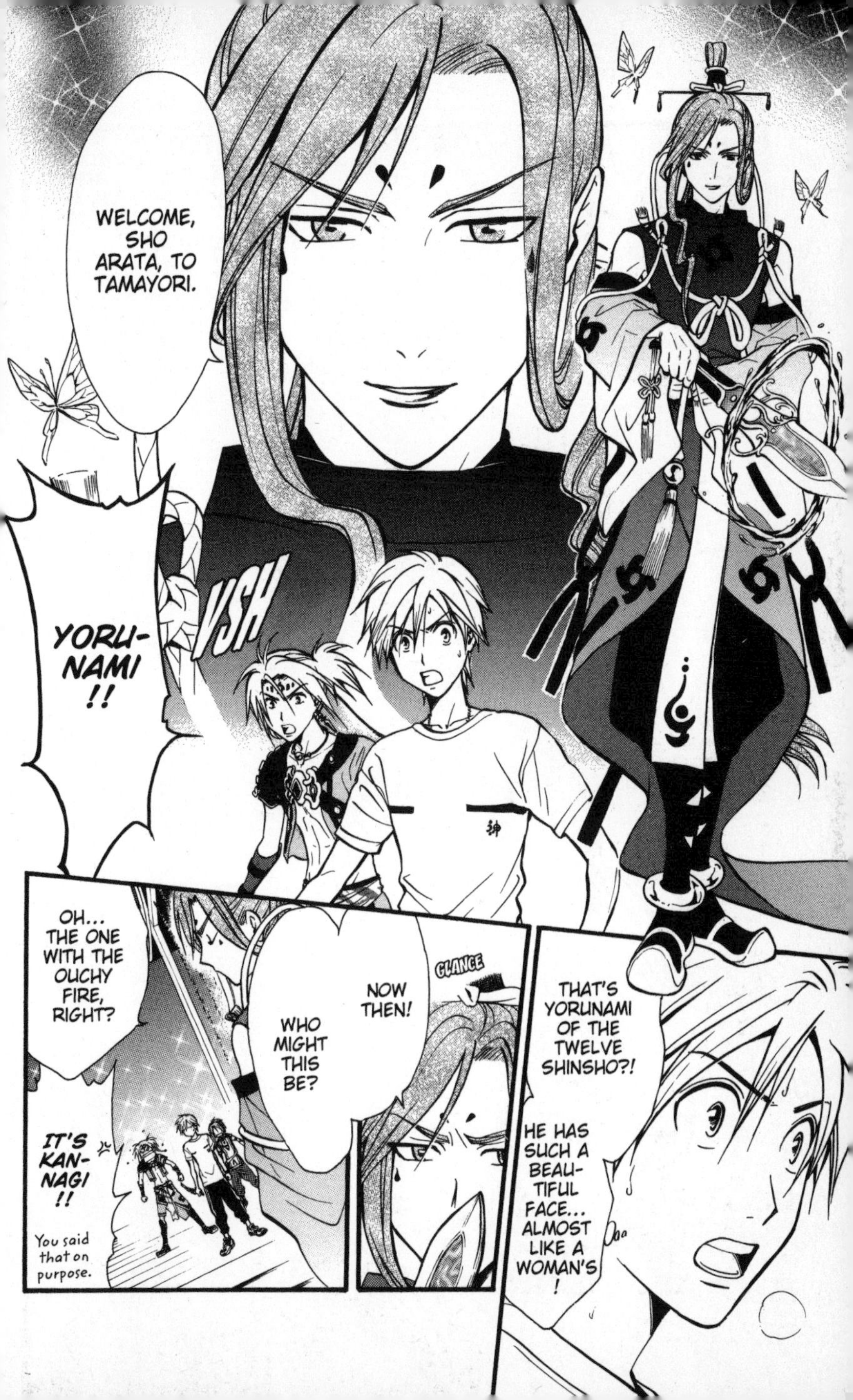
WELCOME, SHO ARATA, TO TAMAYORI.
VSH
YORU-NAMI!!
THAT'S YORUNAMI OF THE TWELVE SHINSHO?!
HE HAS SUCH A BEAU-TIFUL FACE... ALMOST LIKE A WOMAN'S!
GLANCE
NOW THEN!
WHO MIGHT THIS BE?
OH... THE ONE WITH THE OUCHY FIRE, RIGHT?
IT'S KAN-NAGI!!
You said that on purpose.

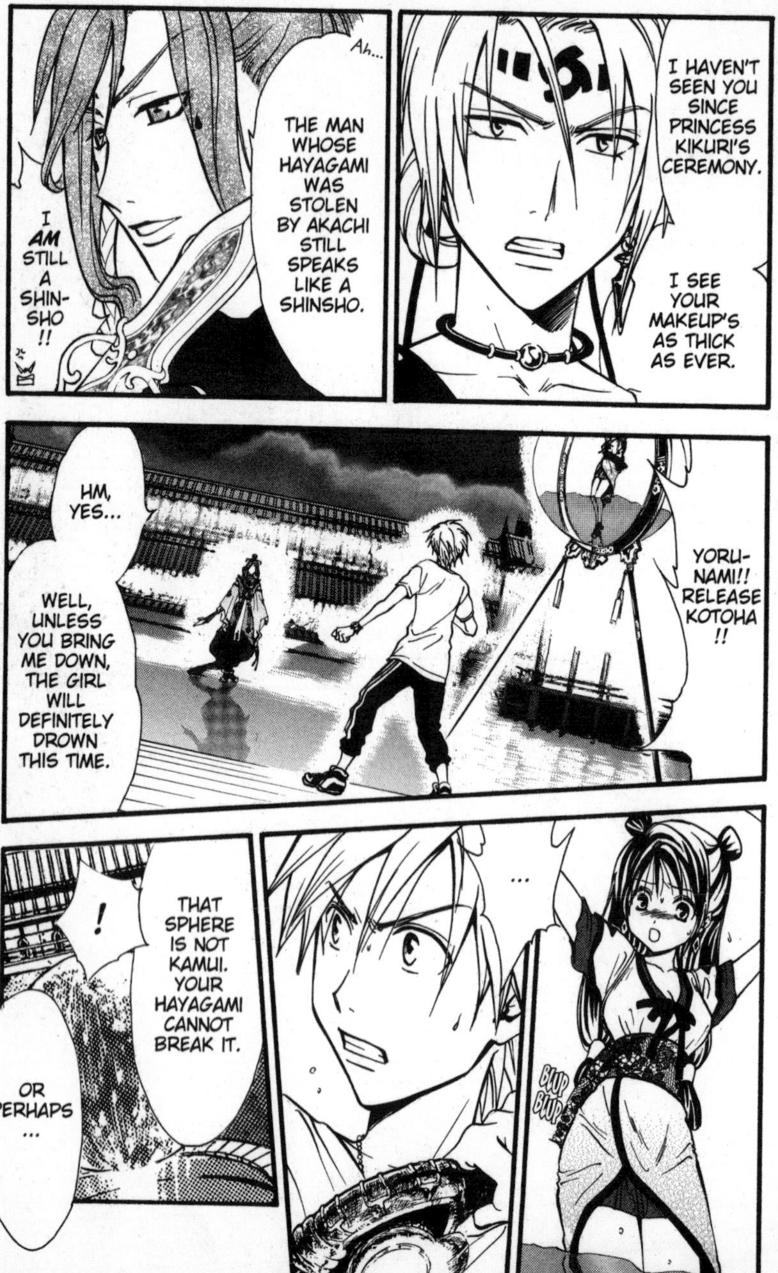
I HAVEN'T SEEN YOU SINCE PRINCESS KIKURI'S CEREMONY.
I SEE YOUR MAKEUP'S AS THICK AS EVER.
Ah...
THE MAN WHOSE HAYAGAMI WAS STOLEN BY AKACHI STILL SPEAKS LIKE A SHINSHO.
I ***AM*** STILL A SHIN-SHO!!
YORU-NAMI!! RELEASE KOTOHA!!
HM, YES...
WELL, UNLESS YOU BRING ME DOWN, THE GIRL WILL DEFINITELY DROWN THIS TIME.
...
BLUP BLUP
!
THAT SPHERE IS NOT KAMUI. YOUR HAYAGAMI CANNOT BREAK IT.
OR PERHAPS ...

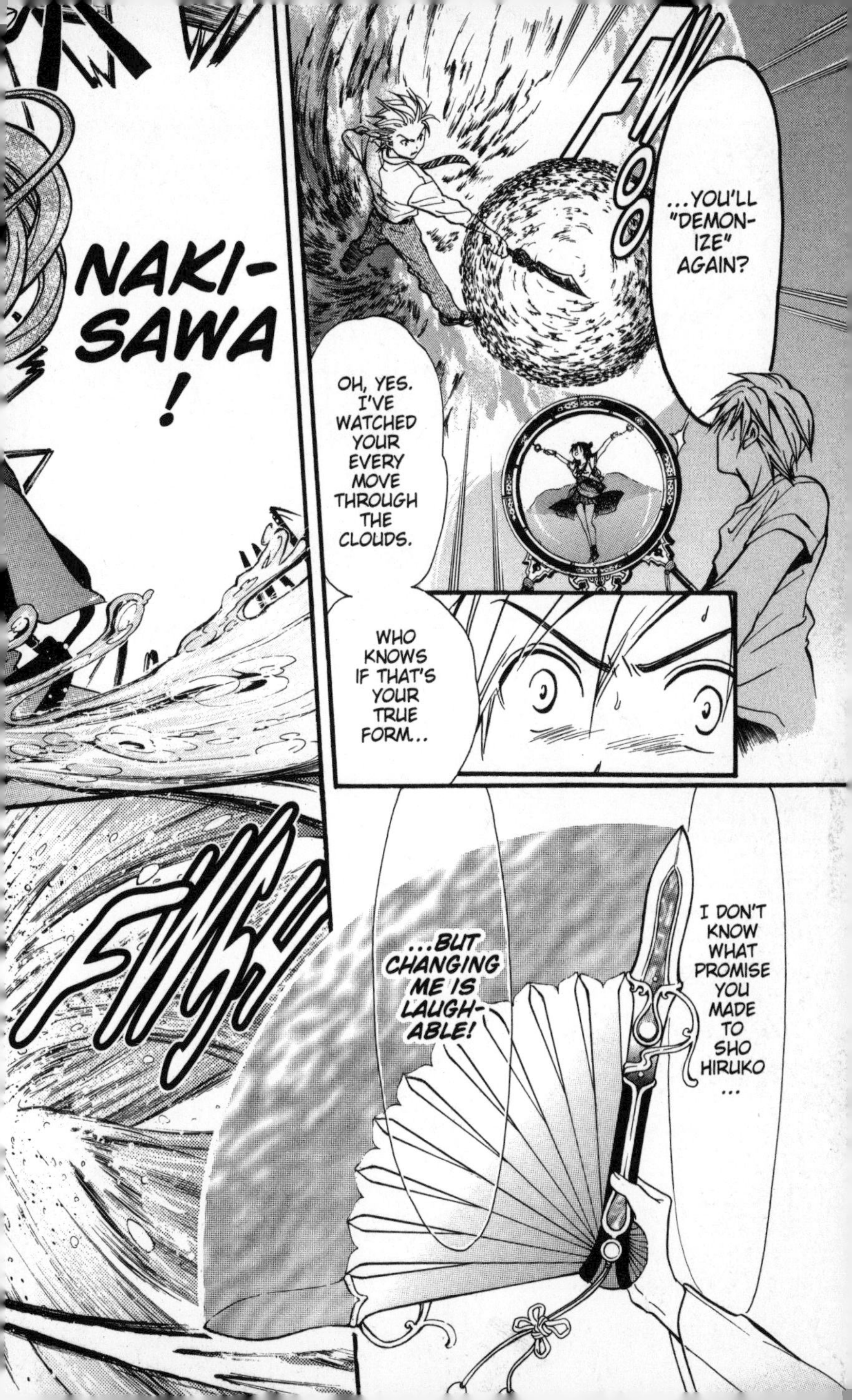
...YOU'LL "DEMON-IZE" AGAIN?
OH, YES. I'VE WATCHED YOUR EVERY MOVE THROUGH THE CLOUDS.
WHO KNOWS IF THAT'S YOUR TRUE FORM...
NAKI-SAWA!
I DON'T KNOW WHAT PROMISE YOU MADE TO SHO HIRUKO ...
...BUT CHANGING ME IS LAUGH-ABLE!

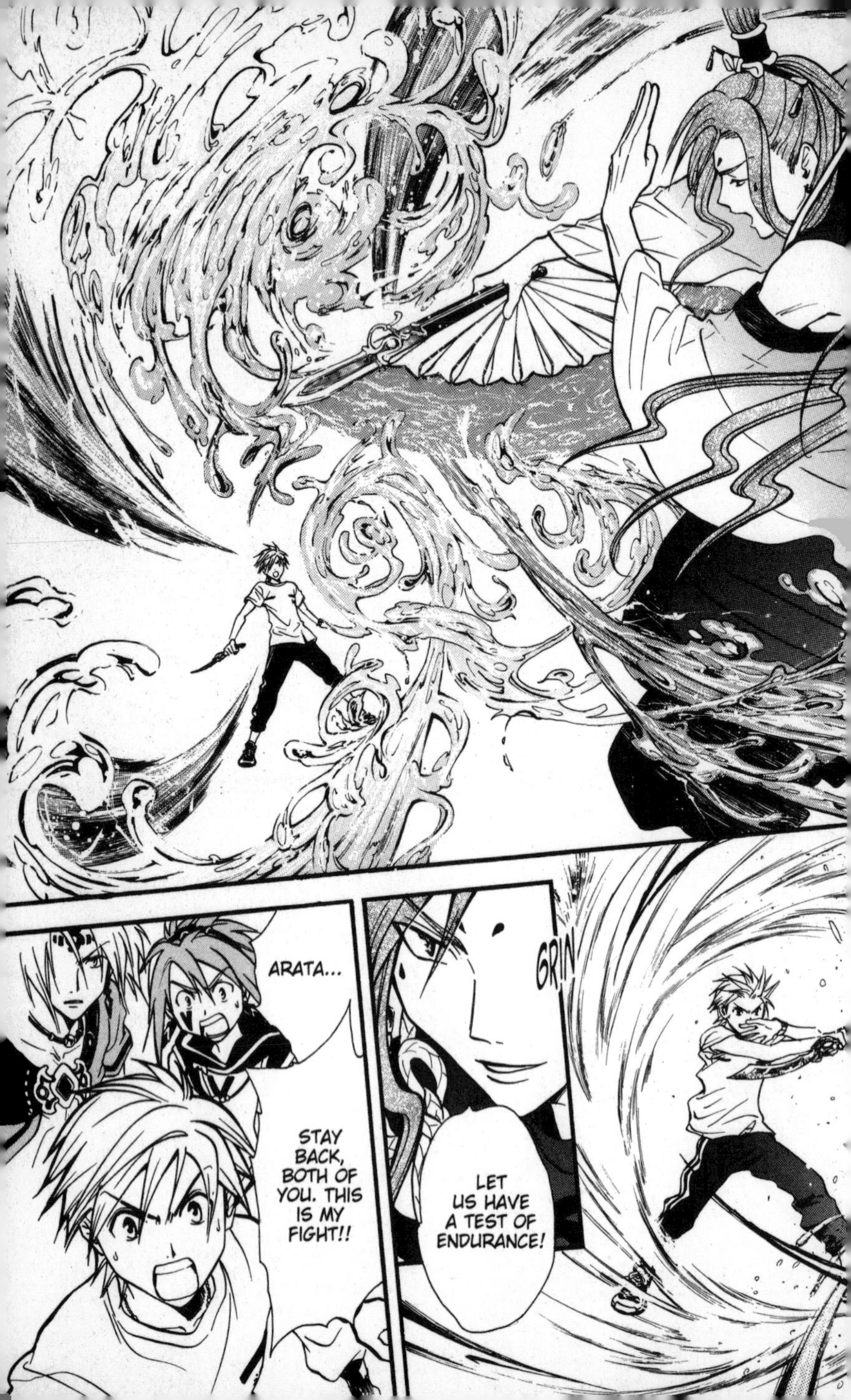
GRIN
LET US HAVE A TEST OF ENDURANCE!
ARATA...
STAY BACK, BOTH OF YOU. THIS IS MY FIGHT!!

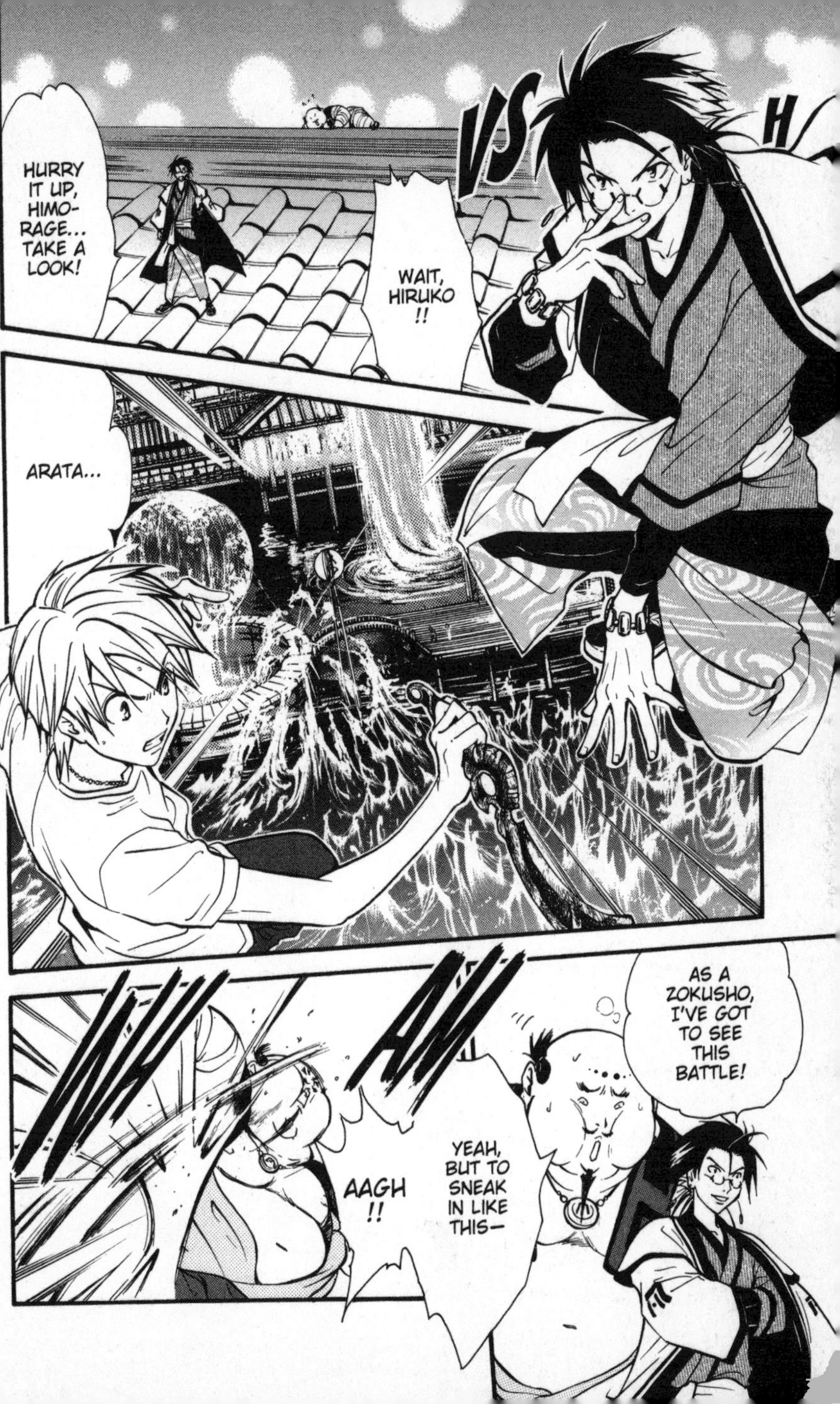
HURRY IT UP, HIMORAGE... TAKE A LOOK!
VS
WAIT, HIRUKO !!
ARATA...
AS A ZOKUSHO, I'VE GOT TO SEE THIS BATTLE!
YEAH, BUT TO SNEAK IN LIKE THIS—
AAGH !!

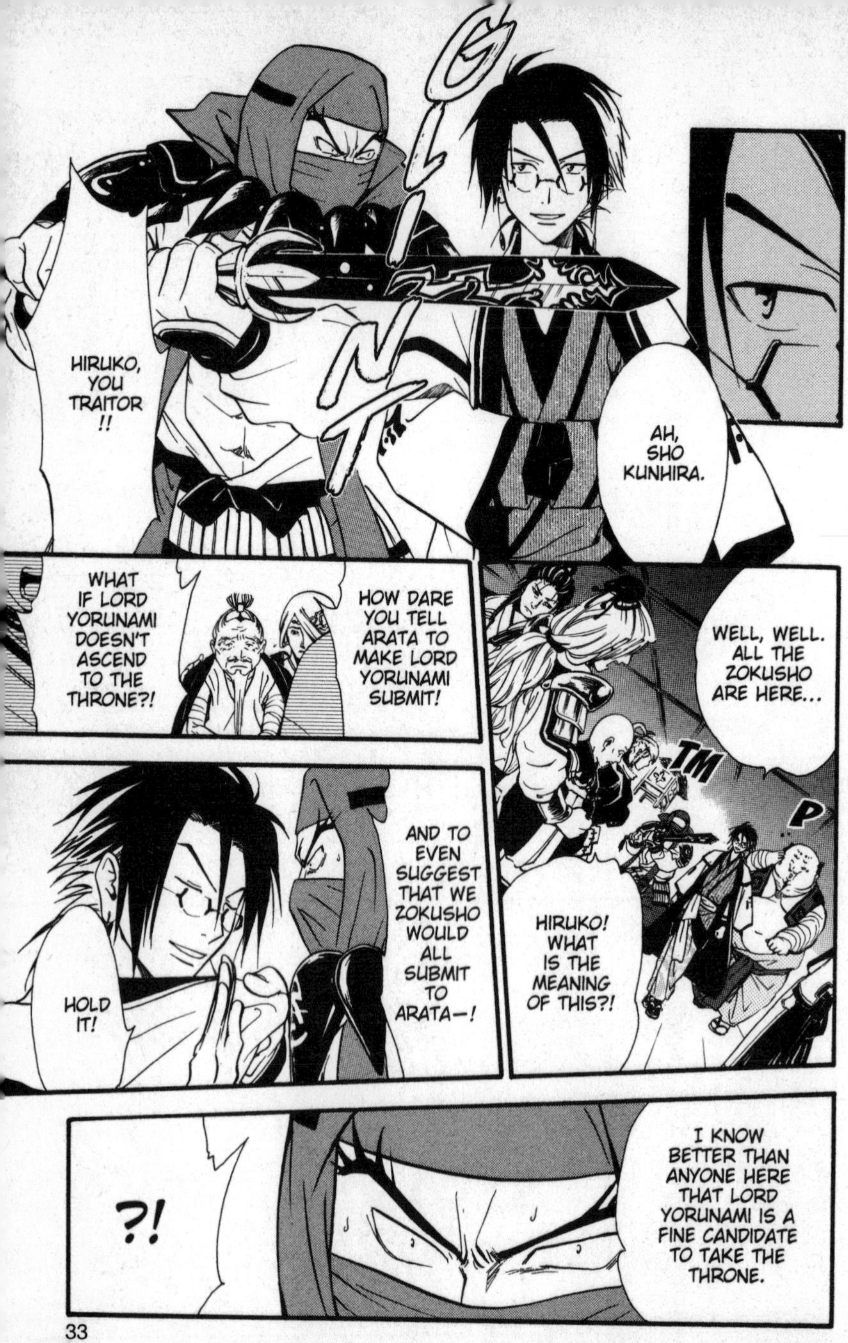
GLINT
AH, SHO KUNHIRA.
HIRUKO, YOU TRAITOR!!
WELL, WELL. ALL THE ZOKUSHO ARE HERE...
TMP
HIRUKO! WHAT IS THE MEANING OF THIS?!
HOW DARE YOU TELL ARATA TO MAKE LORD YORUNAMI SUBMIT!
WHAT IF LORD YORUNAMI DOESN'T ASCEND TO THE THRONE?!
AND TO EVEN SUGGEST THAT WE ZOKUSHO WOULD ALL SUBMIT TO ARATA—!
HOLD IT!
I KNOW BETTER THAN ANYONE HERE THAT LORD YORUNAMI IS A FINE CANDIDATE TO TAKE THE THRONE.
?!

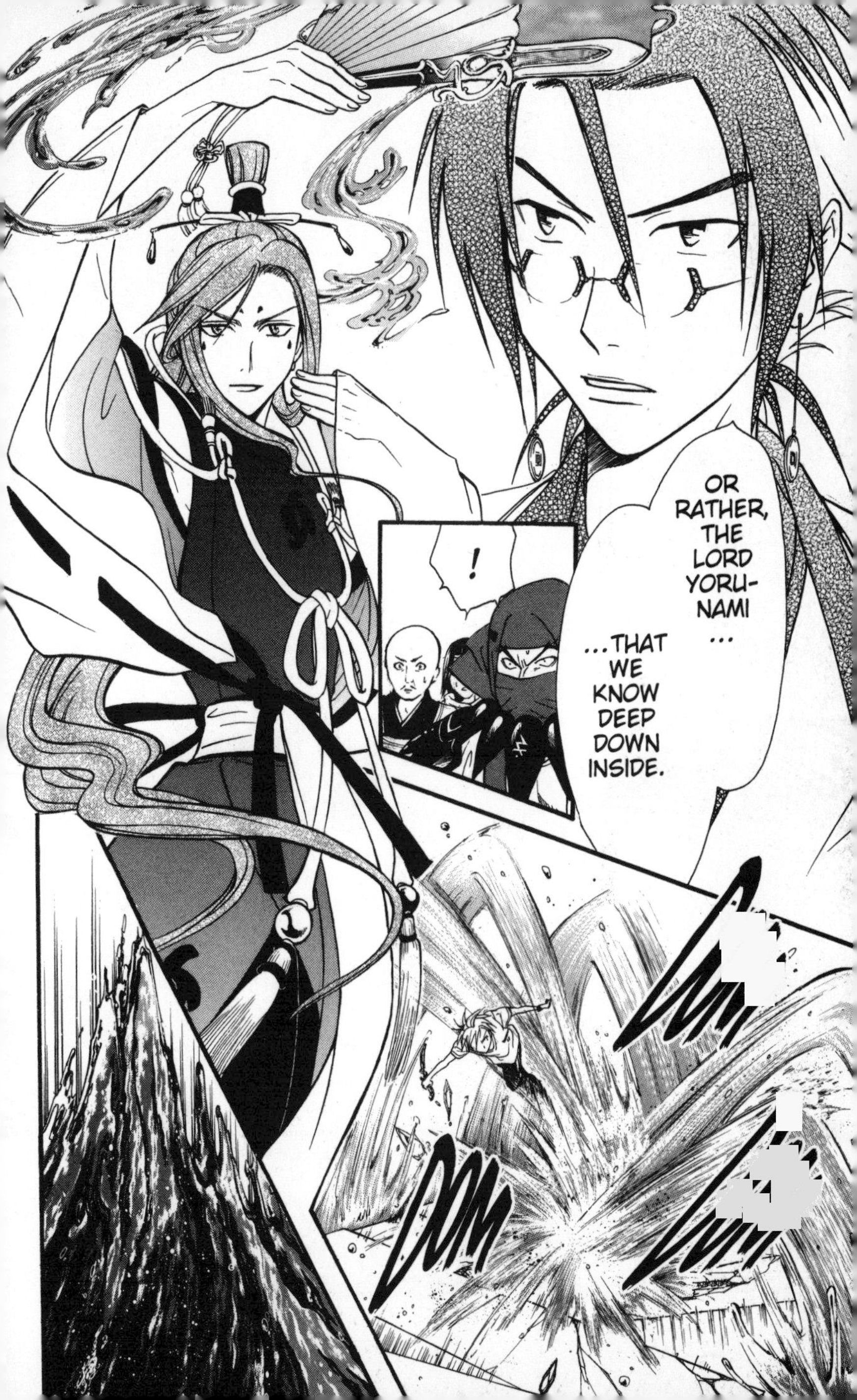
OR RATHER, THE LORD YORU-NAMI...
...THAT WE KNOW DEEP DOWN INSIDE.
!

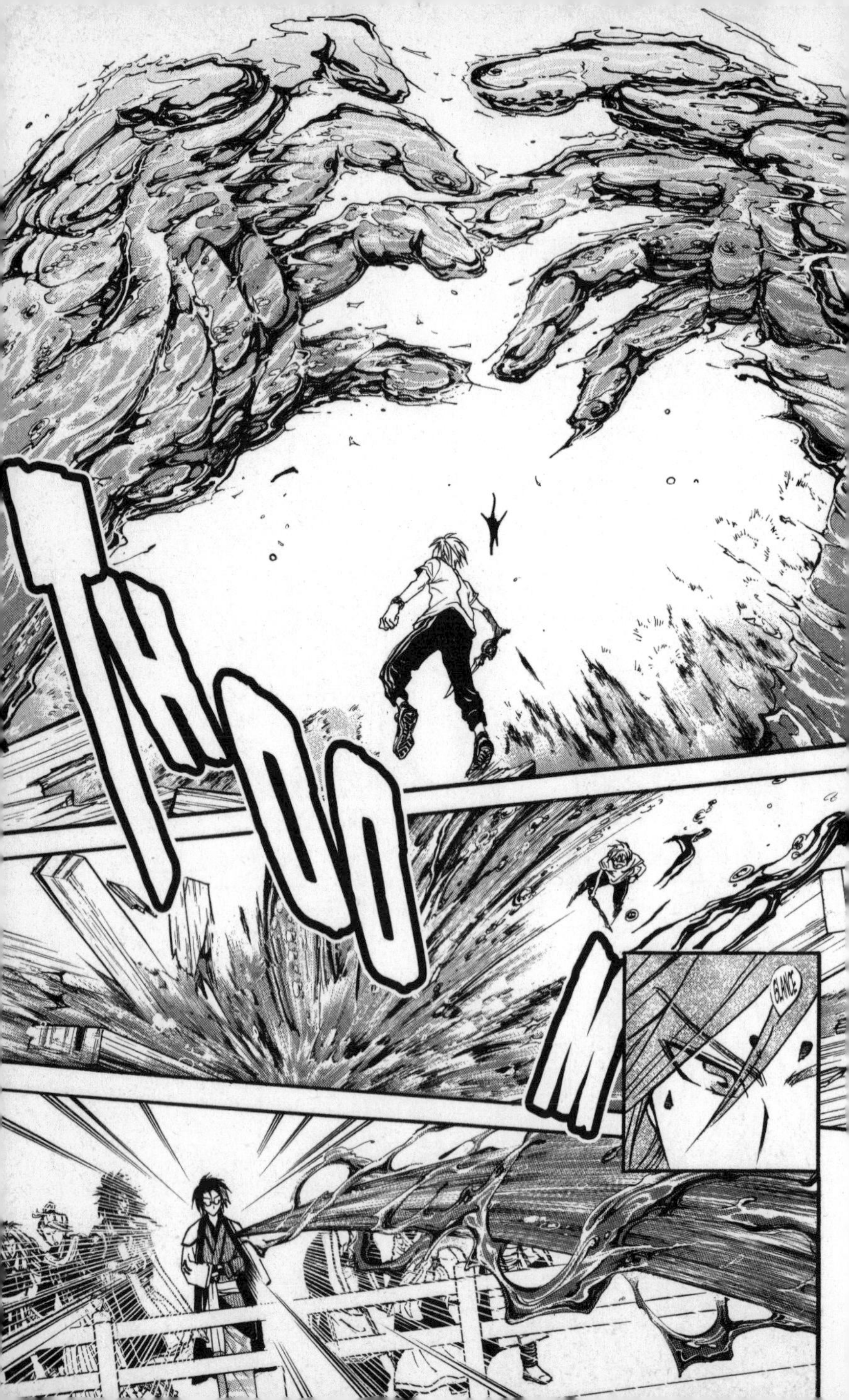
THOOM
GLANCE

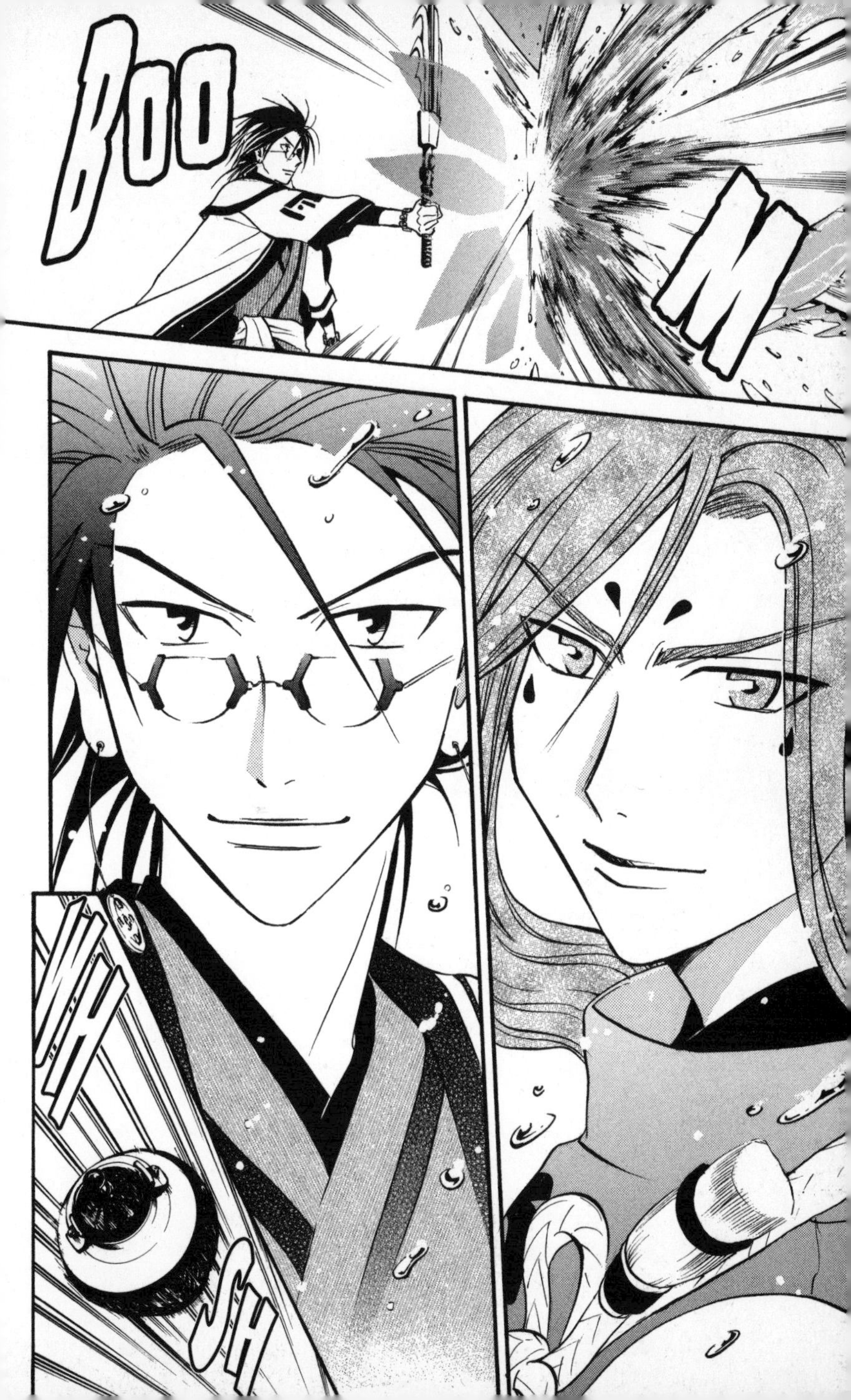
BOOM
WH
SH

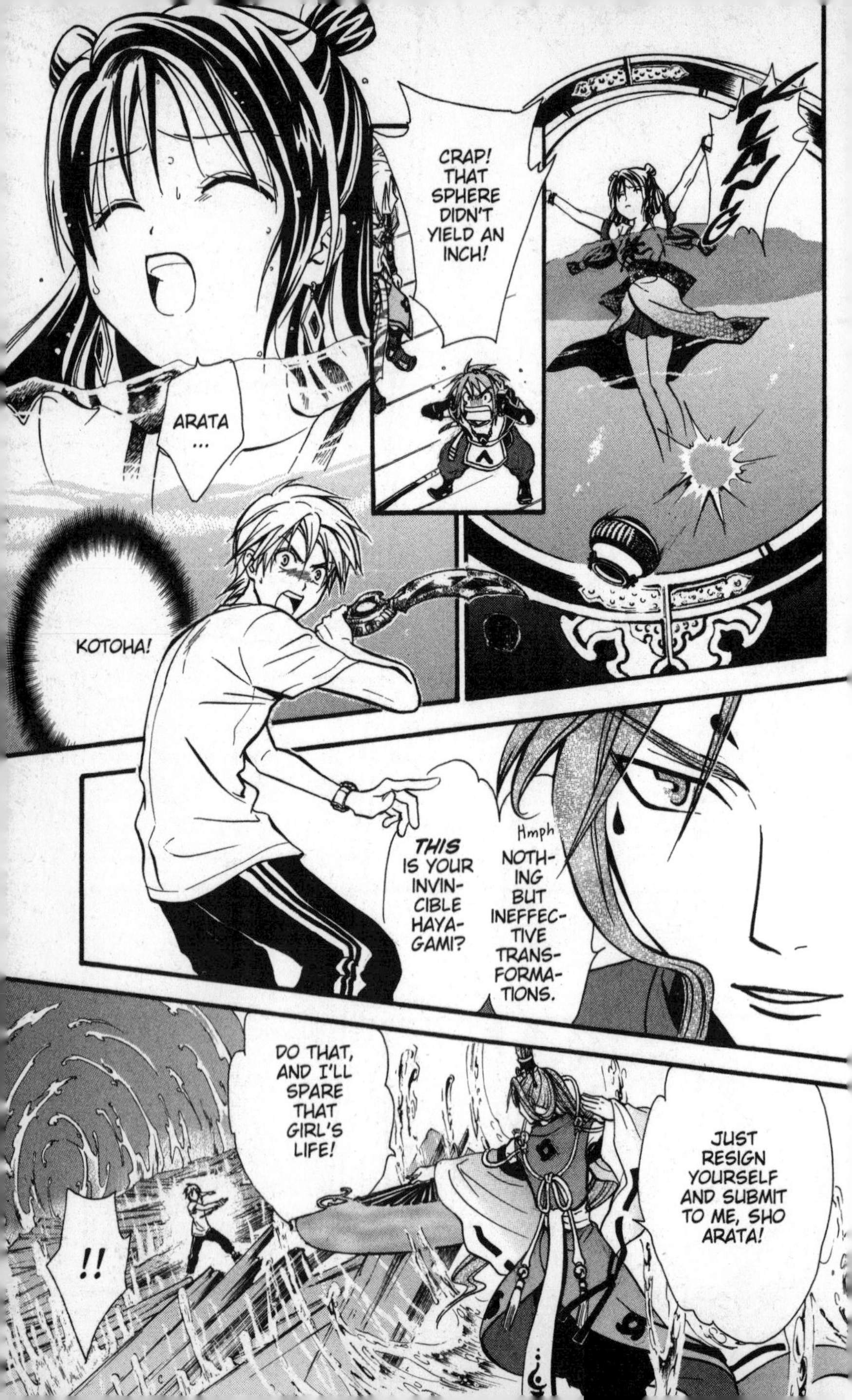
CRAP! THAT SPHERE DIDN'T YIELD AN INCH!
ARATA ...
KOTOHA!
Hmph
NOTHING BUT INEFFECTIVE TRANSFORMATIONS.
THIS IS YOUR INVINCIBLE HAYAGAMI?
JUST RESIGN YOURSELF AND SUBMIT TO ME, SHO ARATA!
DO THAT, AND I'LL SPARE THAT GIRL'S LIFE!
!!

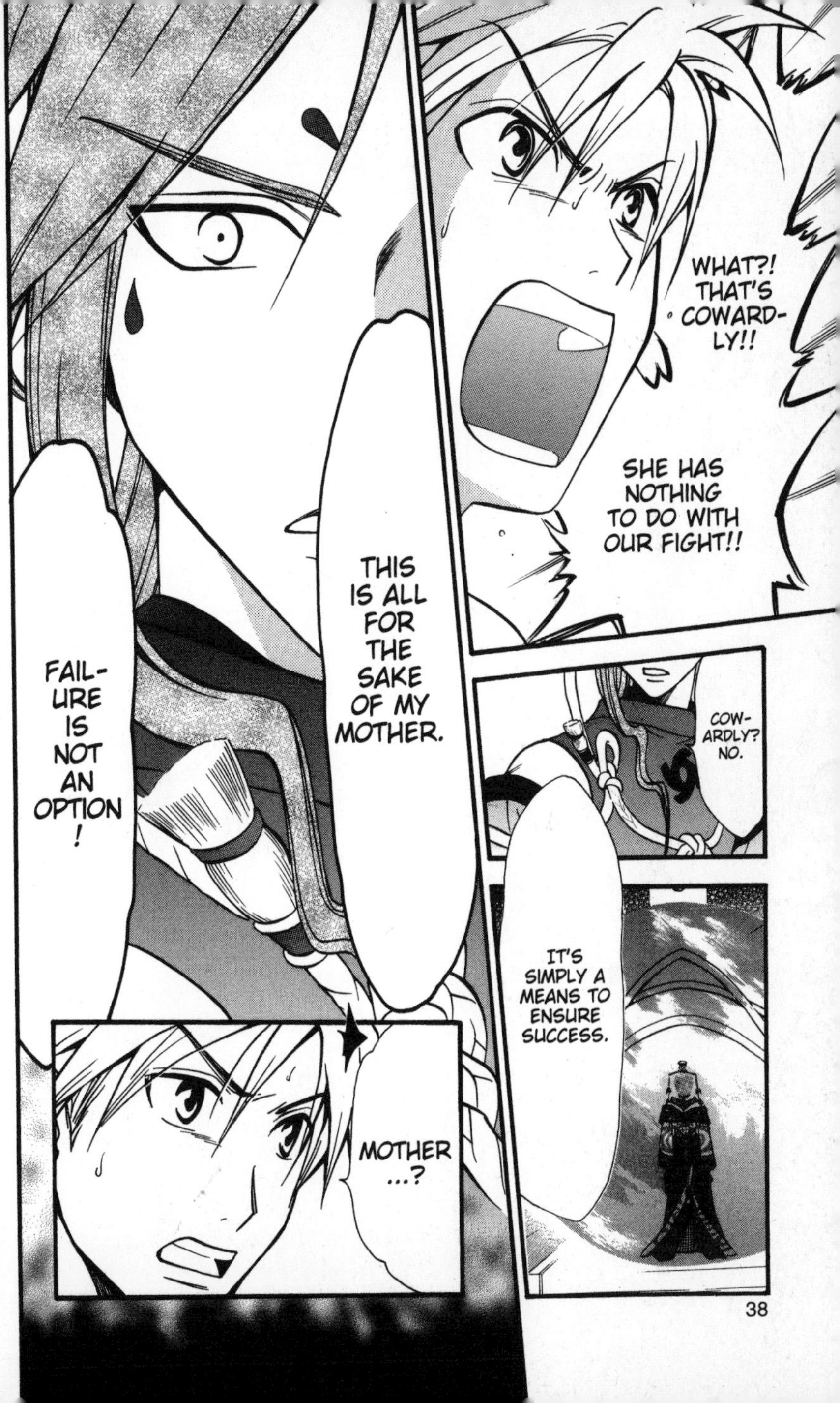

WHAT?! THAT'S COWARDLY!!
SHE HAS NOTHING TO DO WITH OUR FIGHT!!
COWARDLY? NO.
IT'S SIMPLY A MEANS TO ENSURE SUCCESS.
THIS IS ALL FOR THE SAKE OF MY MOTHER.
FAILURE IS NOT AN OPTION!
MOTHER...?

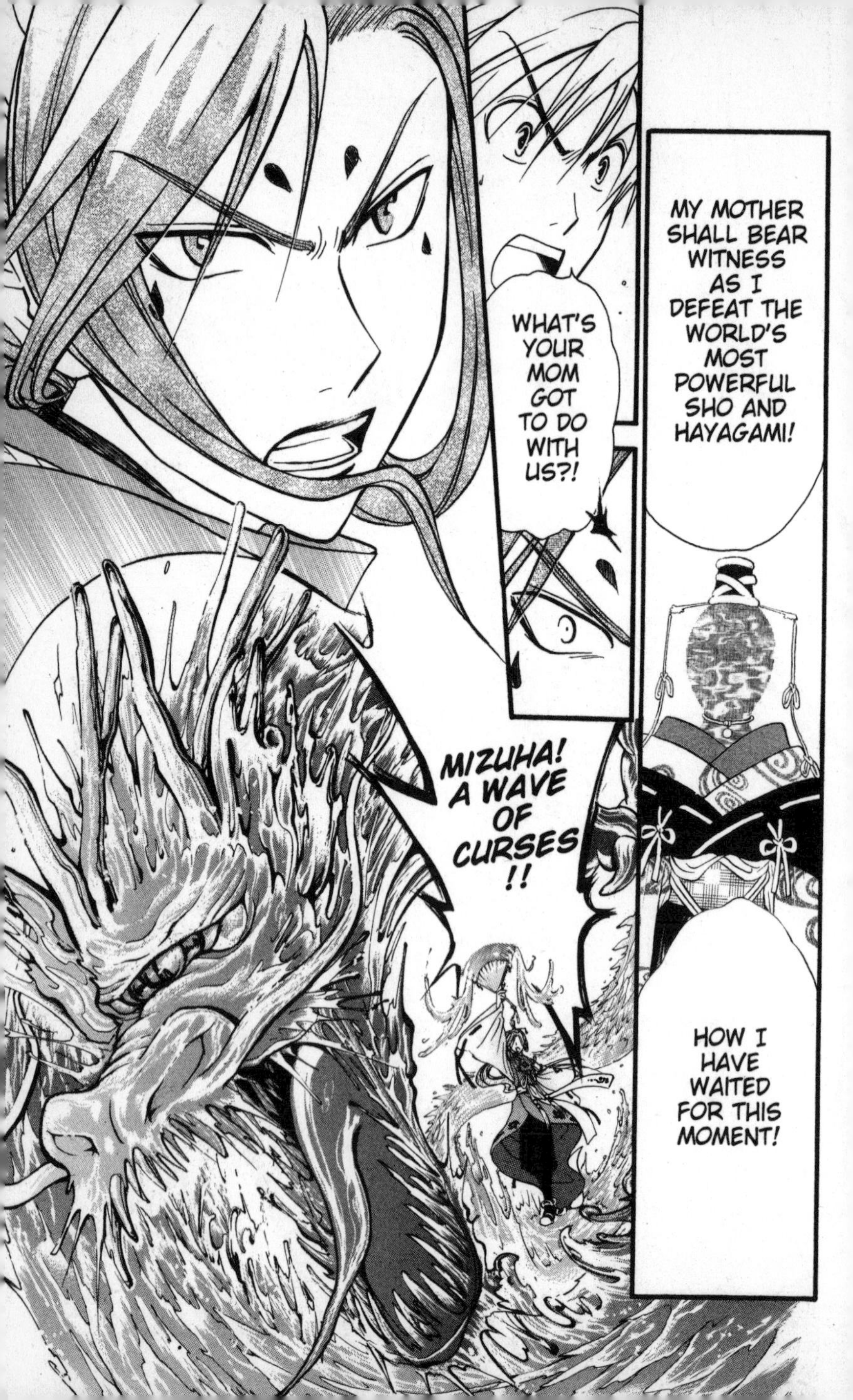

MY MOTHER SHALL BEAR WITNESS AS I DEFEAT THE WORLD'S MOST POWERFUL SHO AND HAYAGAMI!
HOW I HAVE WAITED FOR THIS MOMENT!
WHAT'S YOUR MOM GOT TO DO WITH US?!
MIZUHA! A WAVE OF CURSES!!

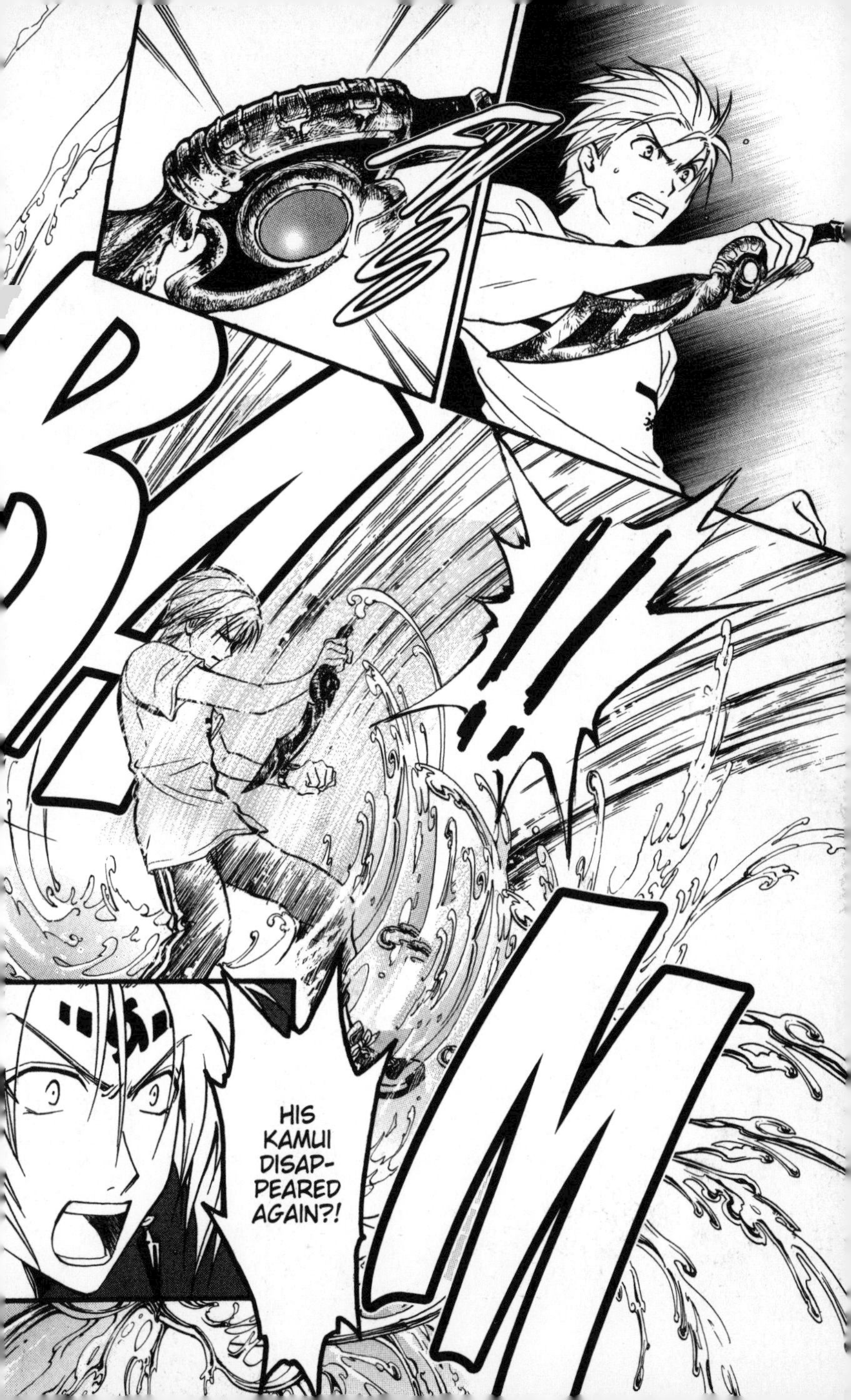
HIS KAMUI DISAP-PEARED AGAIN?!

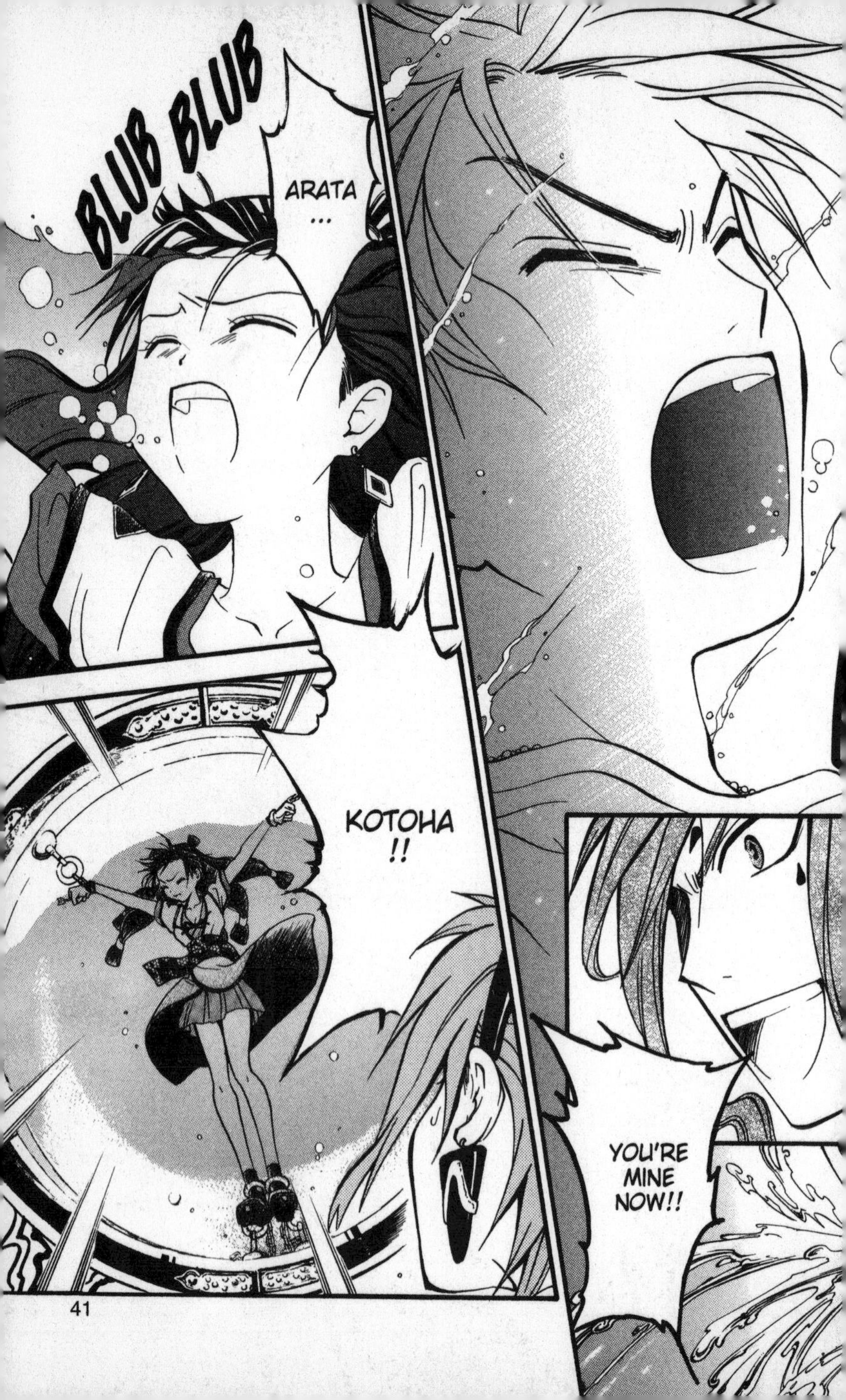
BLUB BLUB
ARATA ...
KOTOHA !!
YOU'RE MINE NOW!!

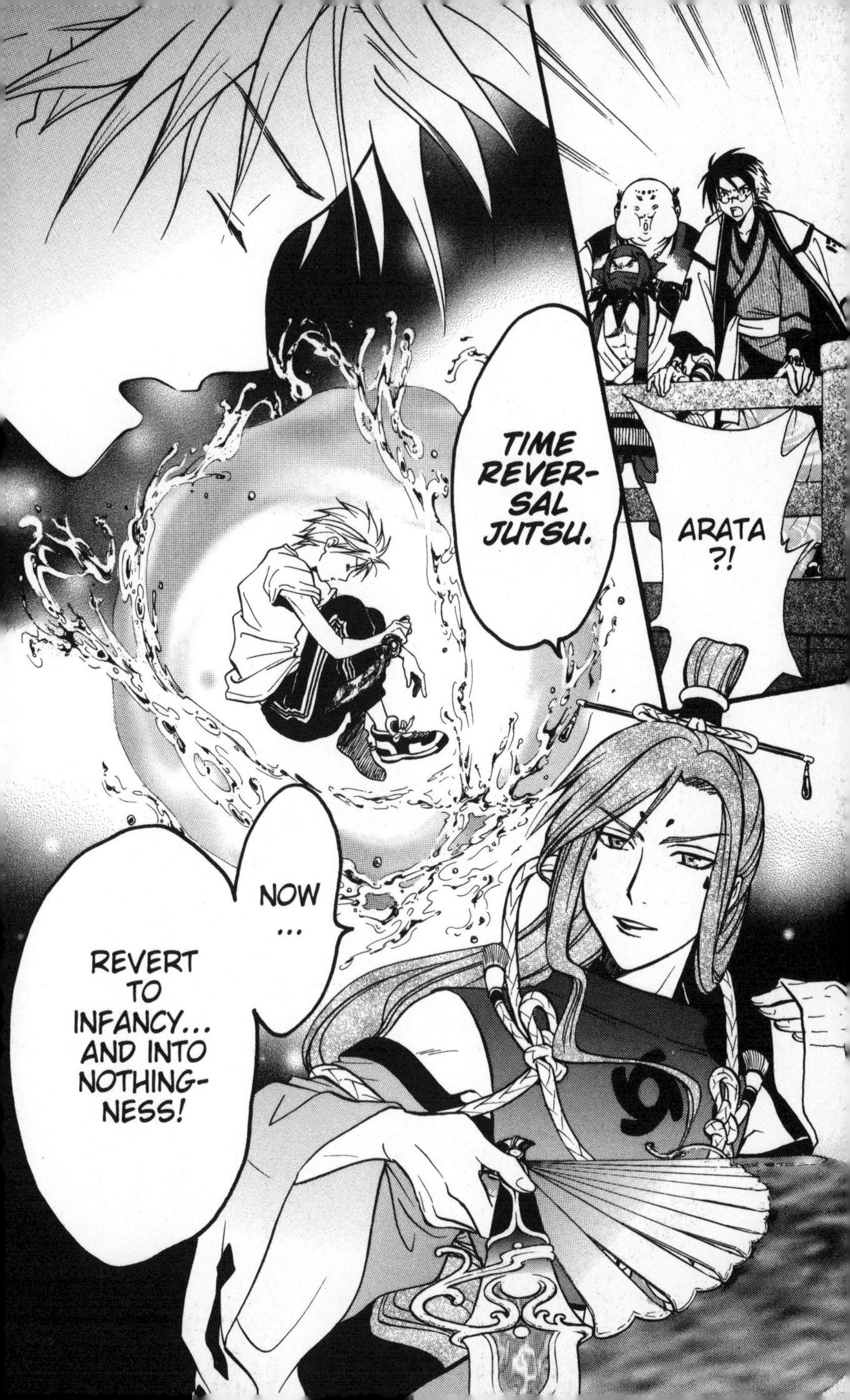
ARATA?!
TIME REVERSAL JUTSU.
NOW...
REVERT TO INFANCY... AND INTO NOTHINGNESS!

CHAPTER 60
TIME REVERSAL JUTSU

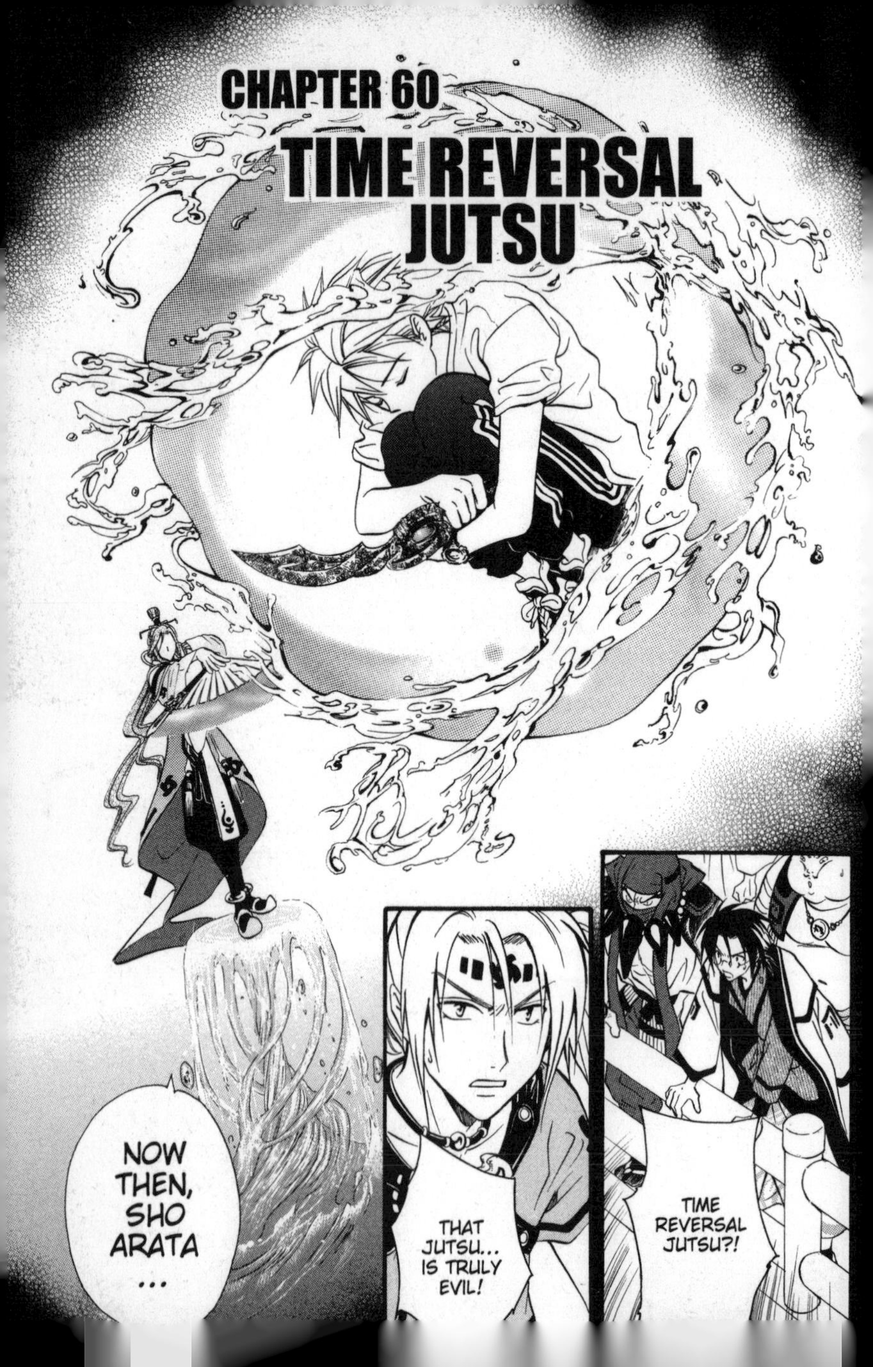
NOW THEN, SHO ARATA ...
TIME REVERSAL JUTSU?!
THAT JUTSU... IS TRULY EVIL!

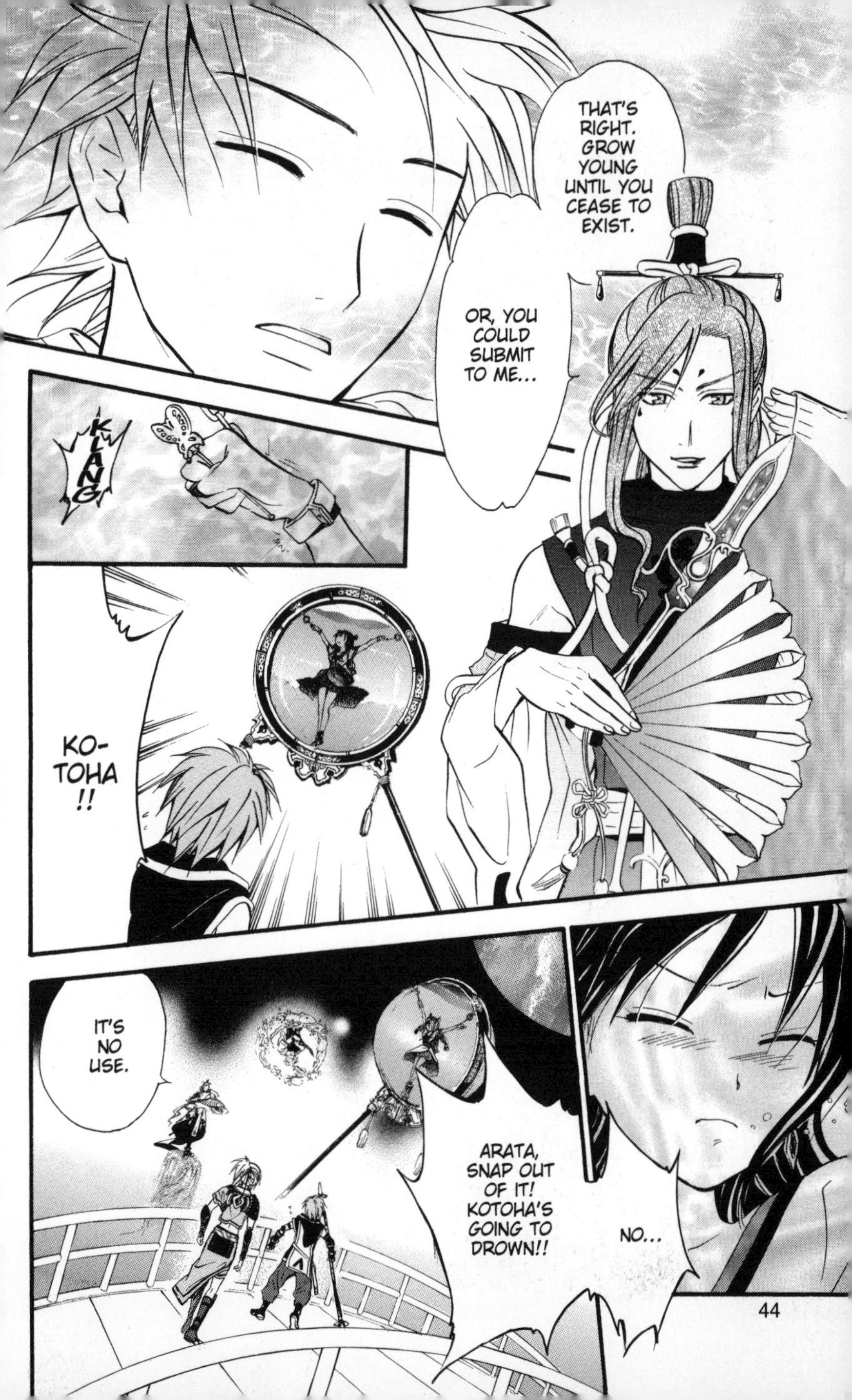
THAT'S RIGHT. GROW YOUNG UNTIL YOU CEASE TO EXIST.
OR, YOU COULD SUBMIT TO ME...
KLANG
KO-TOHA!!
NO...
ARATA, SNAP OUT OF IT! KOTOHA'S GOING TO DROWN!!
IT'S NO USE.

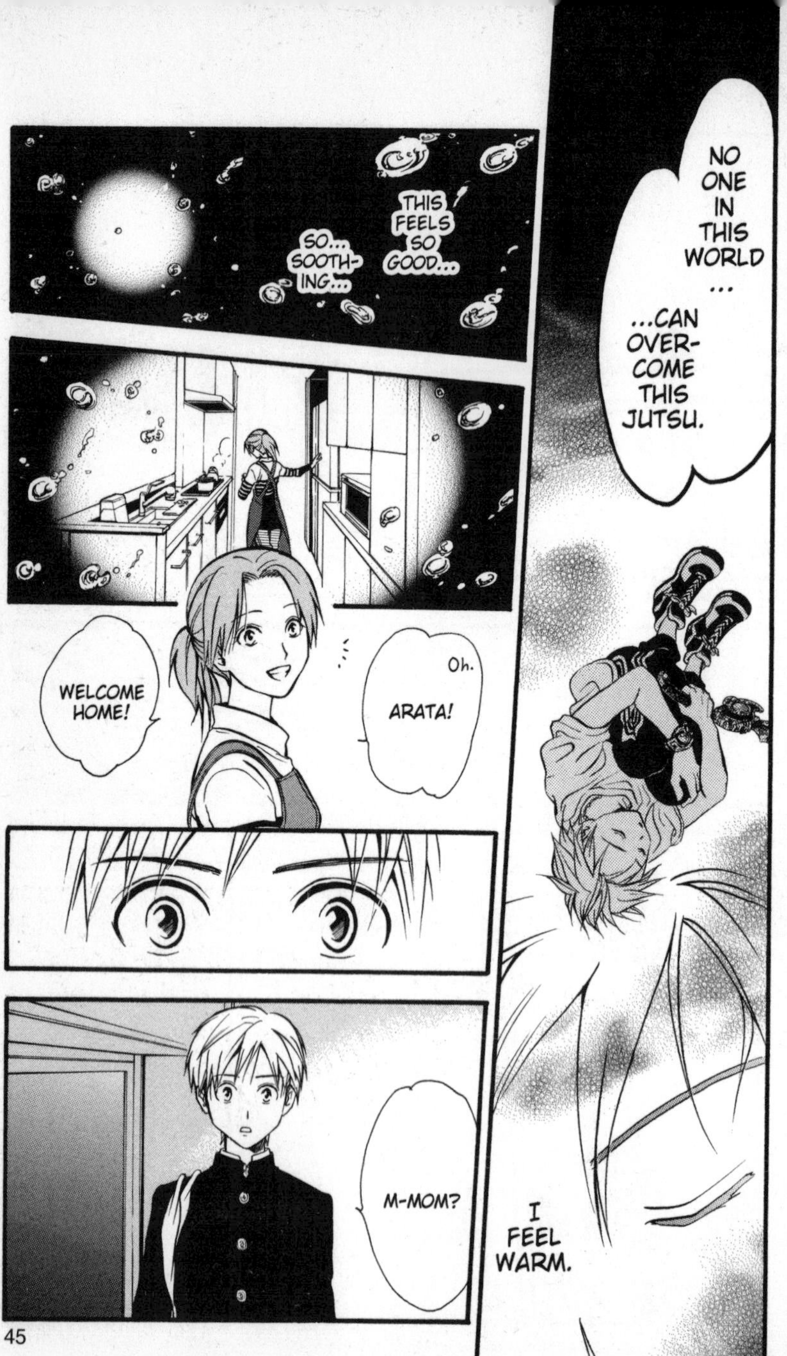
NO ONE IN THIS WORLD...
...CAN OVERCOME THIS JUTSU.
I FEEL WARM.
THIS FEELS SO GOOD...
SO... SOOTHING...
Oh. ARATA!
WELCOME HOME!
M-MOM?

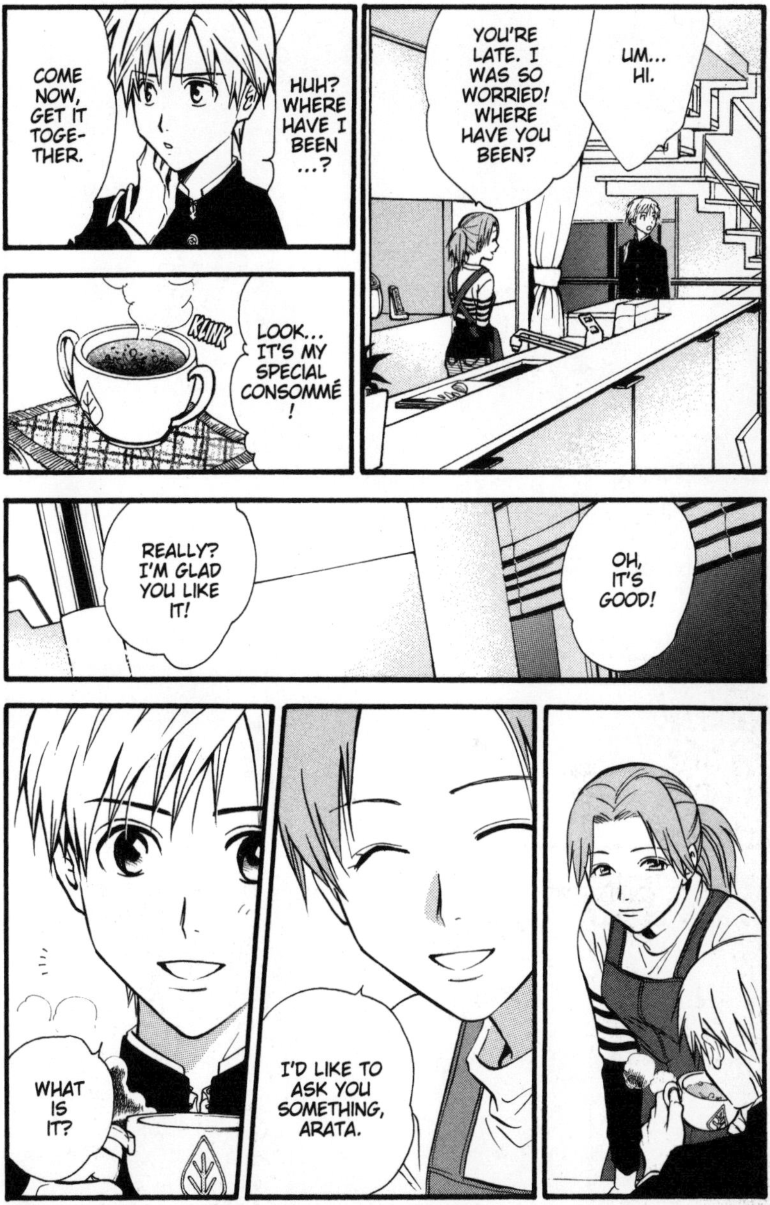
YOU'RE LATE. I WAS SO WORRIED! WHERE HAVE YOU BEEN?
UM... HI.
HUH? WHERE HAVE I BEEN ...?
COME NOW, GET IT TOGE-THER.
LOOK... IT'S MY SPECIAL CONSOMMÉ!
KLINK
OH, IT'S GOOD!
REALLY? I'M GLAD YOU LIKE IT!
I'D LIKE TO ASK YOU SOMETHING, ARATA.
WHAT IS IT?

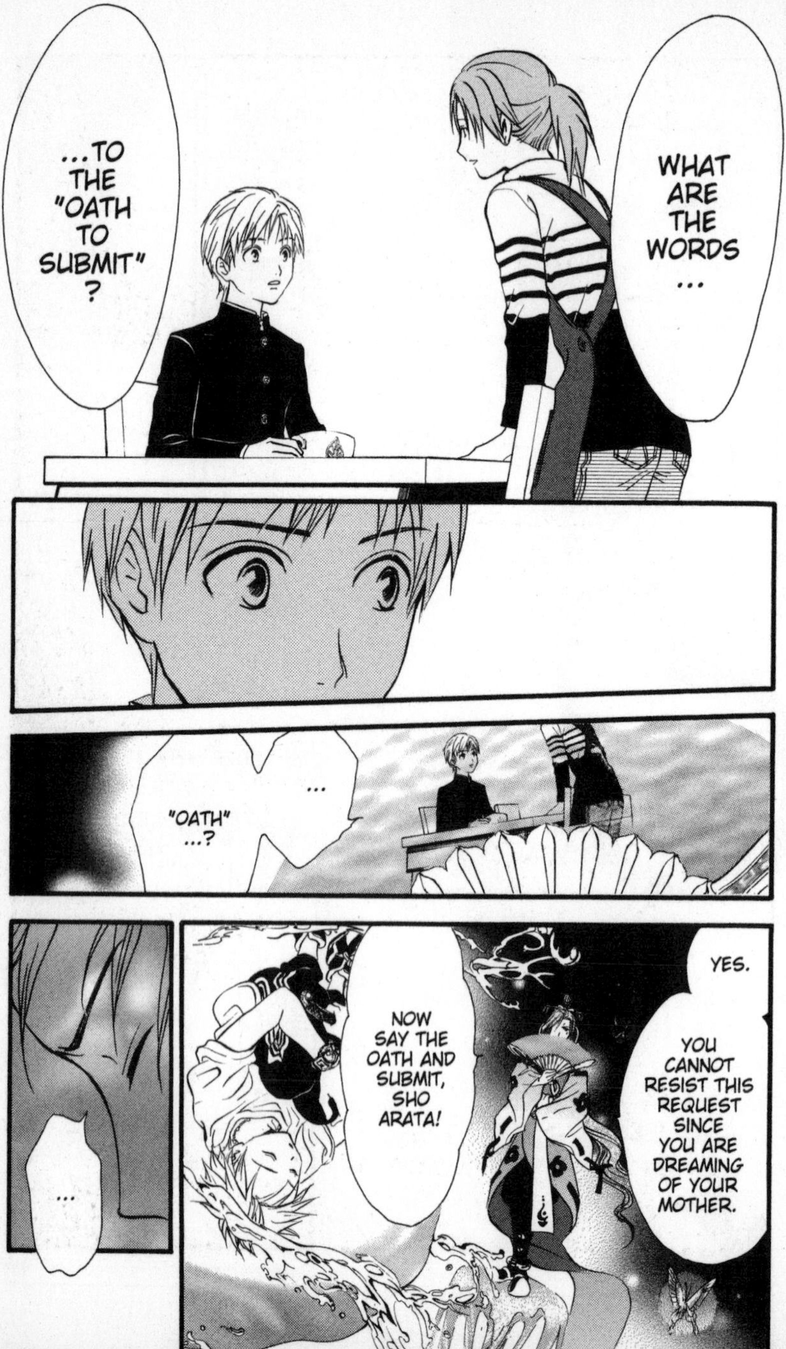
WHAT ARE THE WORDS...
...TO THE "OATH TO SUBMIT"?
...
"OATH" ...?
YES.
YOU CANNOT RESIST THIS REQUEST SINCE YOU ARE DREAMING OF YOUR MOTHER.
NOW SAY THE OATH AND SUBMIT, SHO ARATA!
...

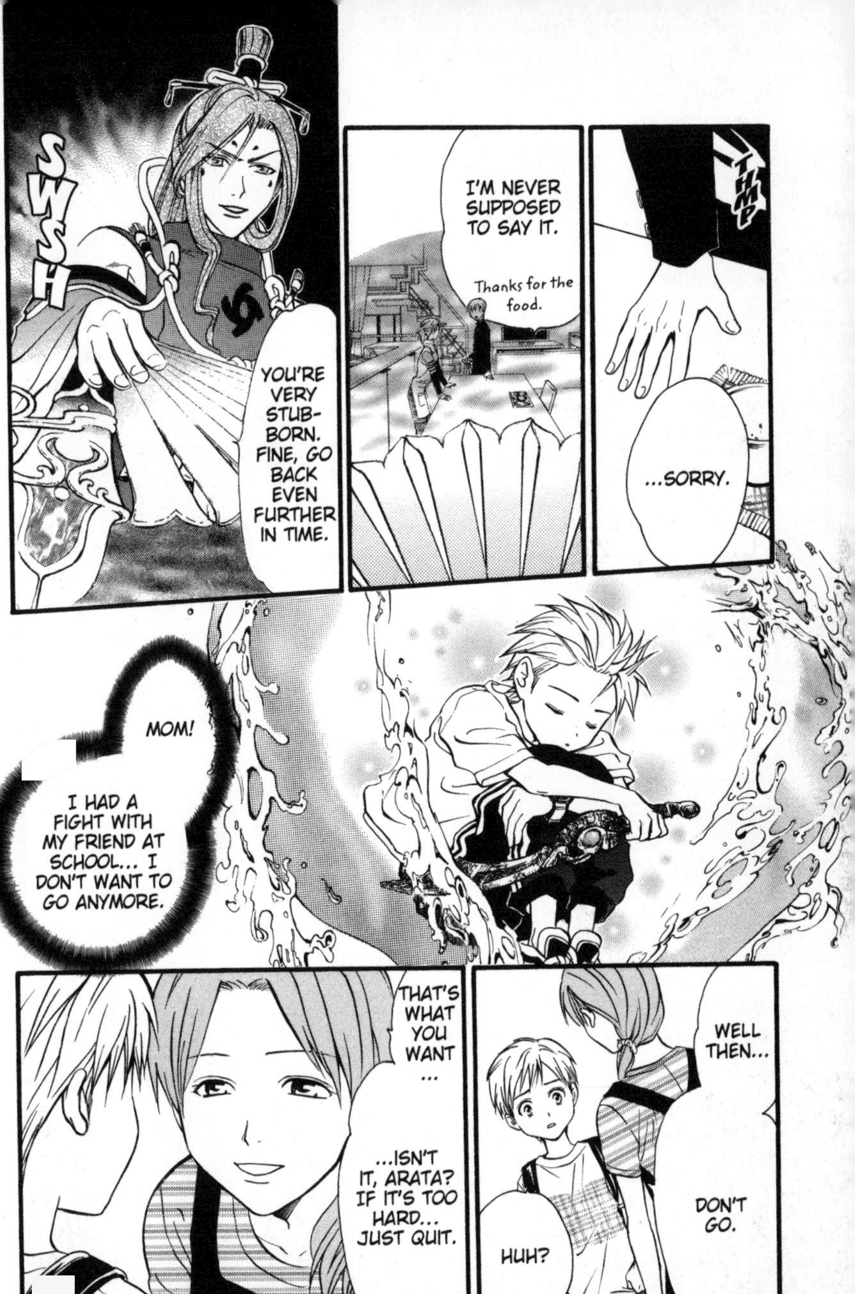
SWSH
YOU'RE VERY STUBBORN. FINE, GO BACK EVEN FURTHER IN TIME.
I'M NEVER SUPPOSED TO SAY IT.
Thanks for the food.
THMP
...SORRY.
MOM!
I HAD A FIGHT WITH MY FRIEND AT SCHOOL... I DON'T WANT TO GO ANYMORE.
THAT'S WHAT YOU WANT...
...ISN'T IT, ARATA? IF IT'S TOO HARD... JUST QUIT.
WELL THEN...
DON'T GO.
HUH?

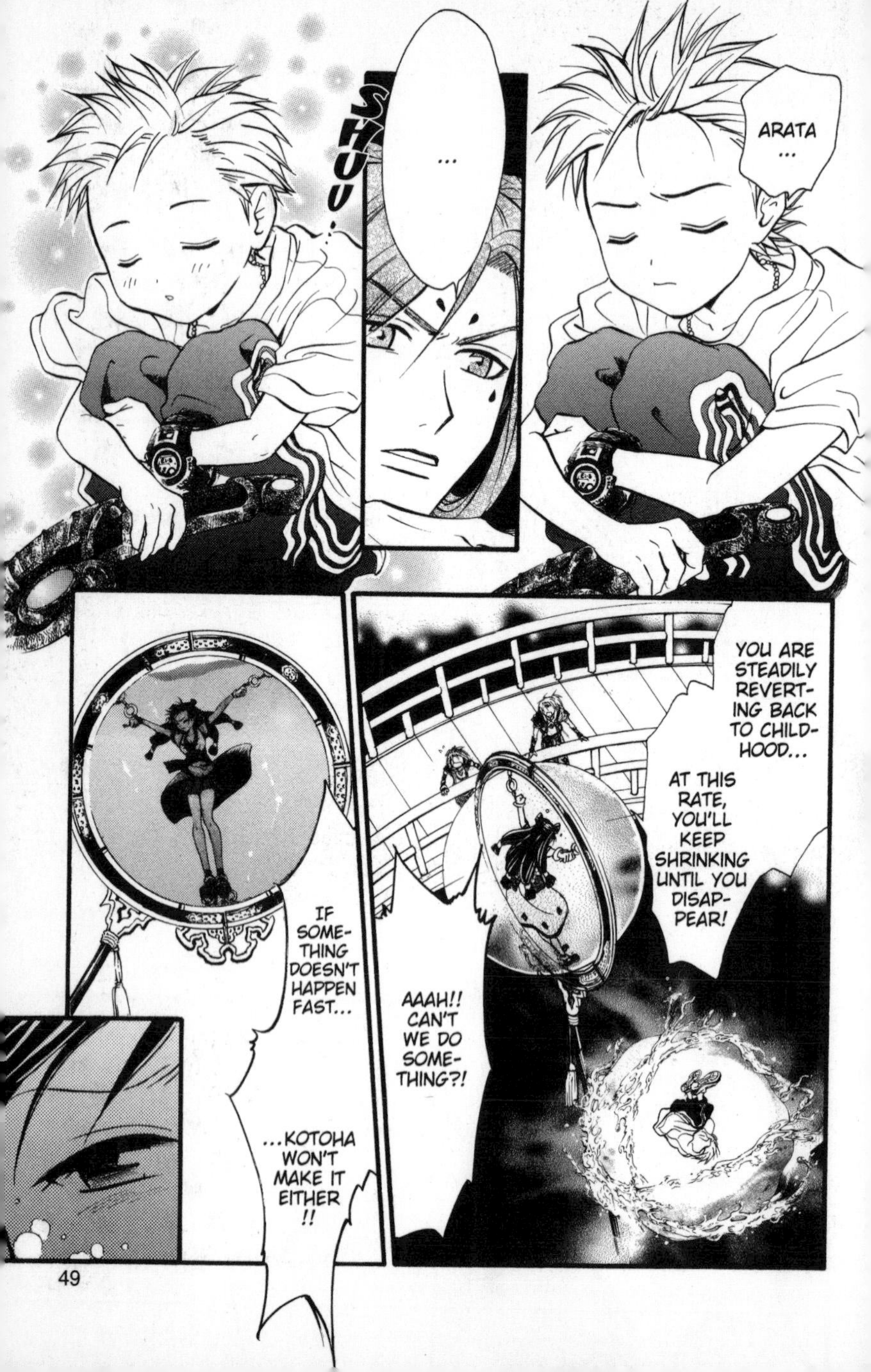
ARATA ...
SHUUU...
...
YOU ARE STEADILY REVERTING BACK TO CHILDHOOD...
AT THIS RATE, YOU'LL KEEP SHRINKING UNTIL YOU DISAPPEAR!
AAAH!! CAN'T WE DO SOMETHING?!
IF SOMETHING DOESN'T HAPPEN FAST...
...KOTOHA WON'T MAKE IT EITHER !!

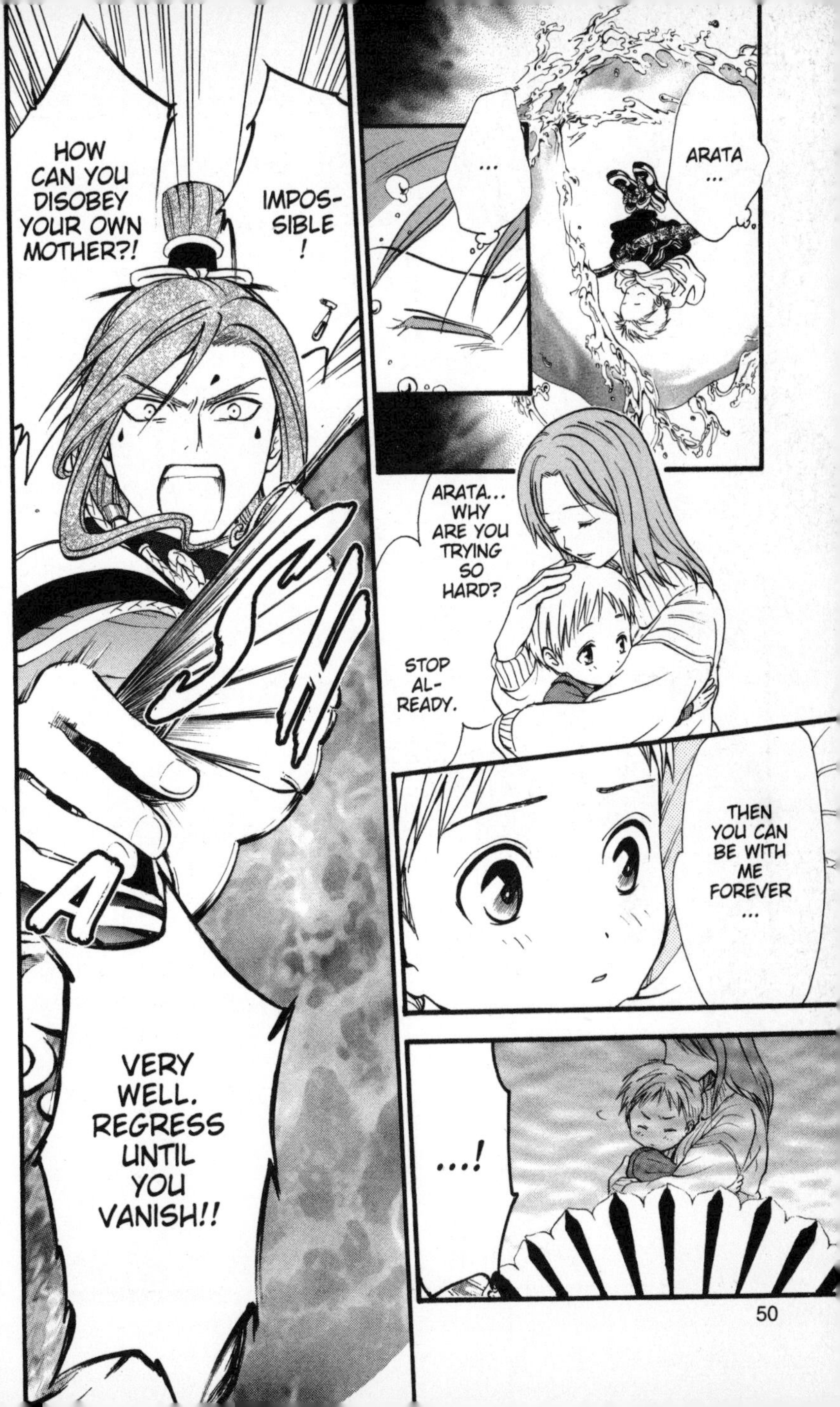
ARATA ...
...
ARATA... WHY ARE YOU TRYING SO HARD?
STOP AL-READY.
THEN YOU CAN BE WITH ME FOREVER ...
...!
IMPOS-SIBLE!
HOW CAN YOU DISOBEY YOUR OWN MOTHER?!
VERY WELL. REGRESS UNTIL YOU VANISH!!

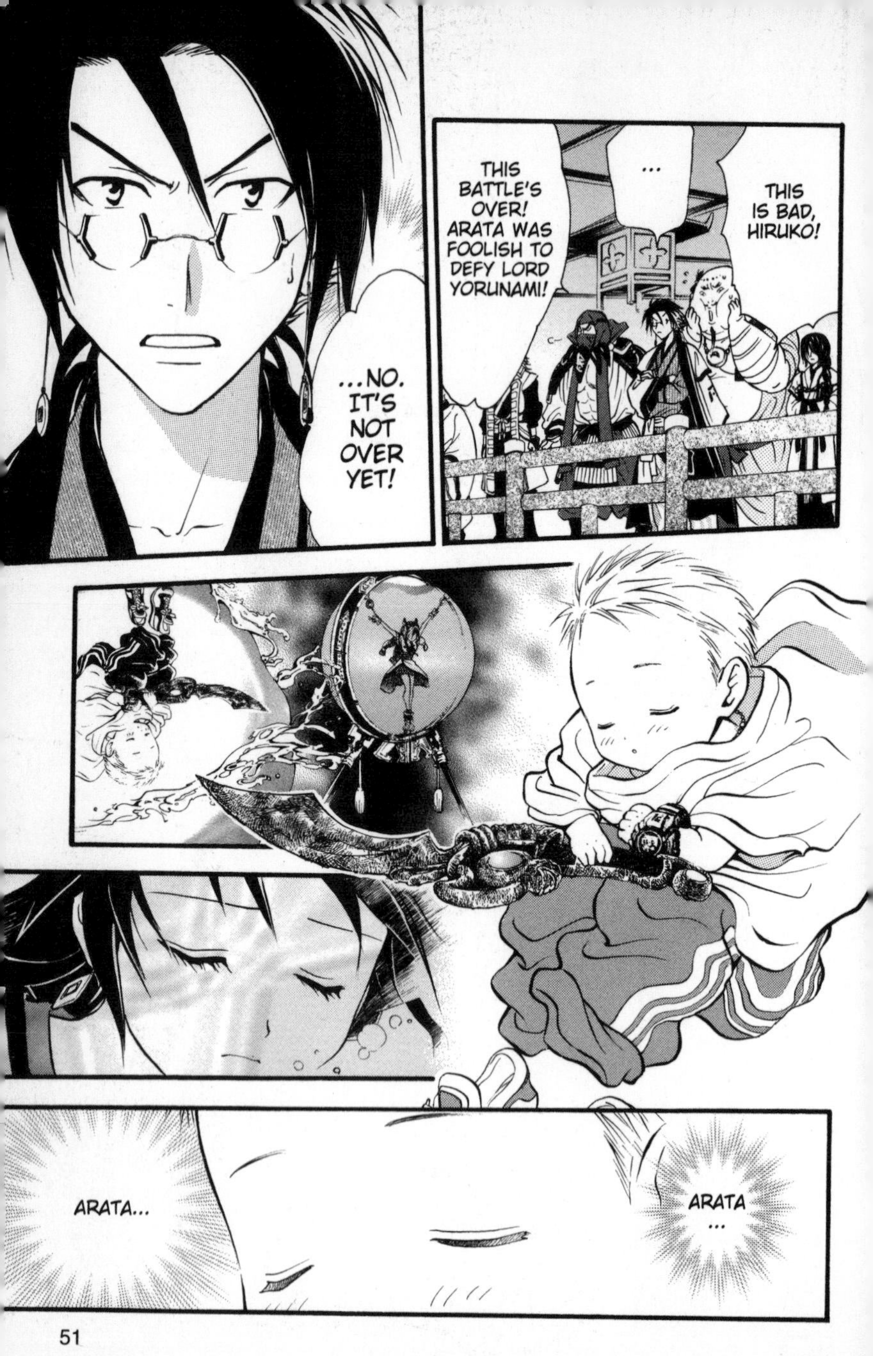
THIS IS BAD, HIRUKO!
...
THIS BATTLE'S OVER! ARATA WAS FOOLISH TO DEFY LORD YORUNAMI!
...NO. IT'S NOT OVER YET!
ARATA ...
ARATA...

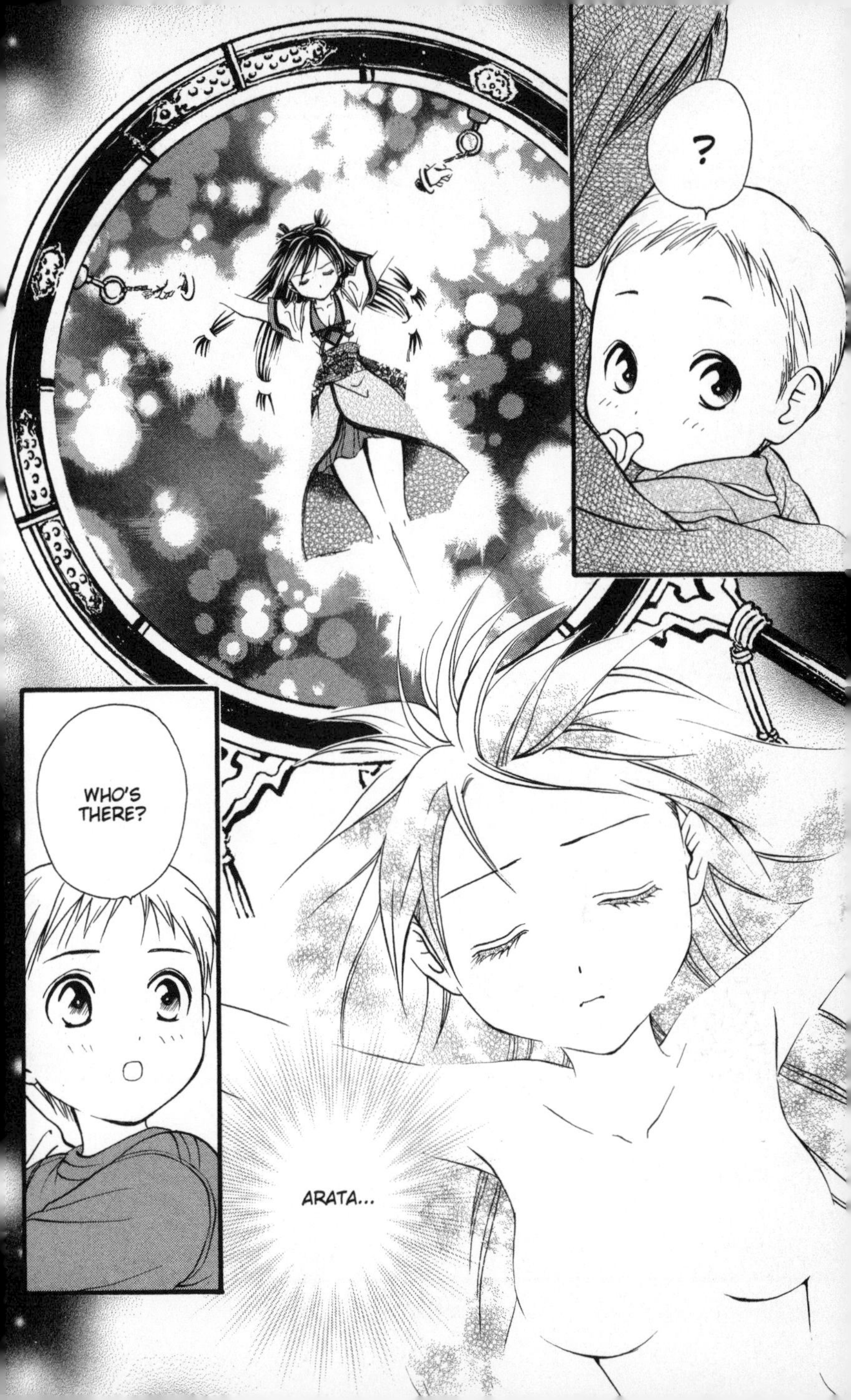
?
WHO'S THERE?
ARATA...

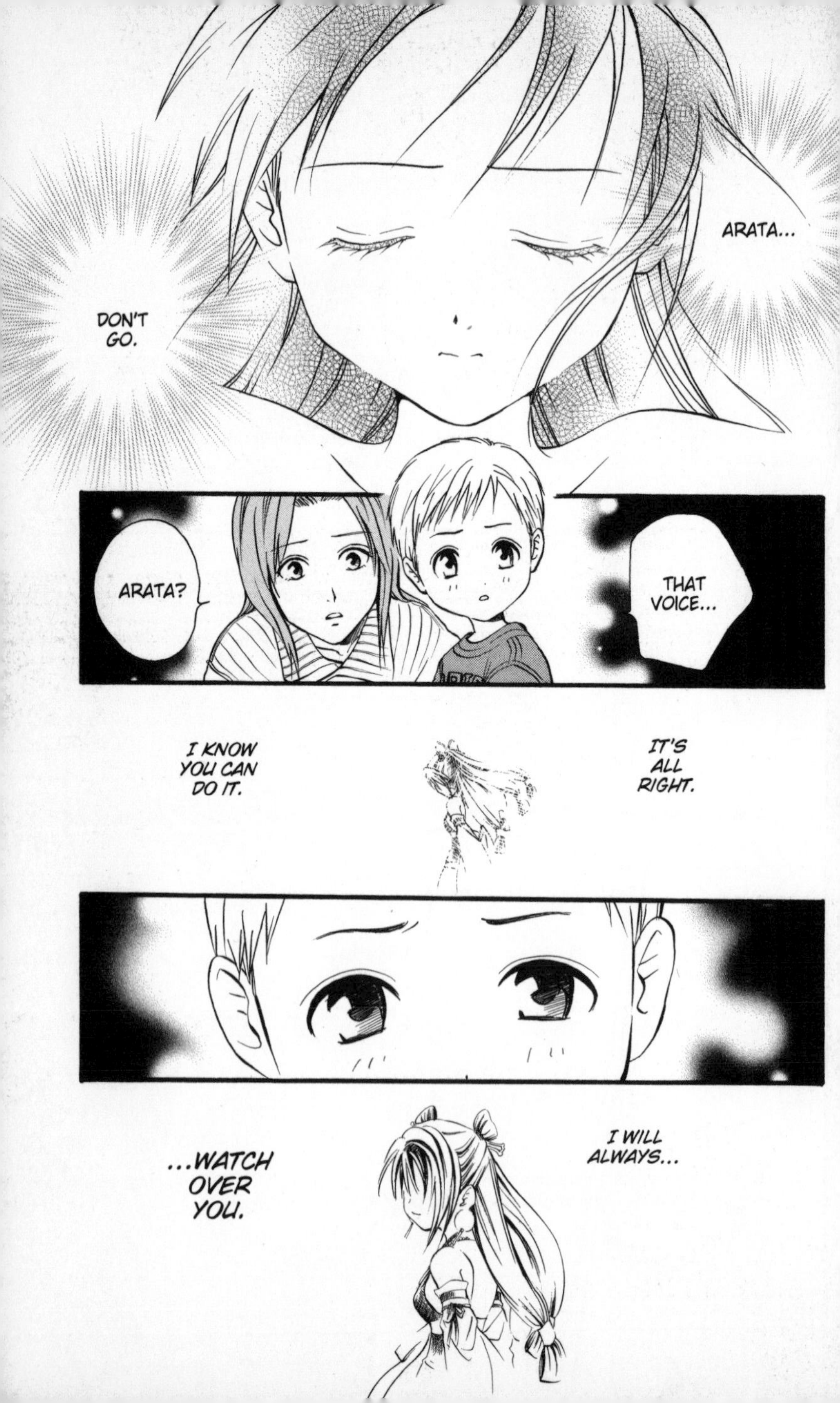
ARATA...
DON'T GO.
THAT VOICE...
ARATA?
IT'S ALL RIGHT.
I KNOW YOU CAN DO IT.
I WILL ALWAYS...
...WATCH OVER YOU.

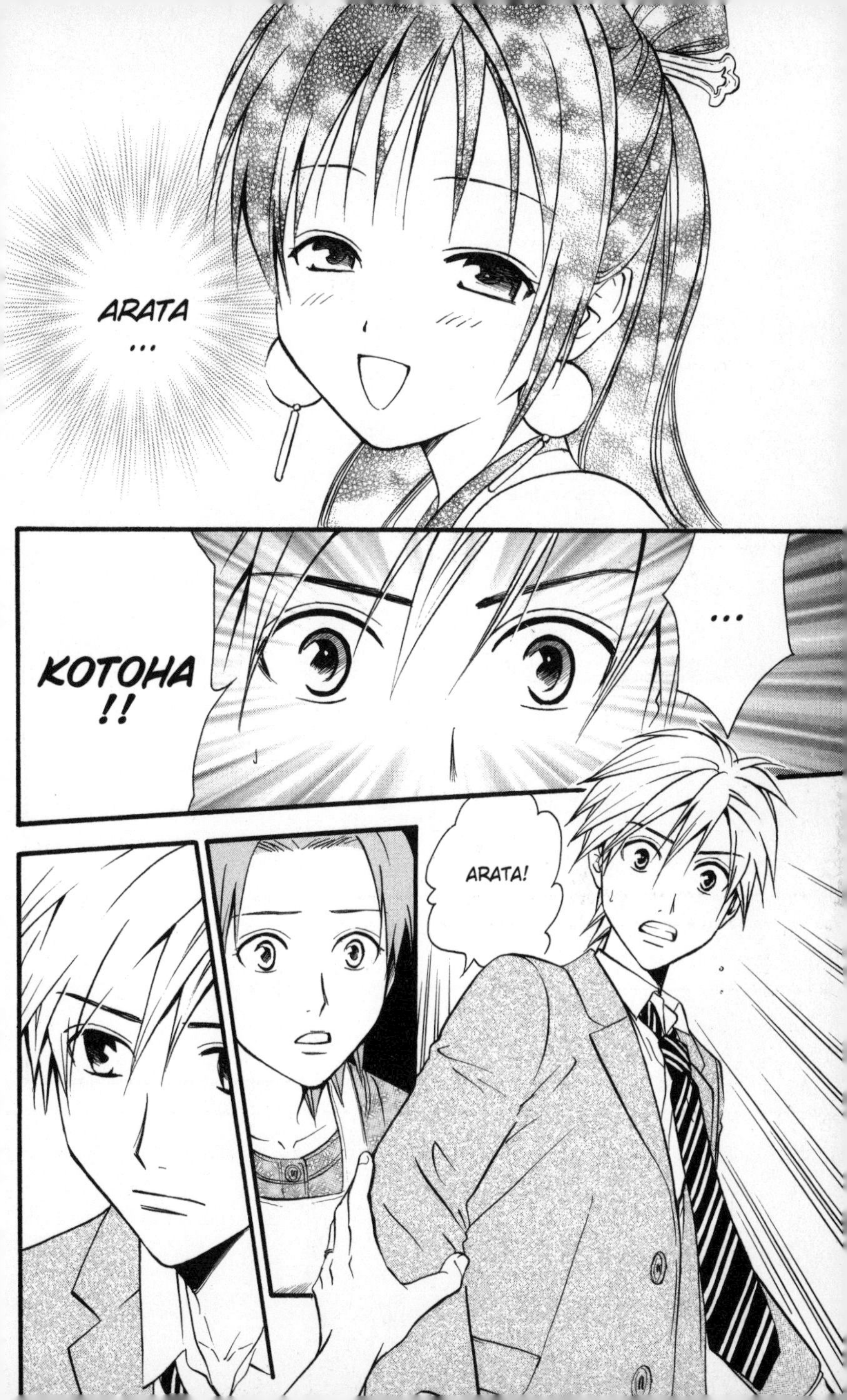
ARATA ...
...
KOTOHA !!
ARATA!

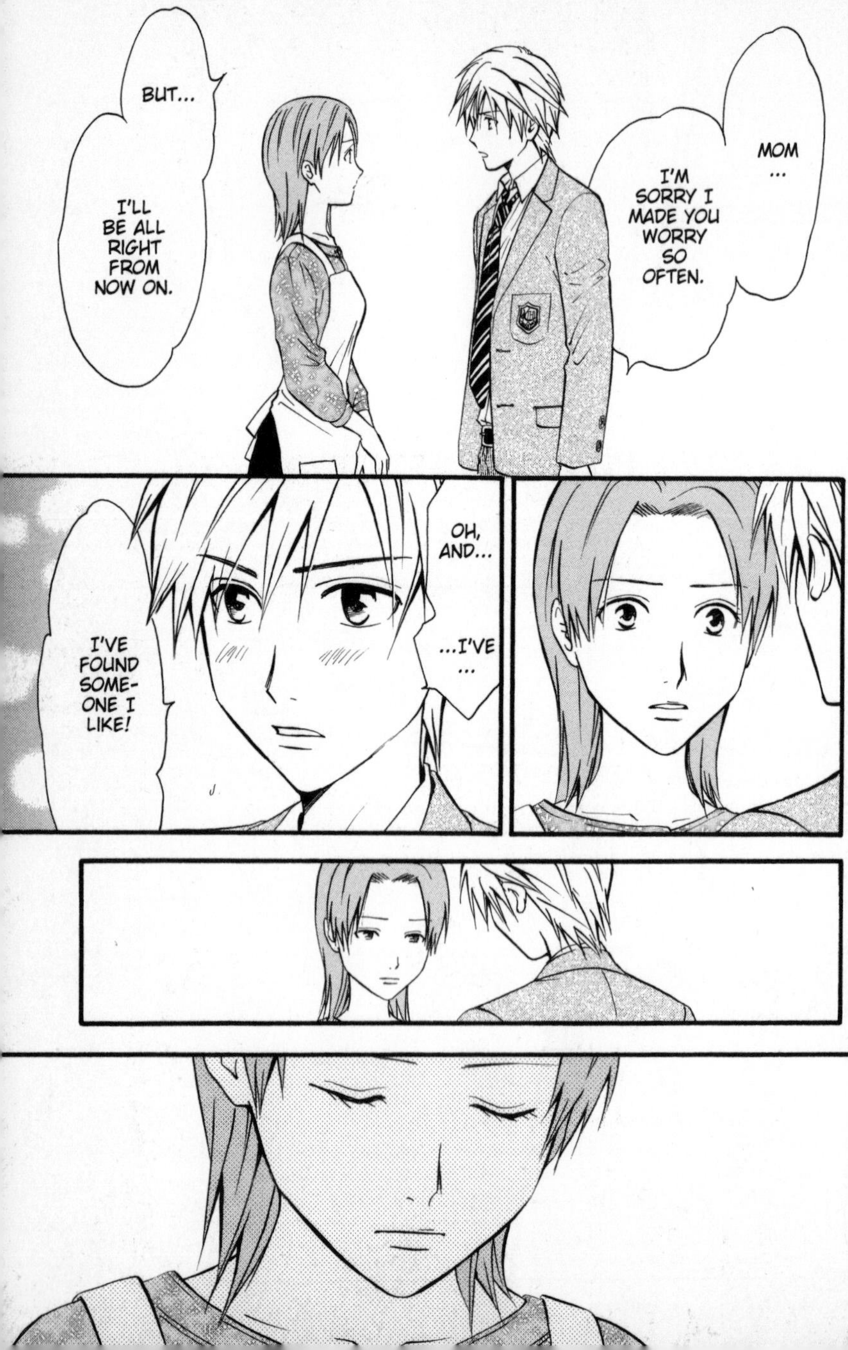
MOM ...
I'M SORRY I MADE YOU WORRY SO OFTEN.
BUT...
I'LL BE ALL RIGHT FROM NOW ON.
OH, AND...
...I'VE ...
I'VE FOUND SOME-ONE I LIKE!

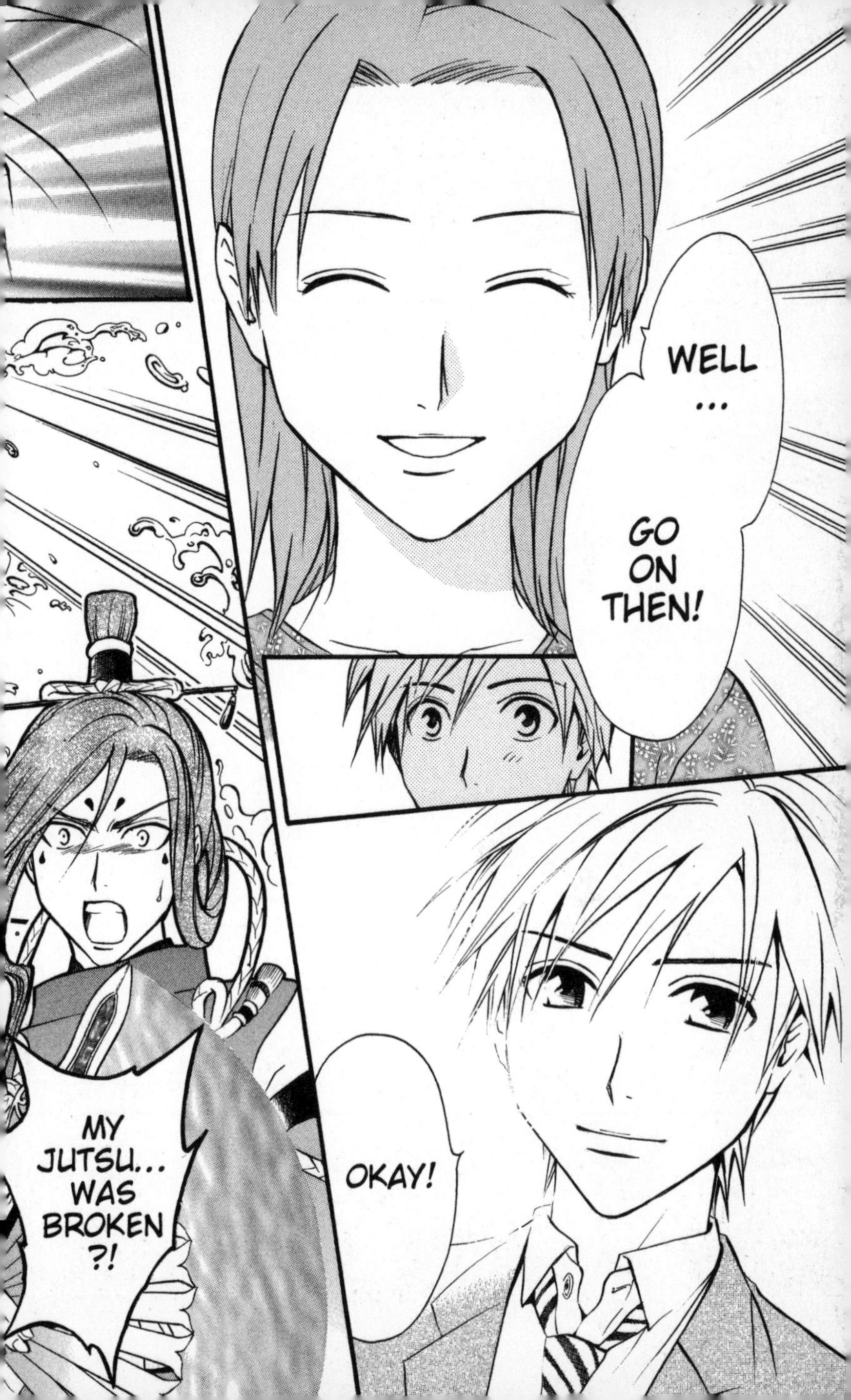
WELL ...
GO ON THEN!
OKAY!
MY JUTSU... WAS BROKEN ?!

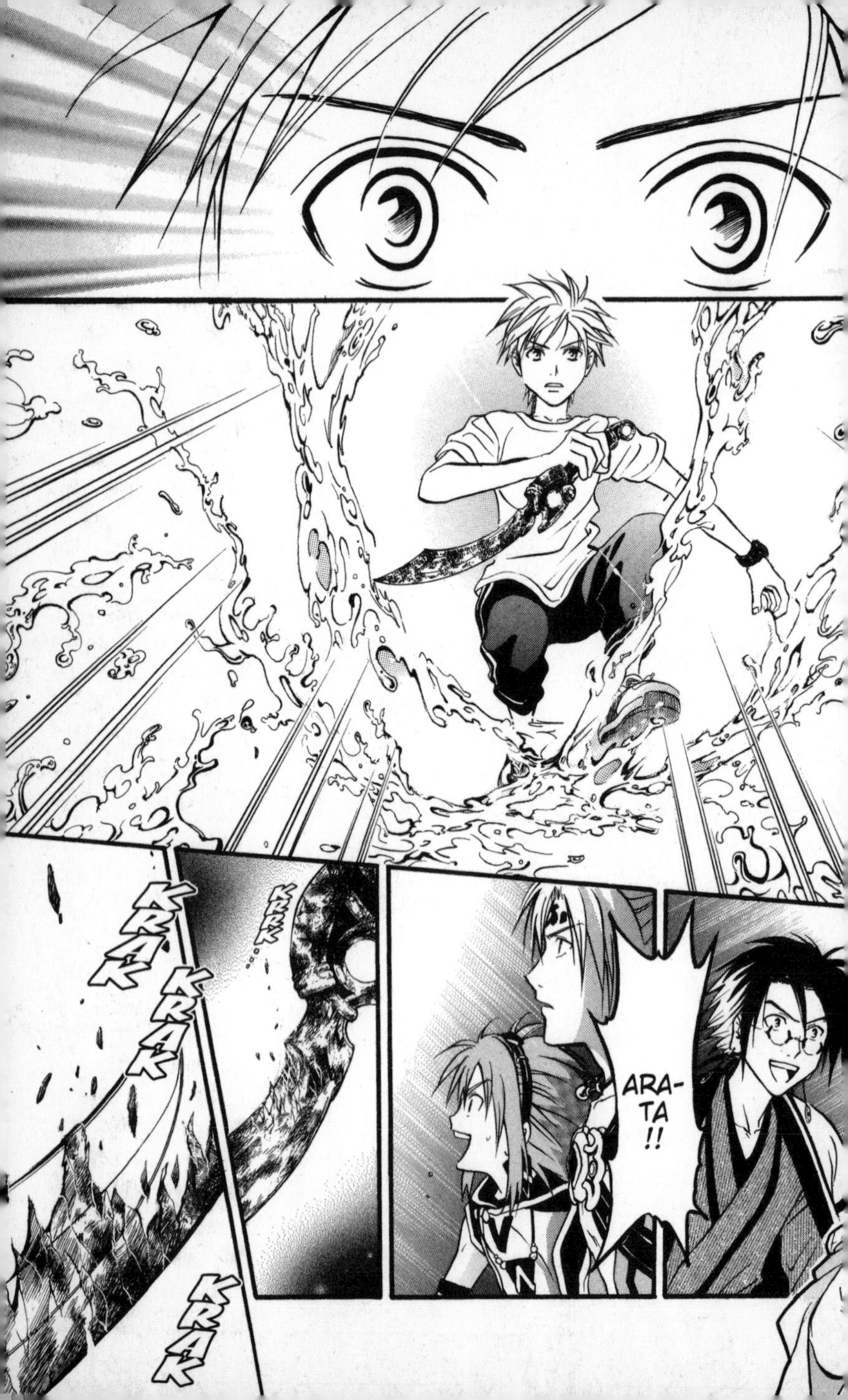
ARA-
TA
!!
KRAK...
KRAK
KRAK
KRAK

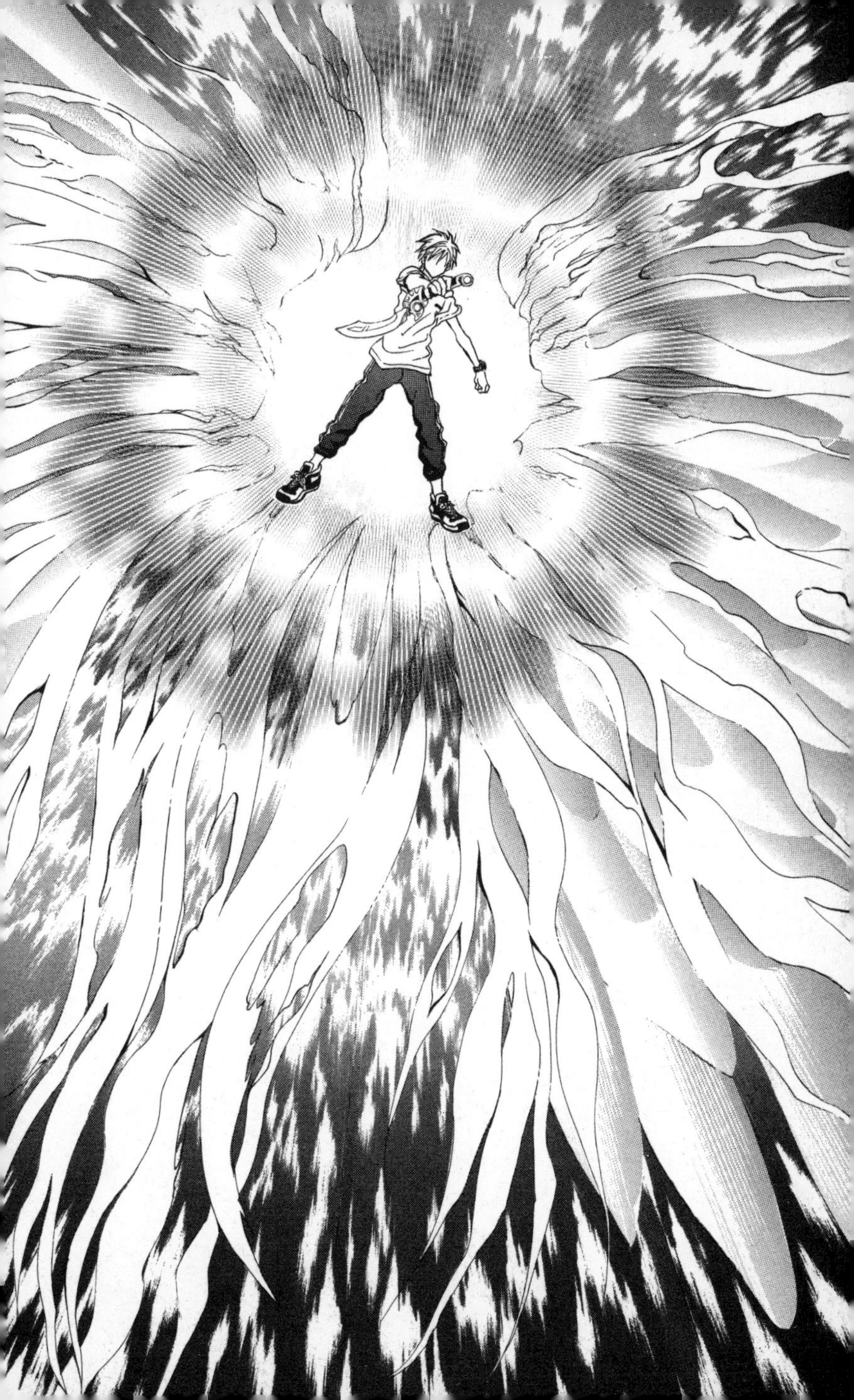

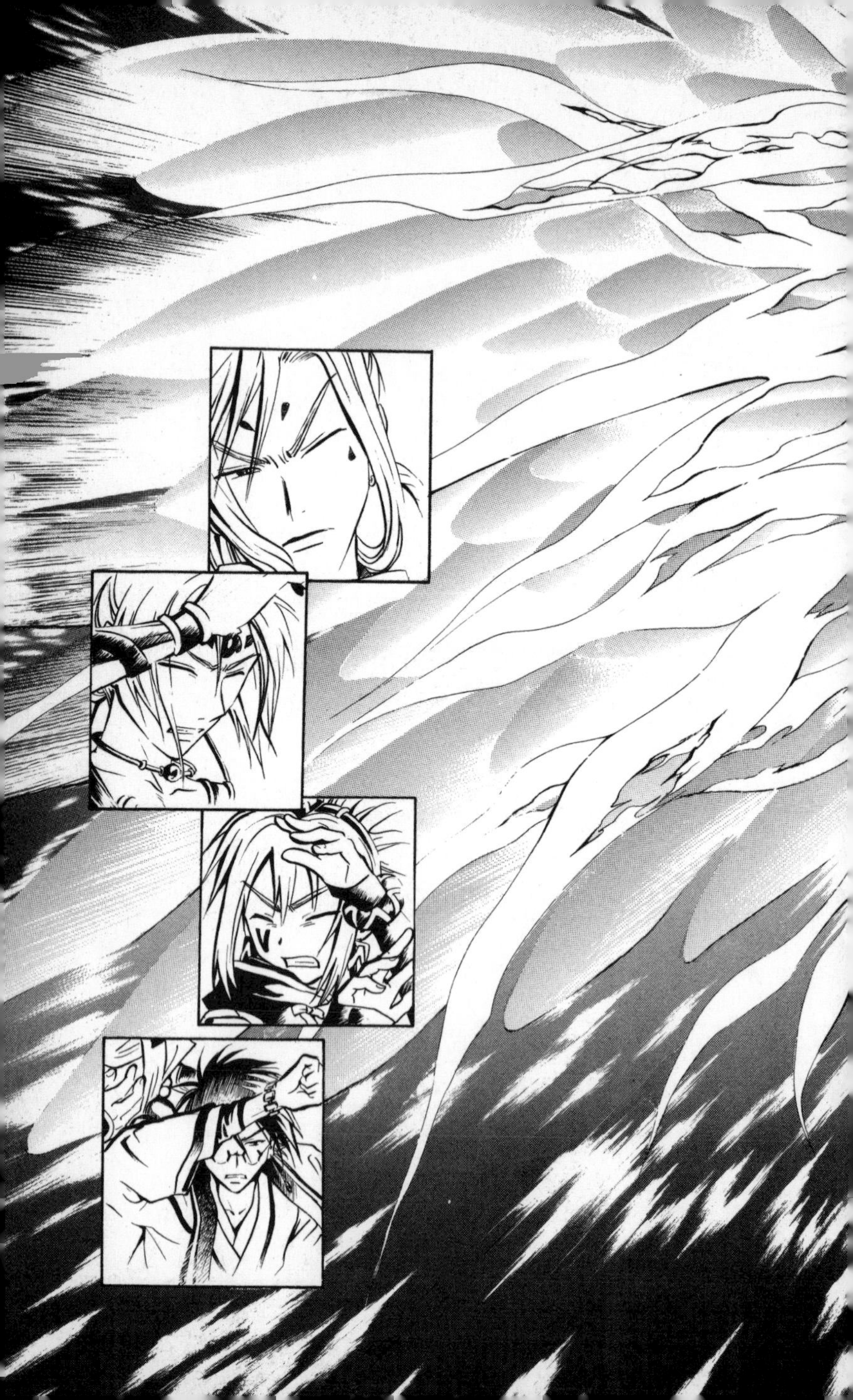

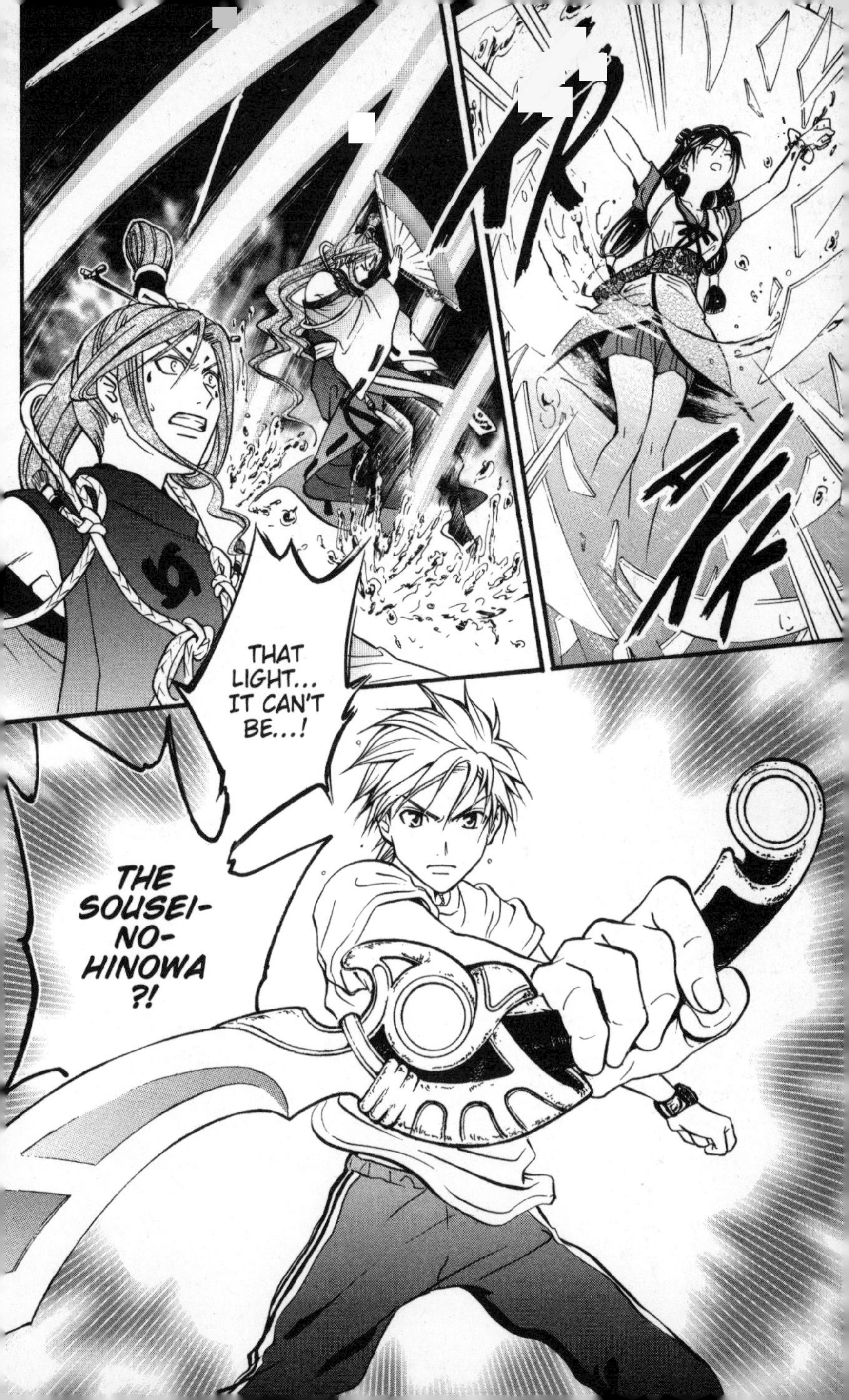
THAT LIGHT... IT CAN'T BE...!
THE SOUSEI-NO-HINOWA?!

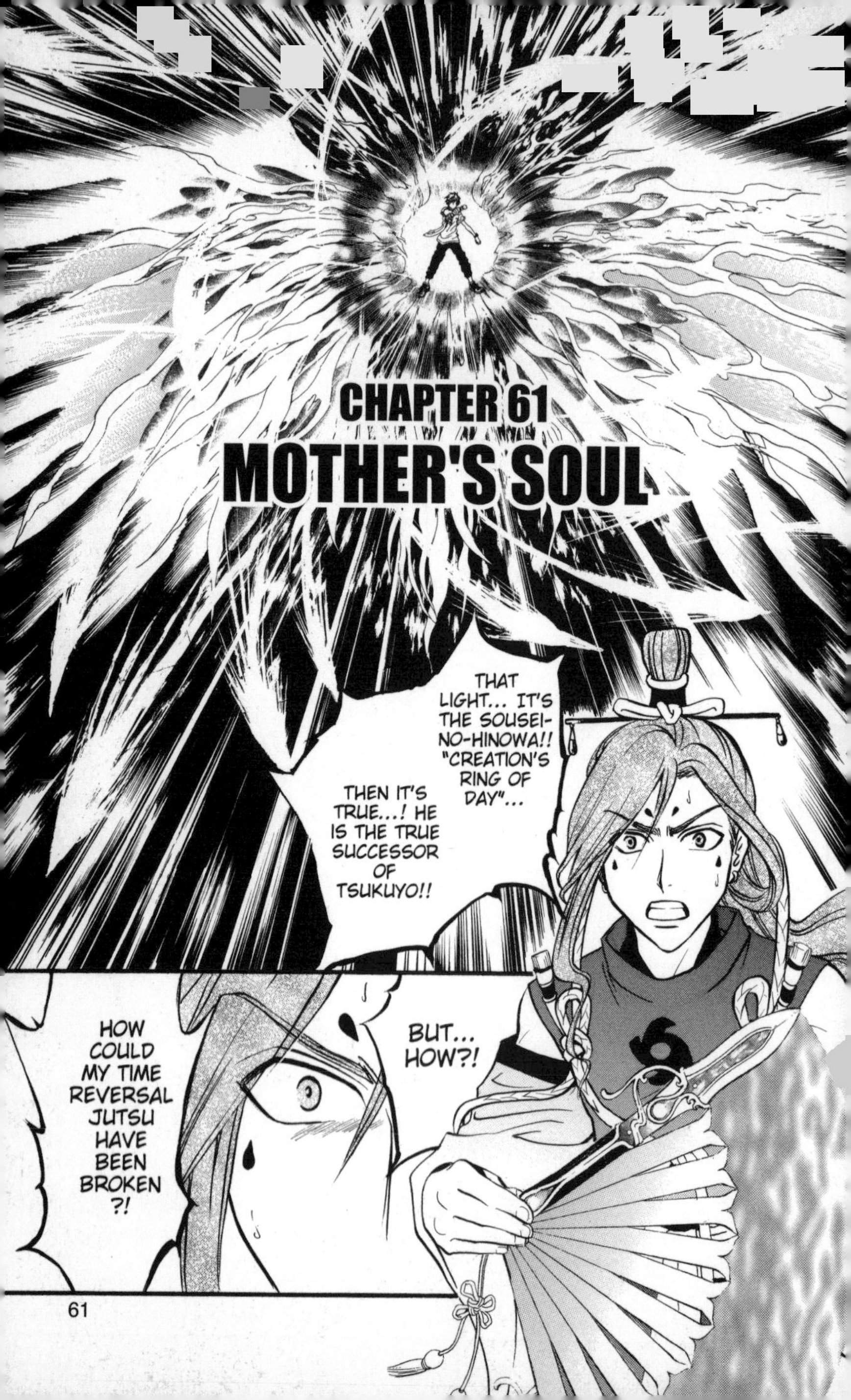
CHAPTER 61
MOTHER'S SOUL
THAT LIGHT... IT'S THE SOUSEI-NO-HINOWA!! "CREATION'S RING OF DAY"...
THEN IT'S TRUE...! HE IS THE TRUE SUCCESSOR OF TSUKUYO!!
BUT... HOW?!
HOW COULD MY TIME REVERSAL JUTSU HAVE BEEN BROKEN?!

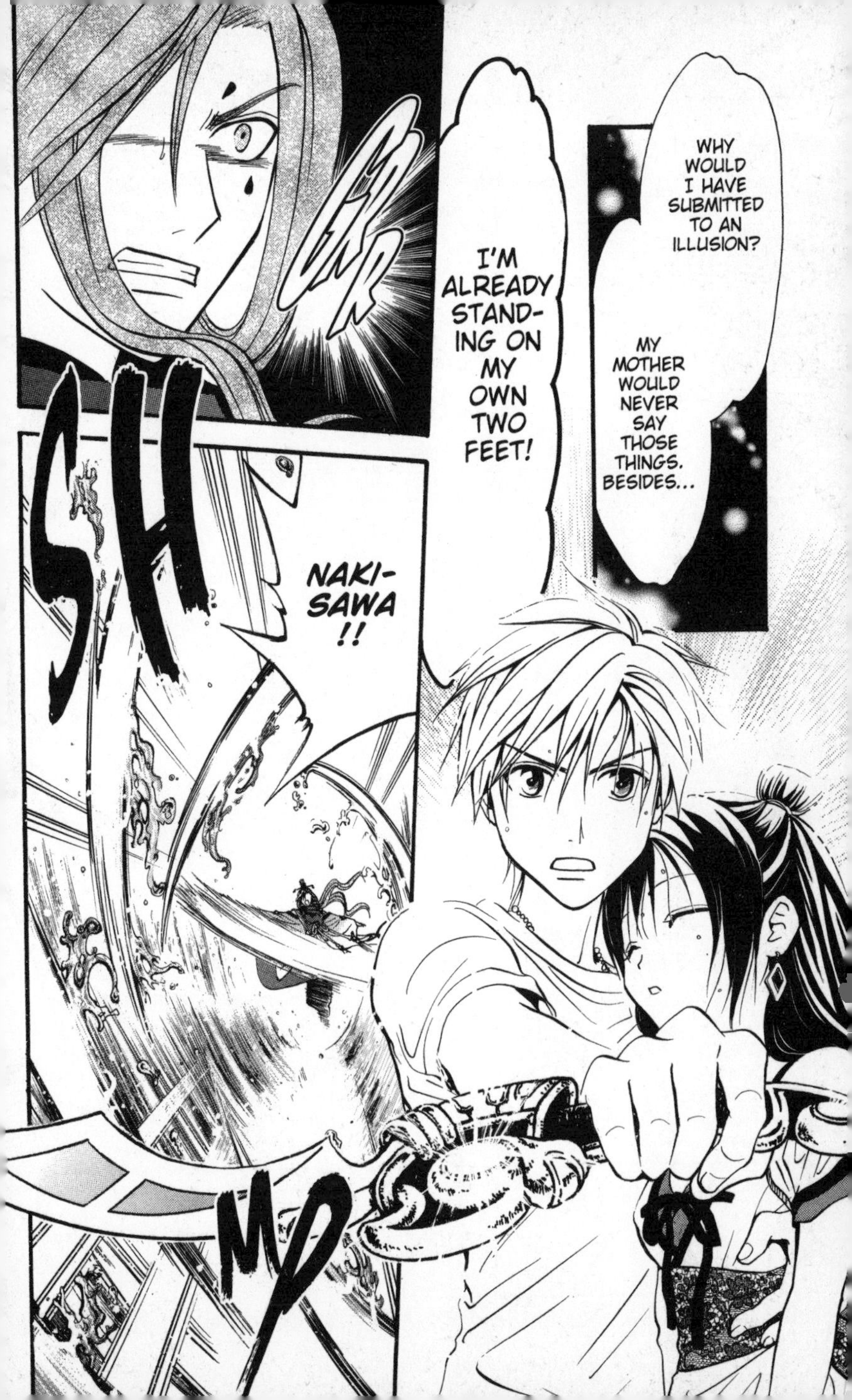
WHY WOULD I HAVE SUBMITTED TO AN ILLUSION?
MY MOTHER WOULD NEVER SAY THOSE THINGS. BESIDES...
I'M ALREADY STANDING ON MY OWN TWO FEET!
NAKI-SAWA!!
SH
MP

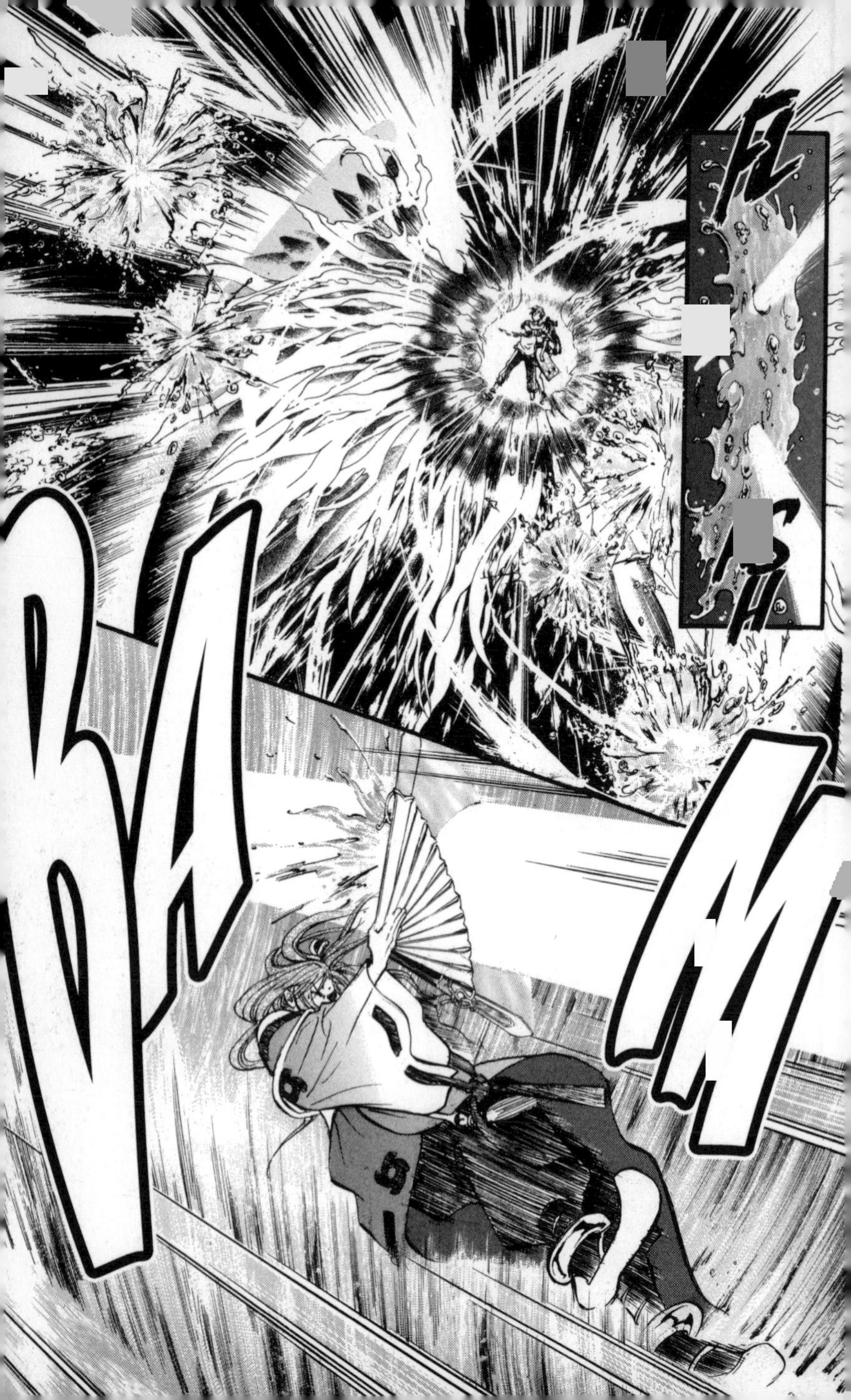
FL
SH
BA
M

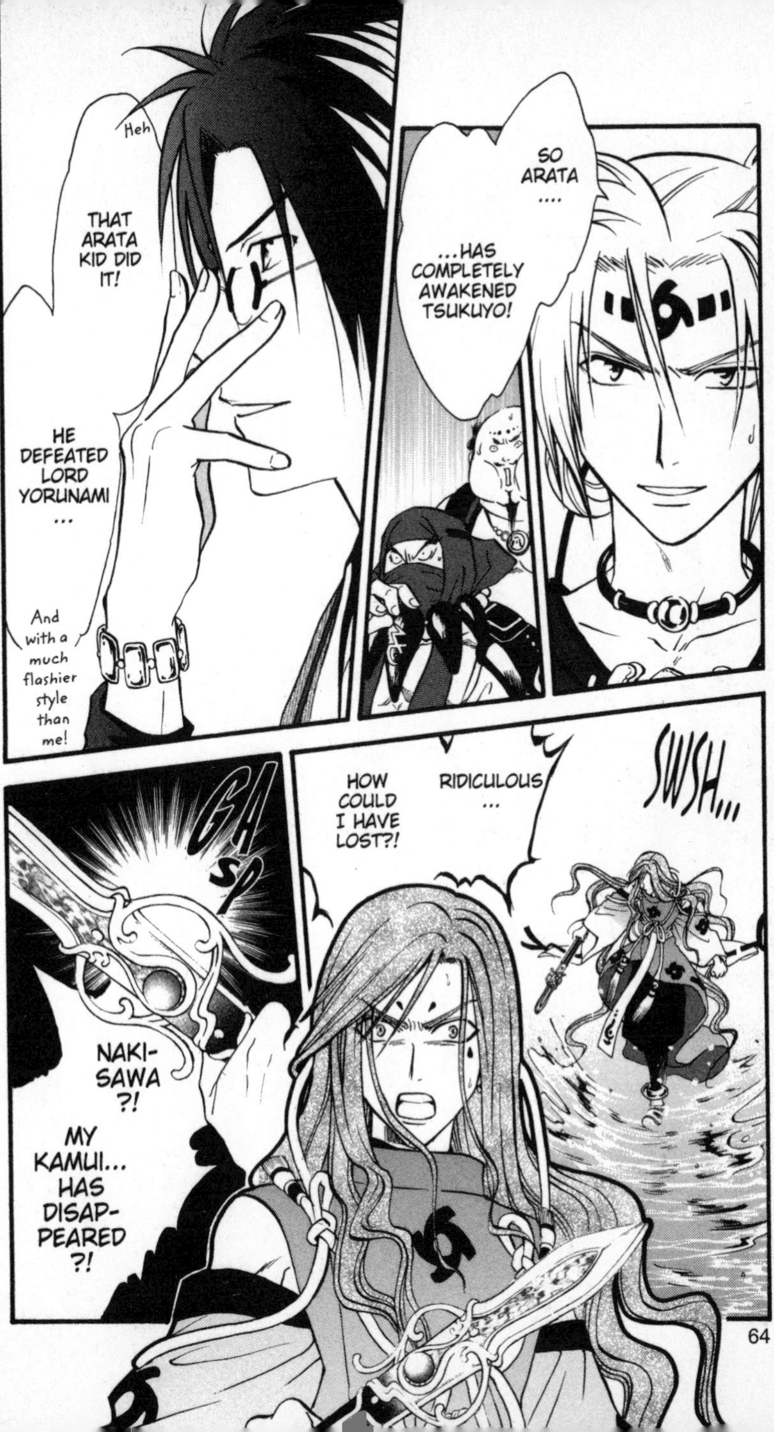
SO ARATA ....
...HAS COMPLETELY AWAKENED TSUKUYO!
Heh
THAT ARATA KID DID IT!
HE DEFEATED LORD YORUNAMI ...
And with a much flashier style than me!
SWSH...
RIDICULOUS ...
HOW COULD I HAVE LOST?!
GASP
NAKI-SAWA ?!
MY KAMUI... HAS DISAP-PEARED ?!

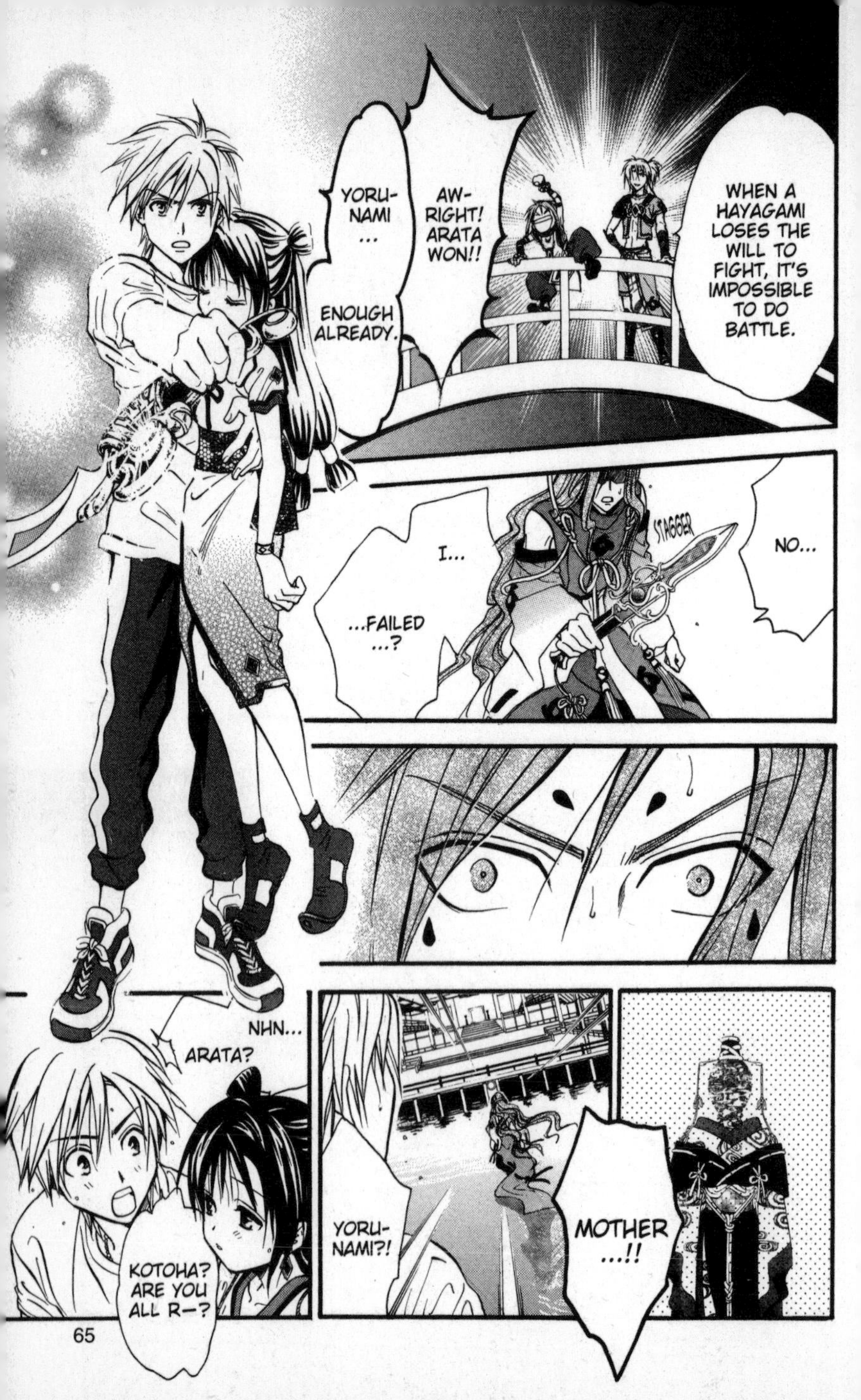

WHEN A HAYAGAMI LOSES THE WILL TO FIGHT, IT'S IMPOSSIBLE TO DO BATTLE.
AW-RIGHT! ARATA WON!!
NO...
STAGGER
I...
...FAILED ...?
YORU-NAMI ...
ENOUGH ALREADY.
MOTHER ...!!
YORU-NAMI?!
NHN...
ARATA?
KOTOHA? ARE YOU ALL R—?

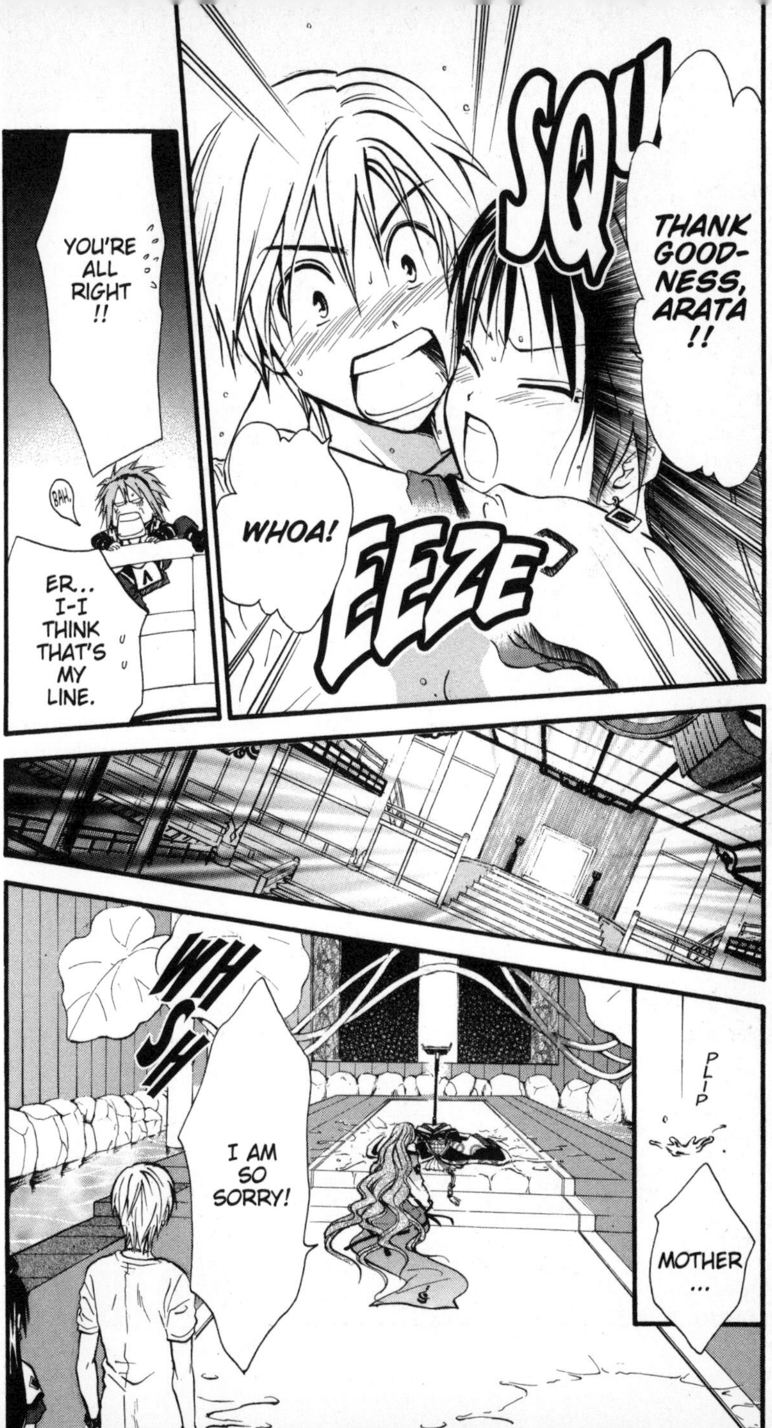
SQ
THANK GOODNESS, ARATA!!
WHOA!
EEZE
YOU'RE ALL RIGHT!!
BAH.
ER... I-I THINK THAT'S MY LINE.
PLIP
MOTHER...
WHSH
I AM SO SORRY!

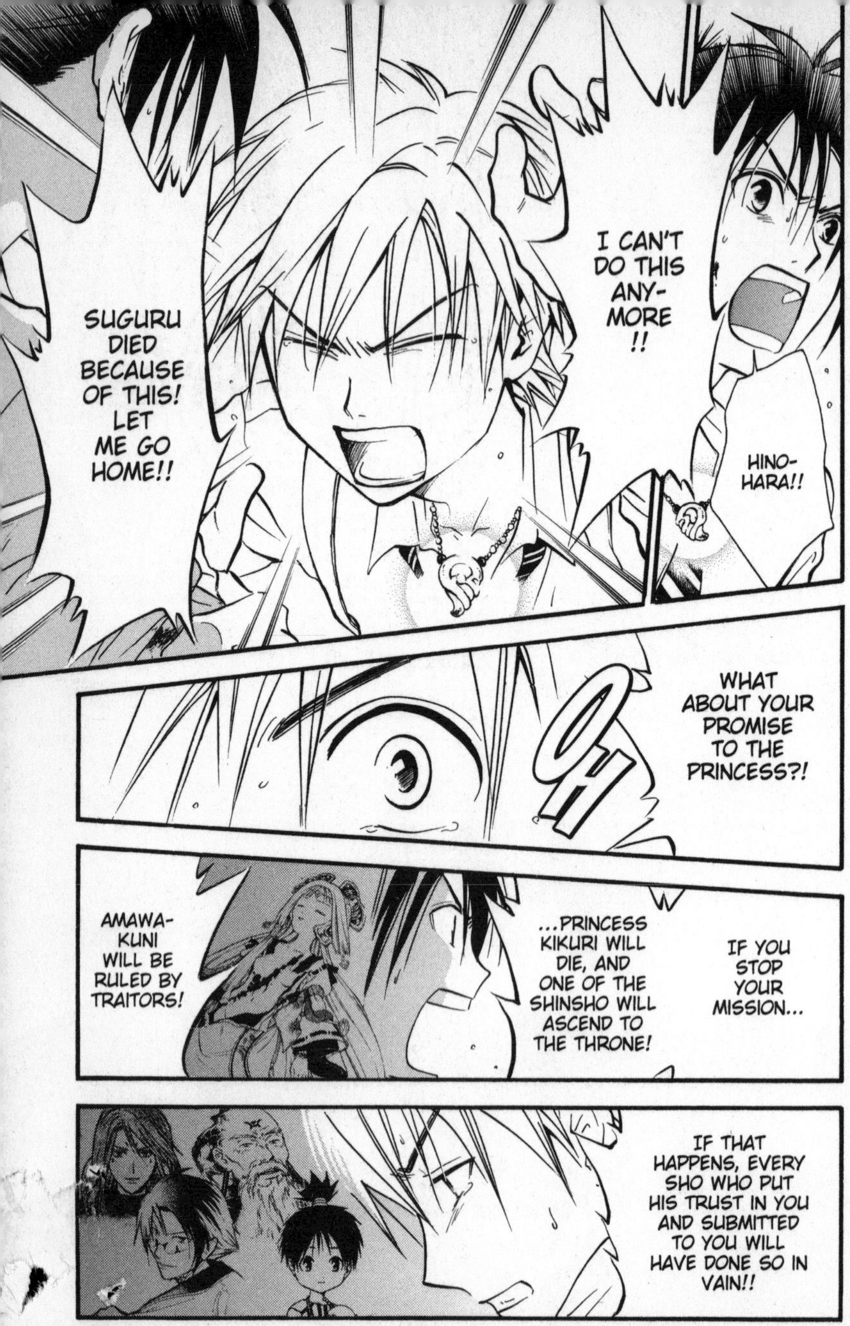
I CAN'T DO THIS ANY-MORE!!
SUGURU DIED BECAUSE OF THIS! LET ME GO HOME!!
HINO-HARA!!
WHAT ABOUT YOUR PROMISE TO THE PRINCESS?!
IF YOU STOP YOUR MISSION...
...PRINCESS KIKURI WILL DIE, AND ONE OF THE SHINSHO WILL ASCEND TO THE THRONE!
AMAWA-KUNI WILL BE RULED BY TRAITORS!
IF THAT HAPPENS, EVERY SHO WHO PUT HIS TRUST IN YOU AND SUBMITTED TO YOU WILL HAVE DONE SO IN VAIN!!

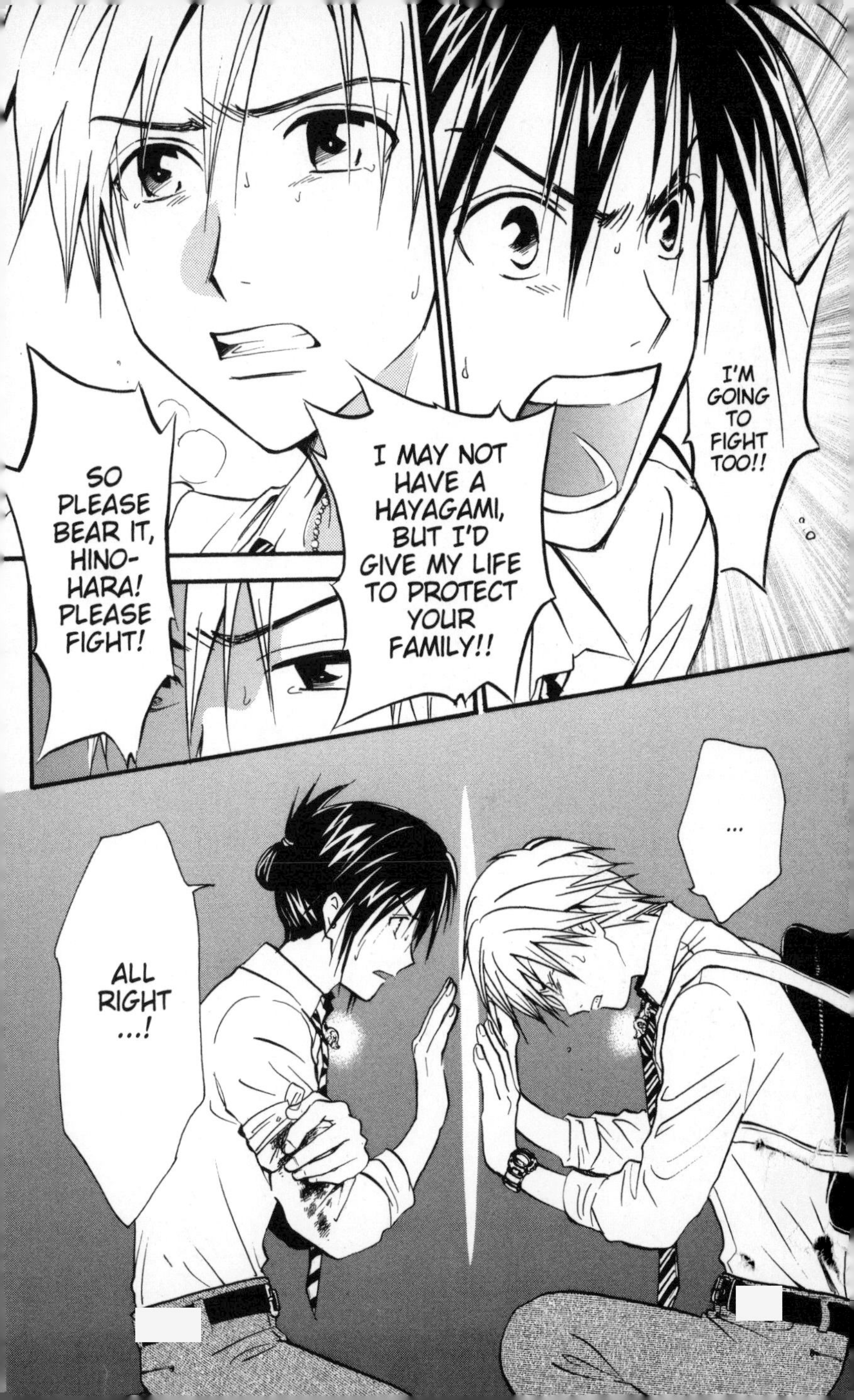
I'M GOING TO FIGHT TOO!!
I MAY NOT HAVE A HAYAGAMI, BUT I'D GIVE MY LIFE TO PROTECT YOUR FAMILY!!
SO PLEASE BEAR IT, HINO-HARA! PLEASE FIGHT!
...
ALL RIGHT ...!

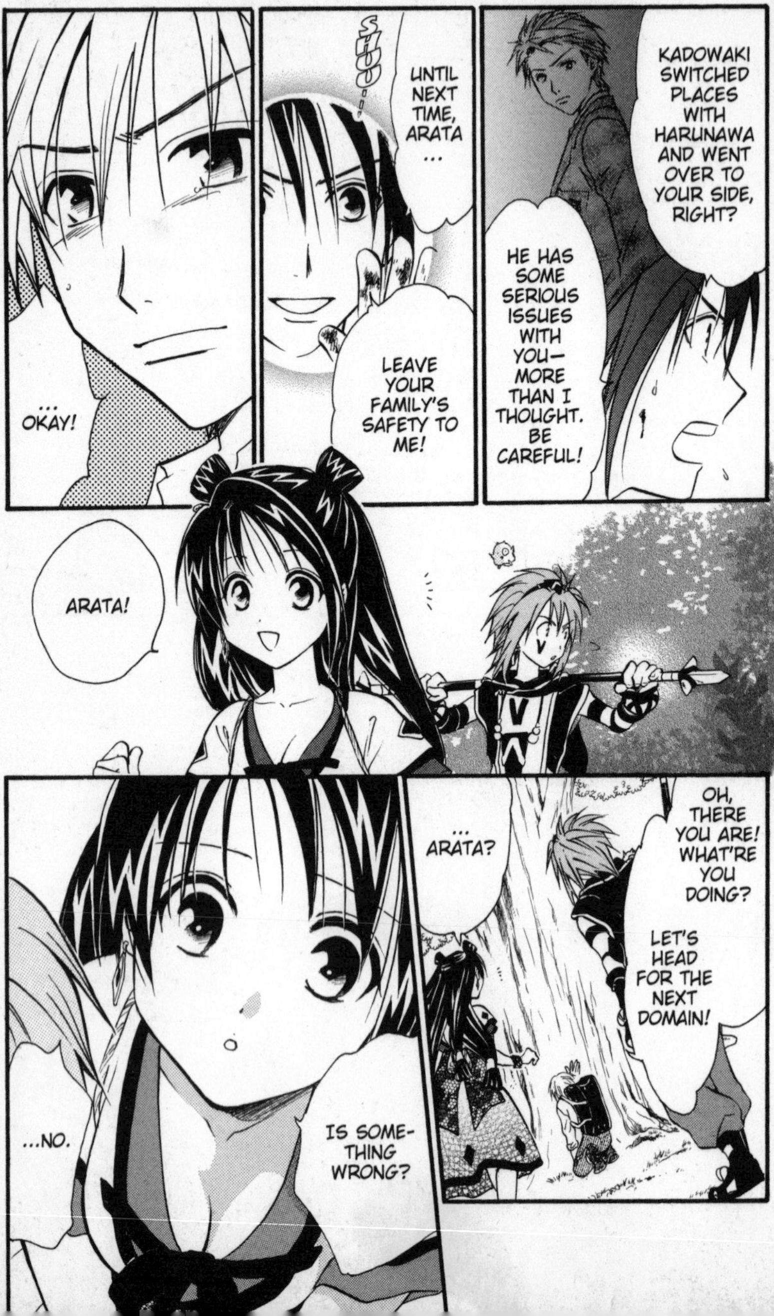

KADOWAKI SWITCHED PLACES WITH HARUNAWA AND WENT OVER TO YOUR SIDE, RIGHT?
HE HAS SOME SERIOUS ISSUES WITH YOU—MORE THAN I THOUGHT. BE CAREFUL!
SHUU...!
UNTIL NEXT TIME, ARATA...
LEAVE YOUR FAMILY'S SAFETY TO ME!
...OKAY!
ARATA!
OH, THERE YOU ARE! WHAT'RE YOU DOING?
LET'S HEAD FOR THE NEXT DOMAIN!
...ARATA?
IS SOME-THING WRONG?
...NO.

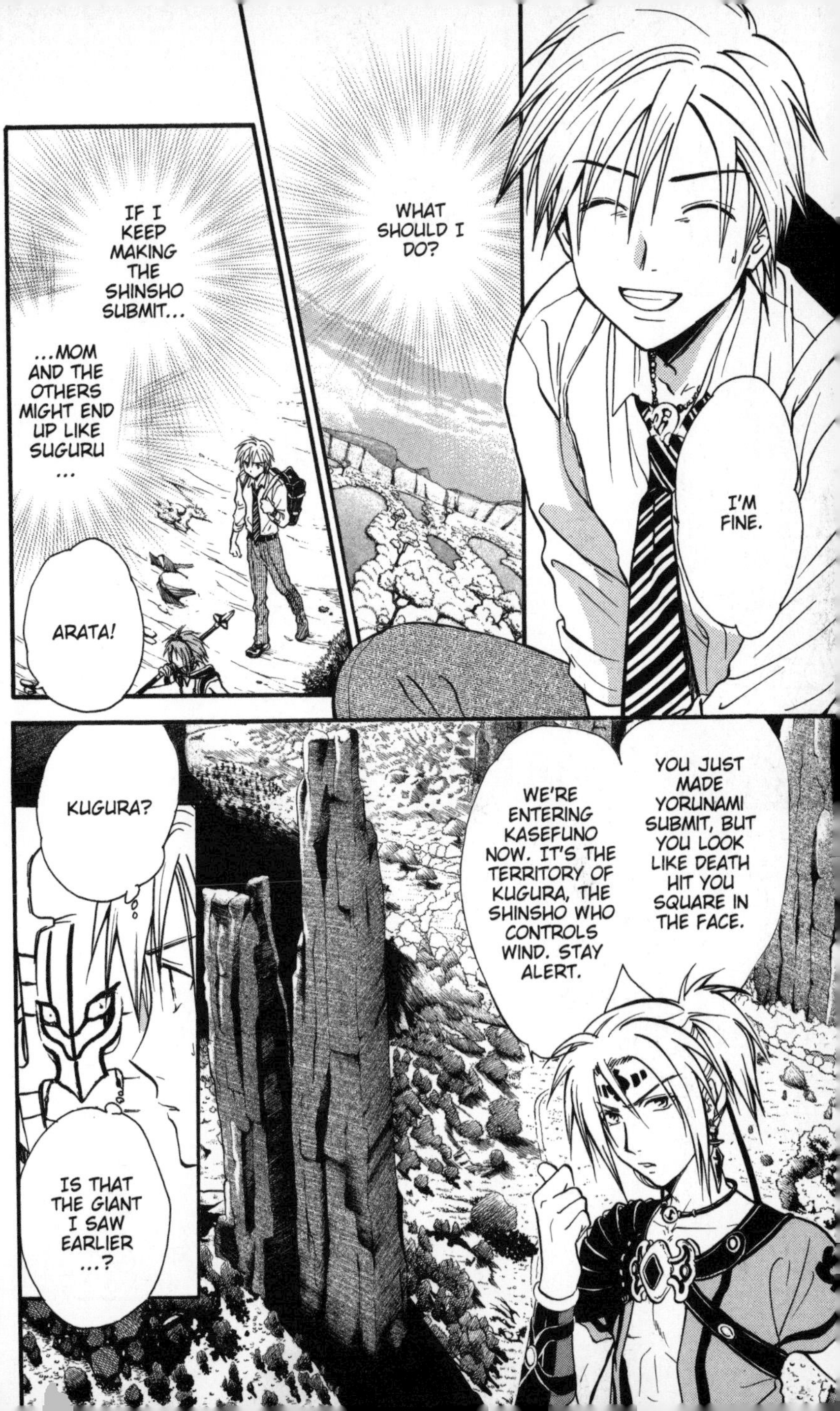
I'M FINE.
WHAT SHOULD I DO?
IF I KEEP MAKING THE SHINSHO SUBMIT...
...MOM AND THE OTHERS MIGHT END UP LIKE SUGURU...
ARATA!
YOU JUST MADE YORUNAMI SUBMIT, BUT YOU LOOK LIKE DEATH HIT YOU SQUARE IN THE FACE.
WE'RE ENTERING KASEFUNO NOW. IT'S THE TERRITORY OF KUGURA, THE SHINSHO WHO CONTROLS WIND. STAY ALERT.
KUGURA?
IS THAT THE GIANT I SAW EARLIER...?

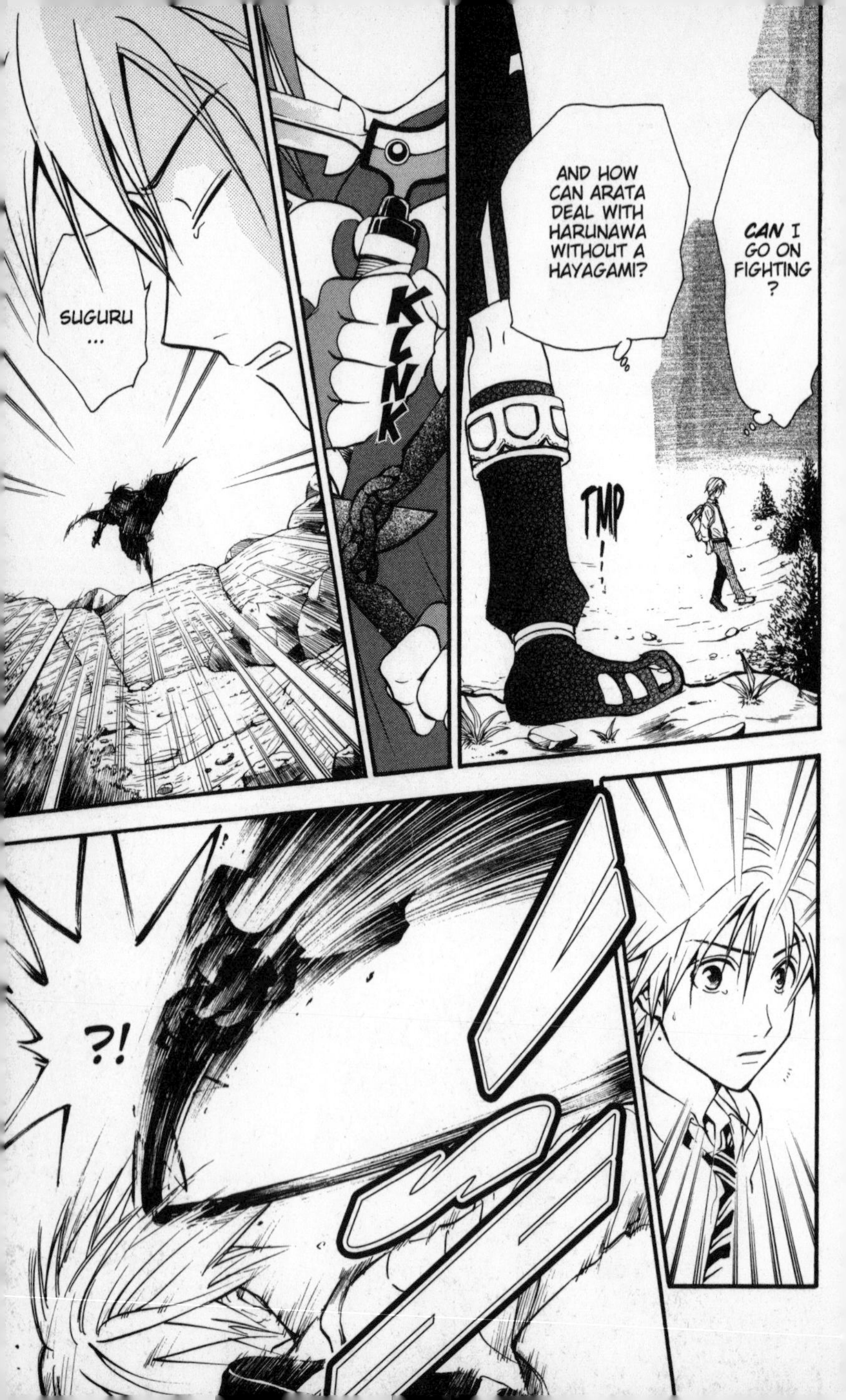
CAN I GO ON FIGHTING?
AND HOW CAN ARATA DEAL WITH HARUNAWA WITHOUT A HAYAGAMI?
TMP
KLNK
SUGURU ...
?!

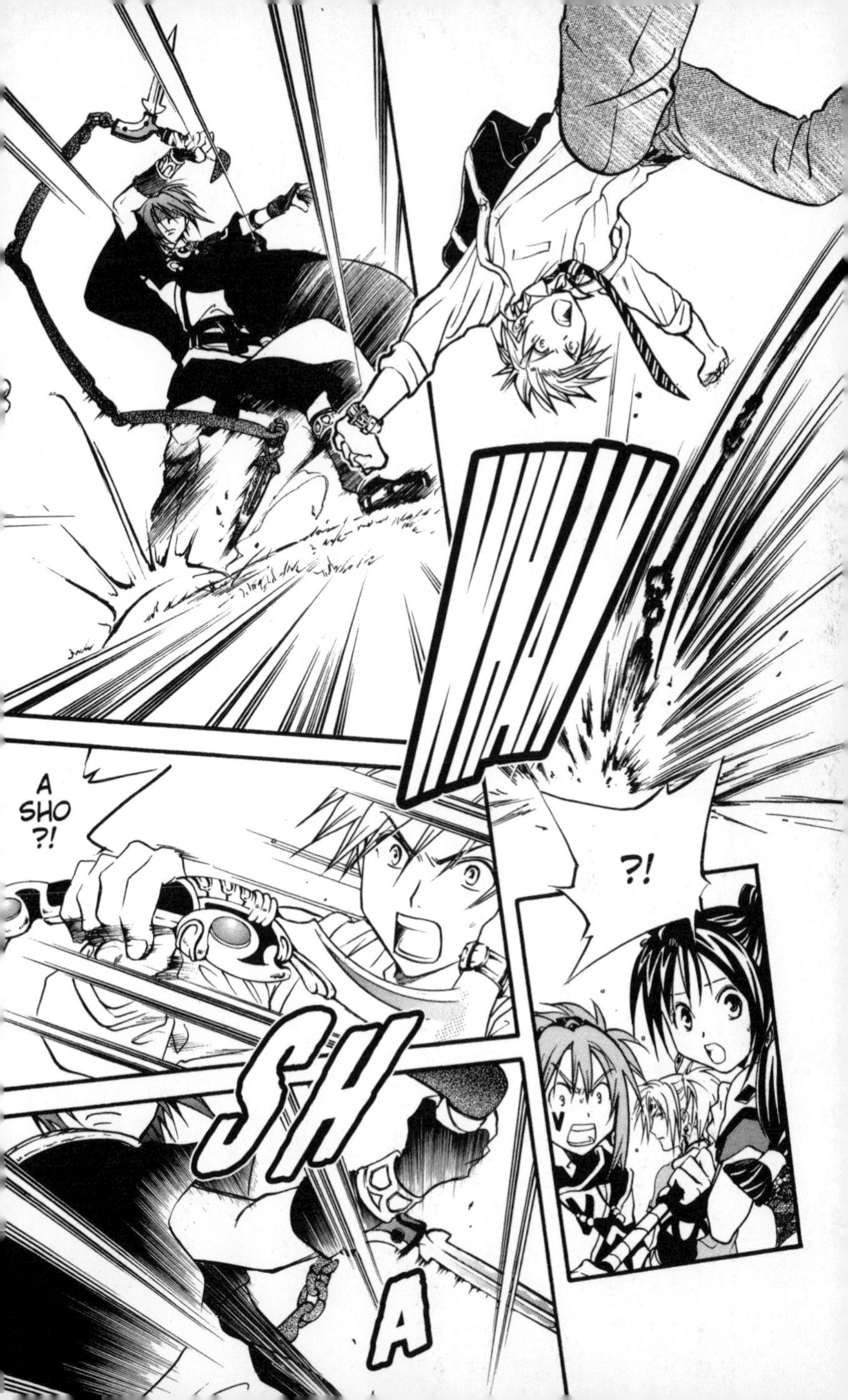
?!
A SHO ?!
SH
A

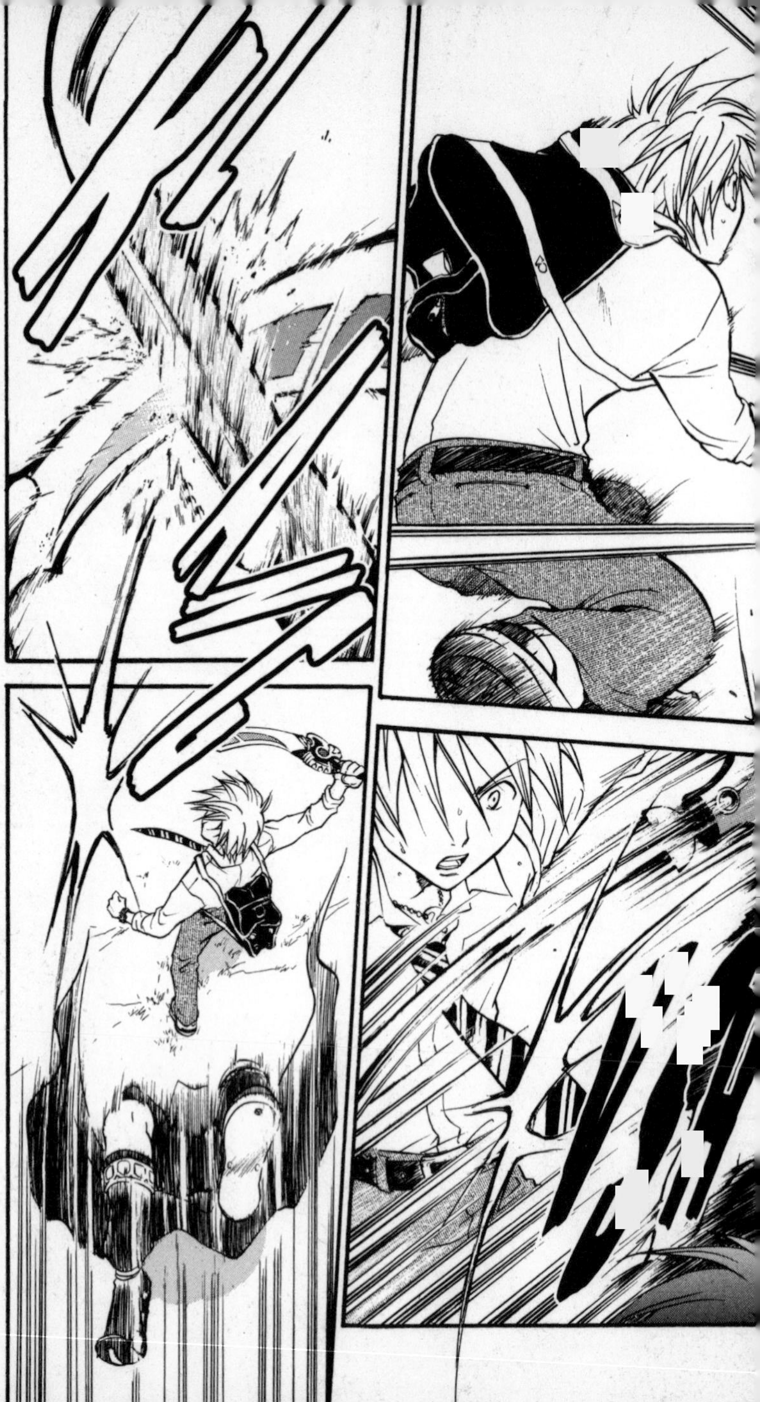

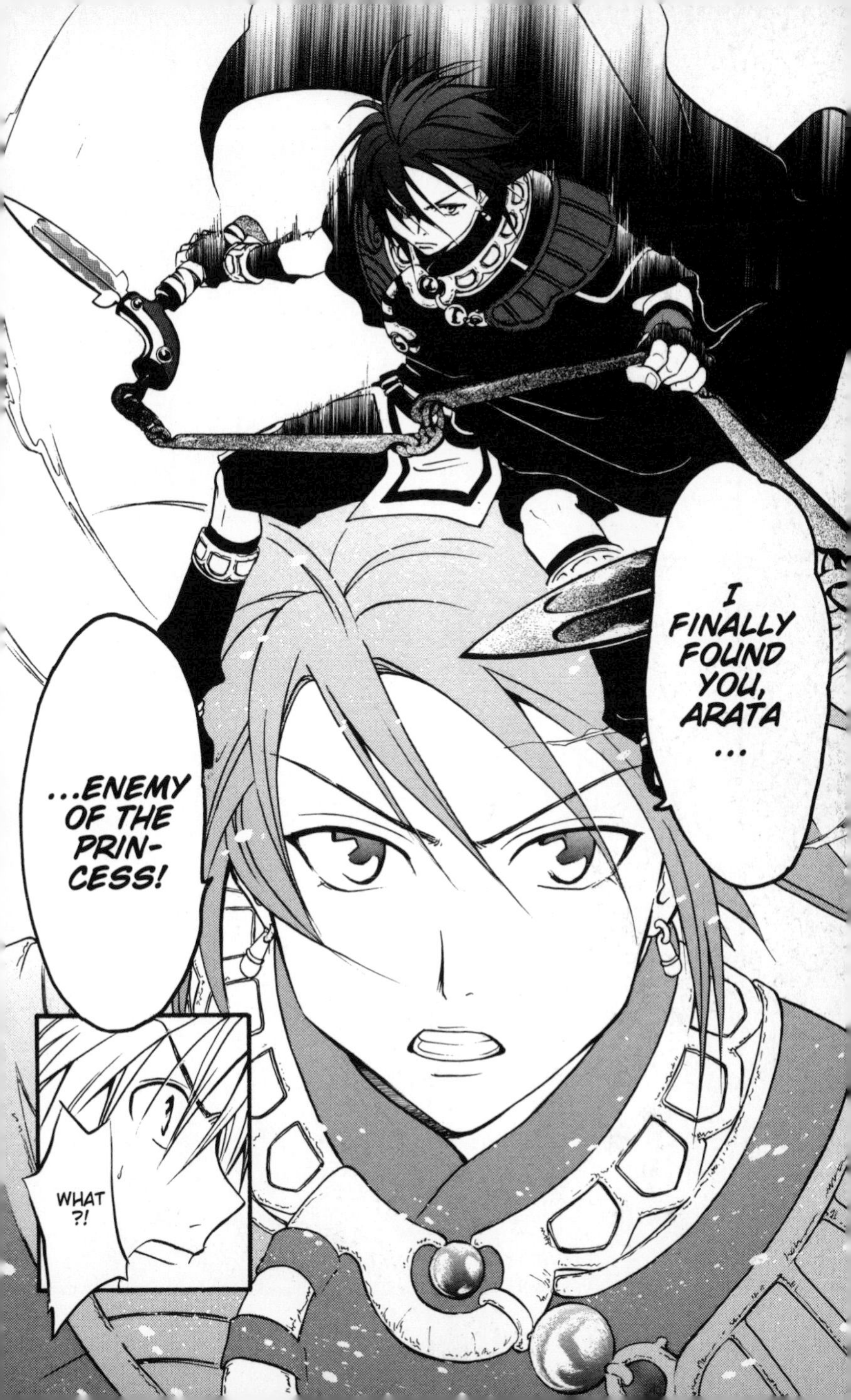
I FINALLY FOUND YOU, ARATA ...
...ENEMY OF THE PRIN-CESS!
WHAT ?!

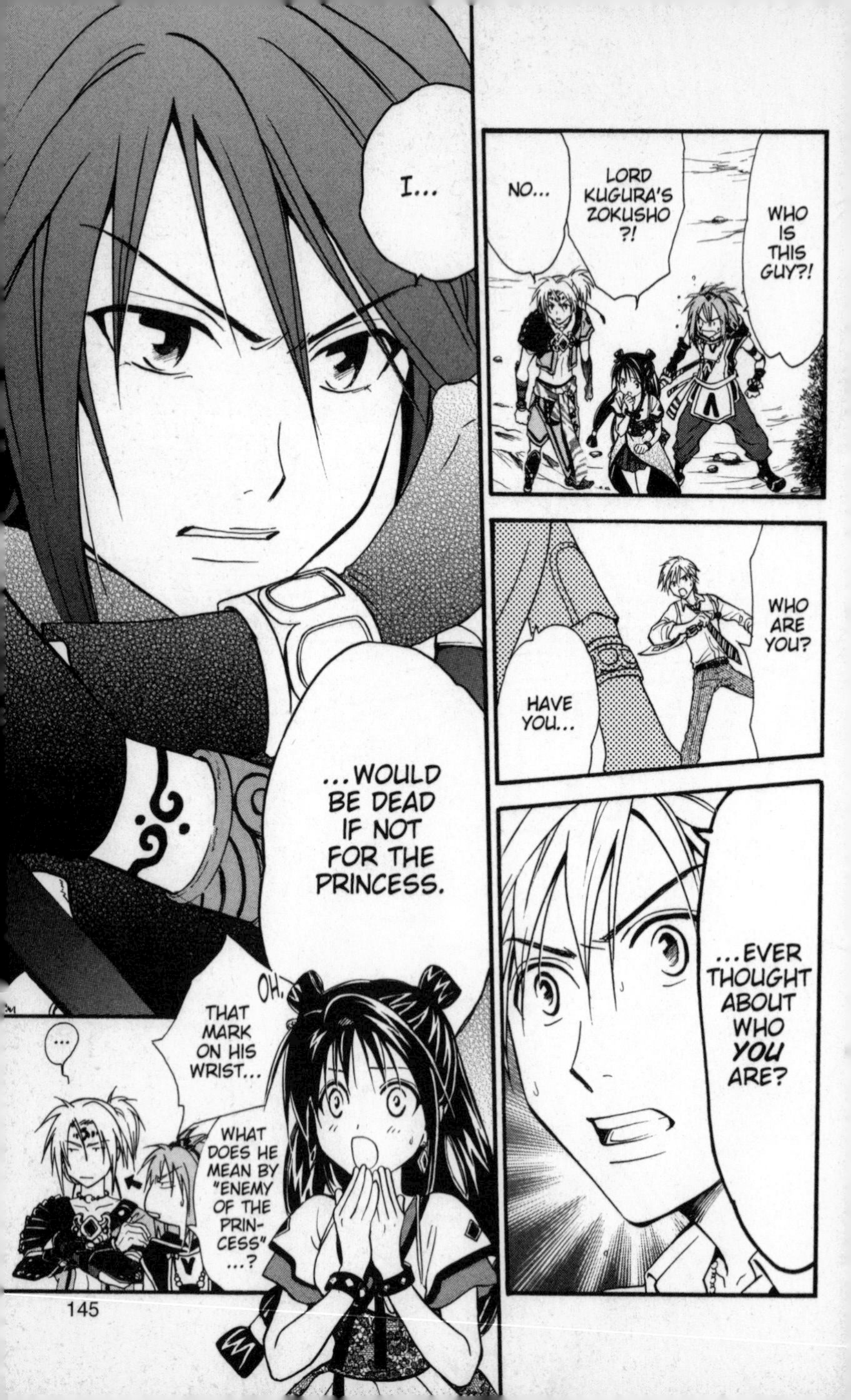
WHO IS THIS GUY?!
LORD KUGURA'S ZOKUSHO?!
NO...
WHO ARE YOU?
HAVE YOU...
...EVER THOUGHT ABOUT WHO *YOU* ARE?
I...
...WOULD BE DEAD IF NOT FOR THE PRINCESS.
OH.
THAT MARK ON HIS WRIST...
WHAT DOES HE MEAN BY "ENEMY OF THE PRIN-CESS"...?
...

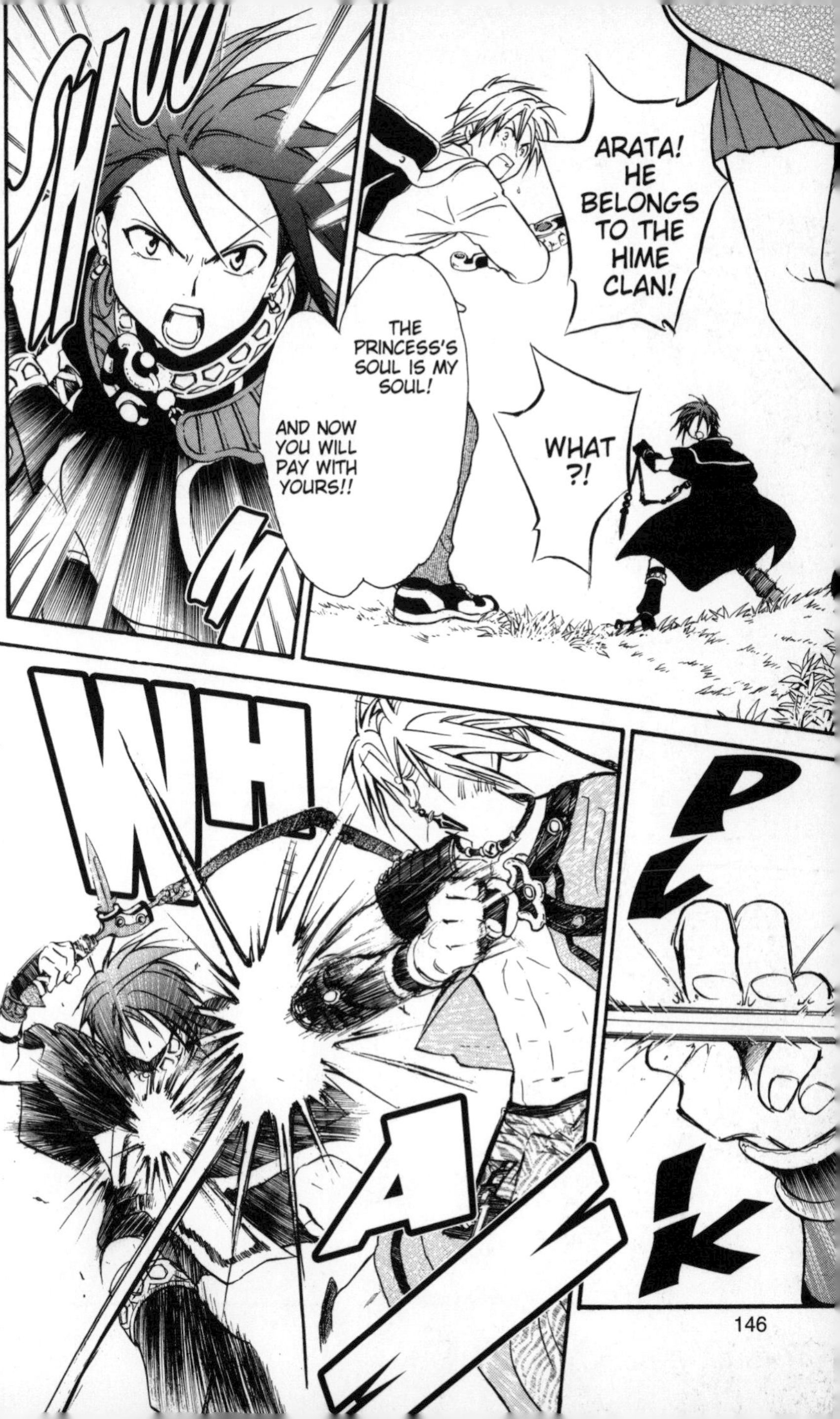
ARATA! HE BELONGS TO THE HIME CLAN!
WHAT ?!
THE PRINCESS'S SOUL IS MY SOUL!
AND NOW YOU WILL PAY WITH YOURS!!

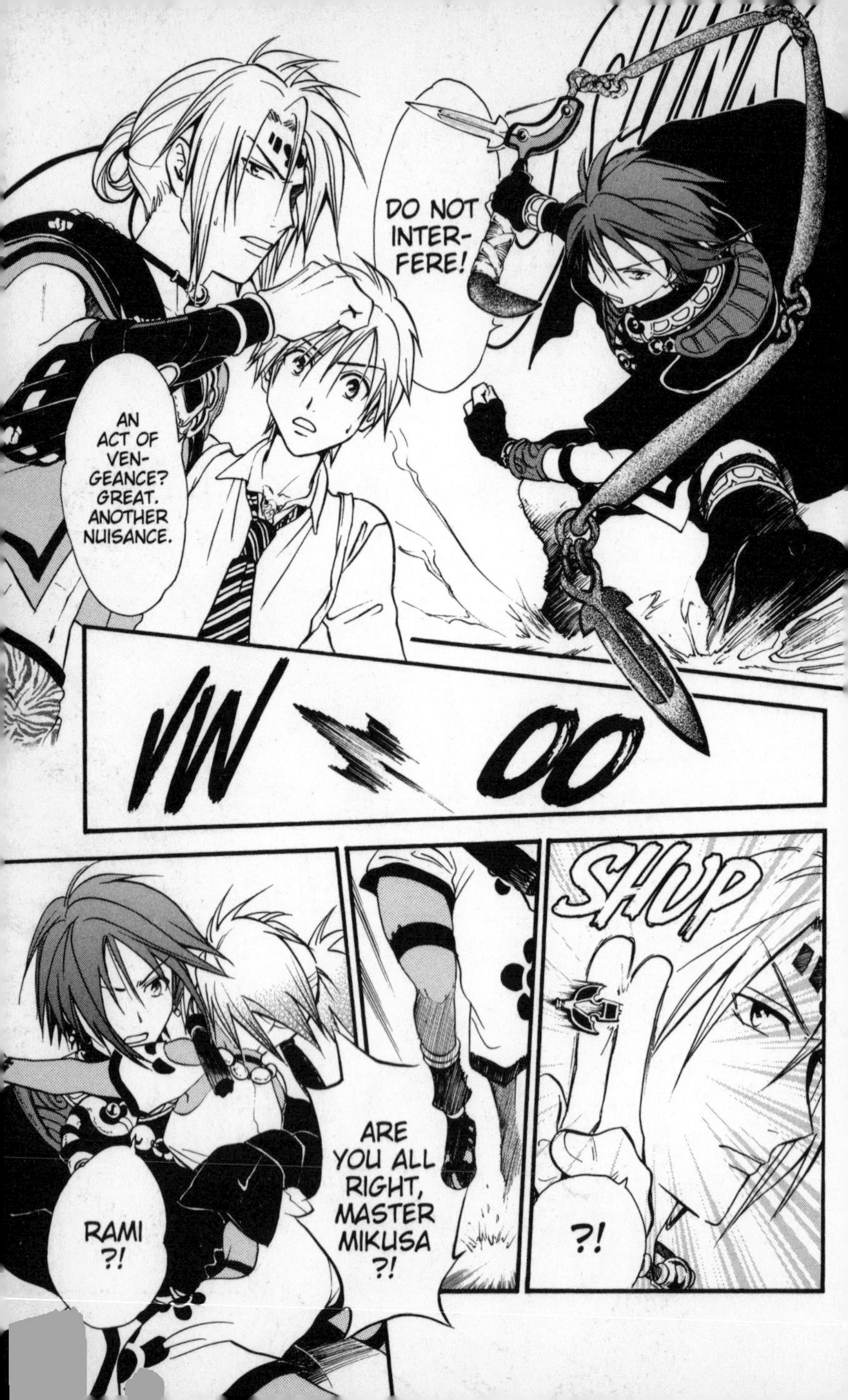
DO NOT INTERFERE!
AN ACT OF VENGEANCE? GREAT. ANOTHER NUISANCE.
VWOO
SHUP
?!
ARE YOU ALL RIGHT, MASTER MIKUSA?!
RAMI?!

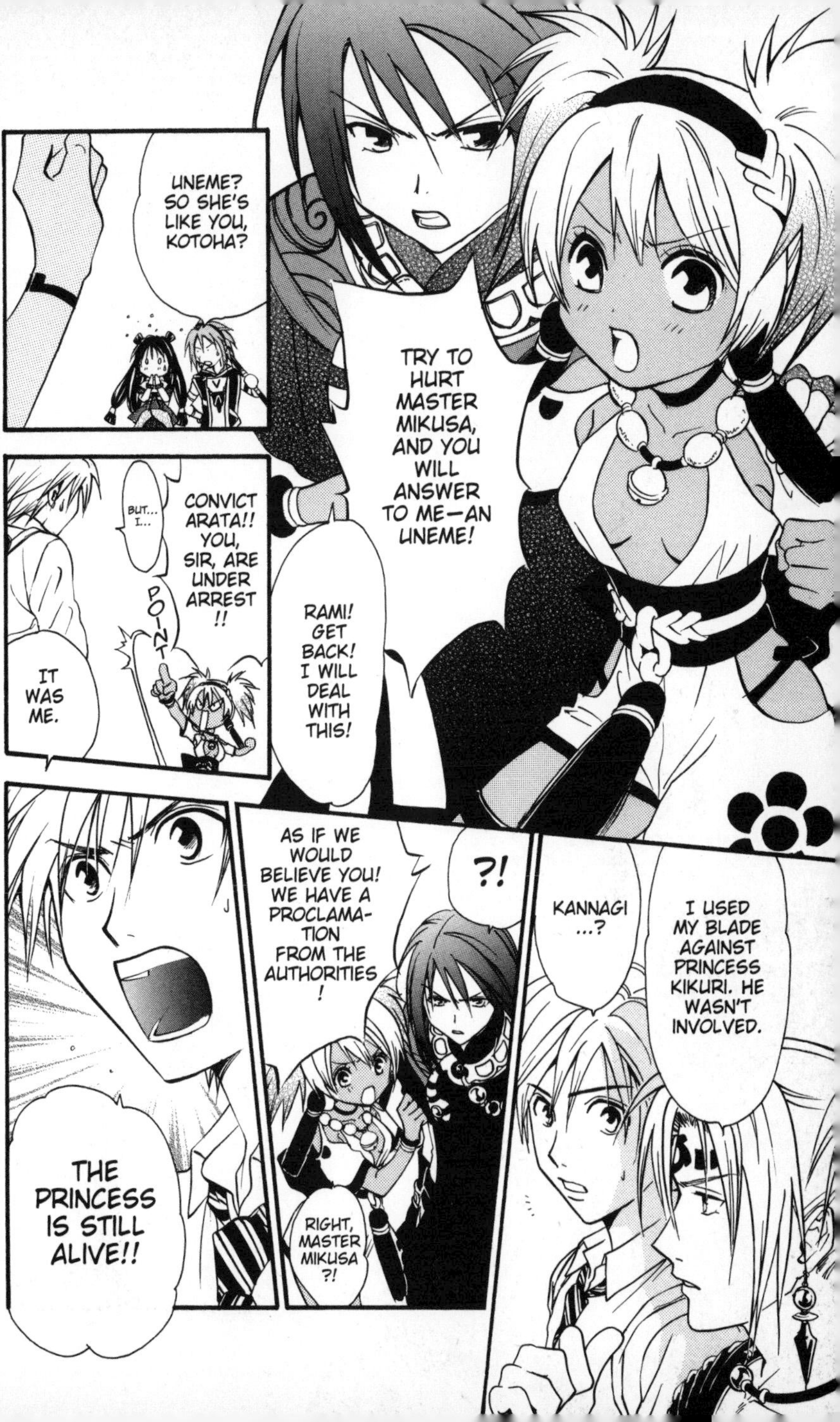
TRY TO HURT MASTER MIKUSA, AND YOU WILL ANSWER TO ME—AN UNEME!
RAMI! GET BACK! I WILL DEAL WITH THIS!
UNEME? SO SHE'S LIKE YOU, KOTOHA?
CONVICT ARATA!! YOU, SIR, ARE UNDER ARREST!!
BUT... I...
POINT
IT WAS ME.
I USED MY BLADE AGAINST PRINCESS KIKURI. HE WASN'T INVOLVED.
KANNAGI ...?
?!
AS IF WE WOULD BELIEVE YOU! WE HAVE A PROCLAMATION FROM THE AUTHORITIES!
RIGHT, MASTER MIKUSA?!
THE PRINCESS IS STILL ALIVE!!

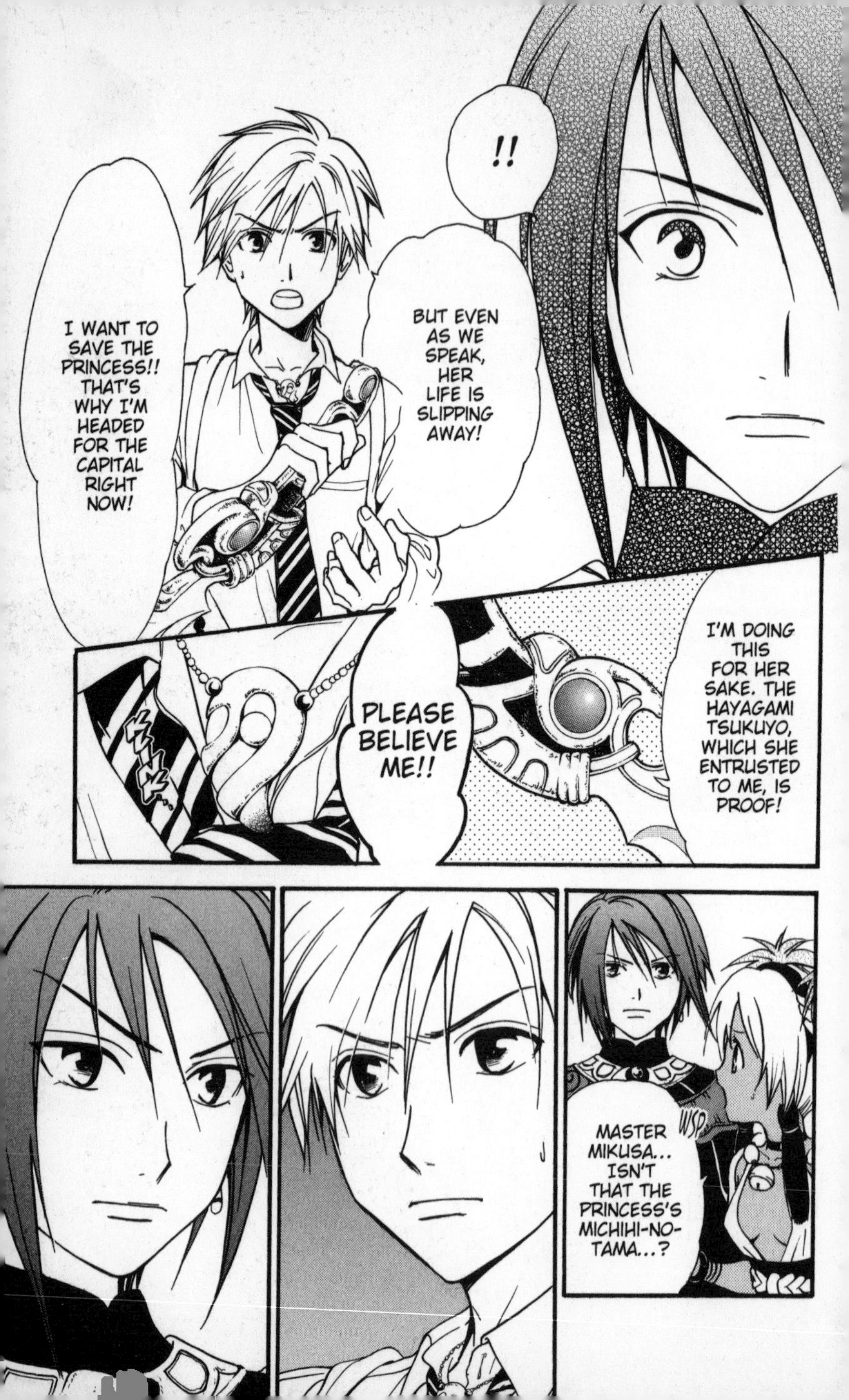
!!
I WANT TO SAVE THE PRINCESS!! THAT'S WHY I'M HEADED FOR THE CAPITAL RIGHT NOW!
BUT EVEN AS WE SPEAK, HER LIFE IS SLIPPING AWAY!
I'M DOING THIS FOR HER SAKE. THE HAYAGAMI TSUKUYO, WHICH SHE ENTRUSTED TO ME, IS PROOF!
PLEASE BELIEVE ME!!
WSP
MASTER MIKUSA... ISN'T THAT THE PRINCESS'S MICHIHI-NO-TAMA...?

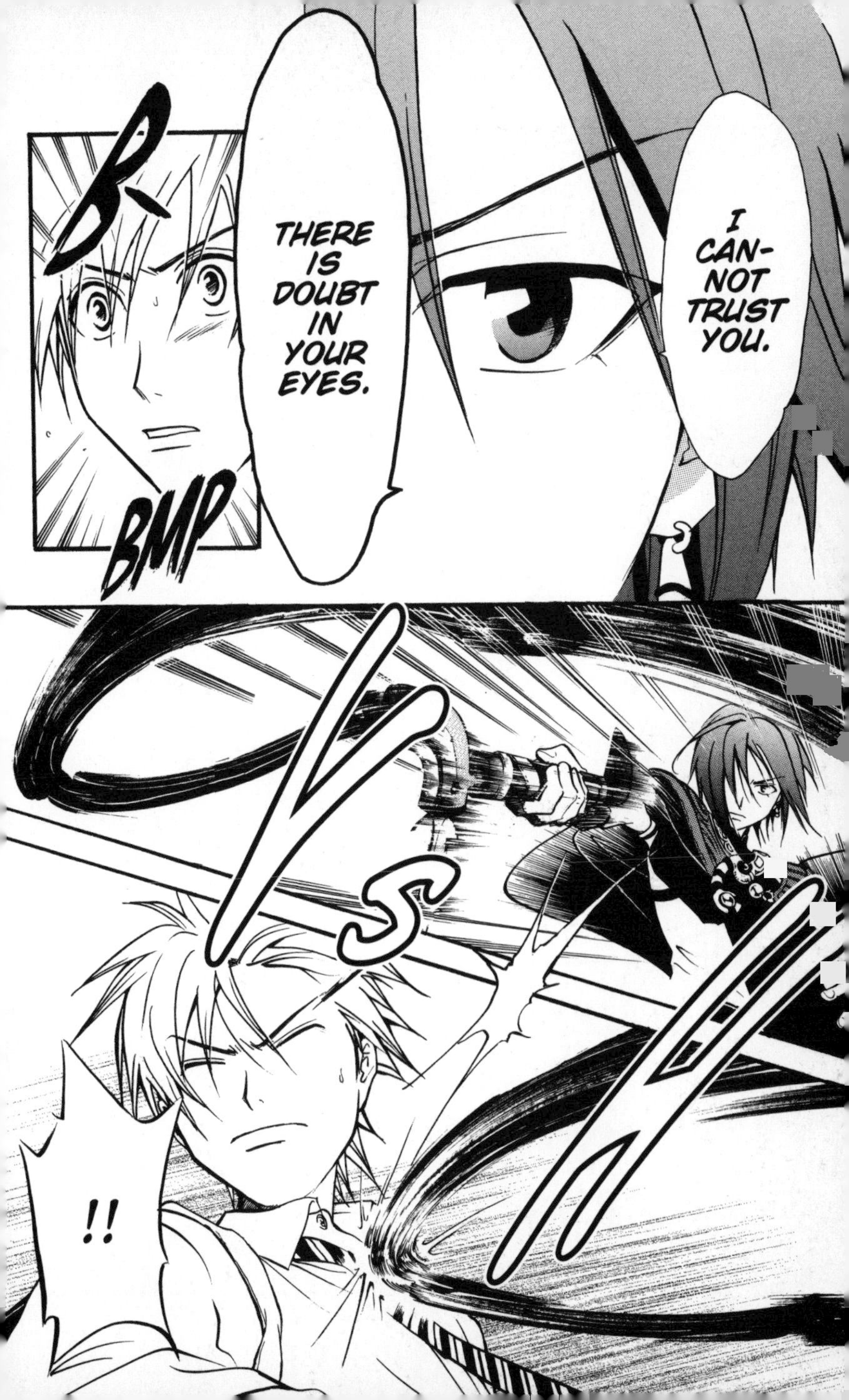
I CAN-NOT TRUST YOU.
THERE IS DOUBT IN YOUR EYES.
B-
BMP
VSH
!!

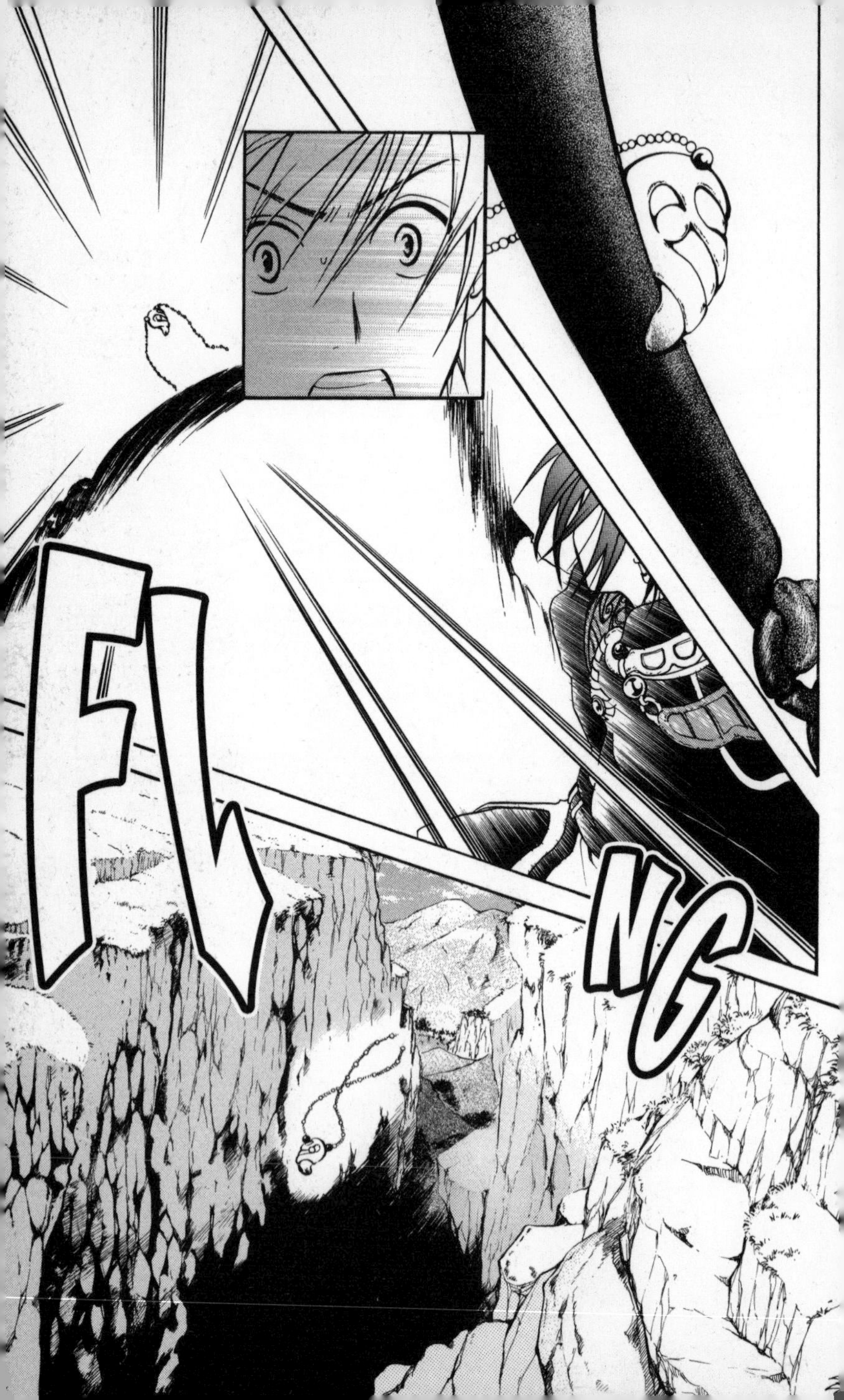
FL
NG

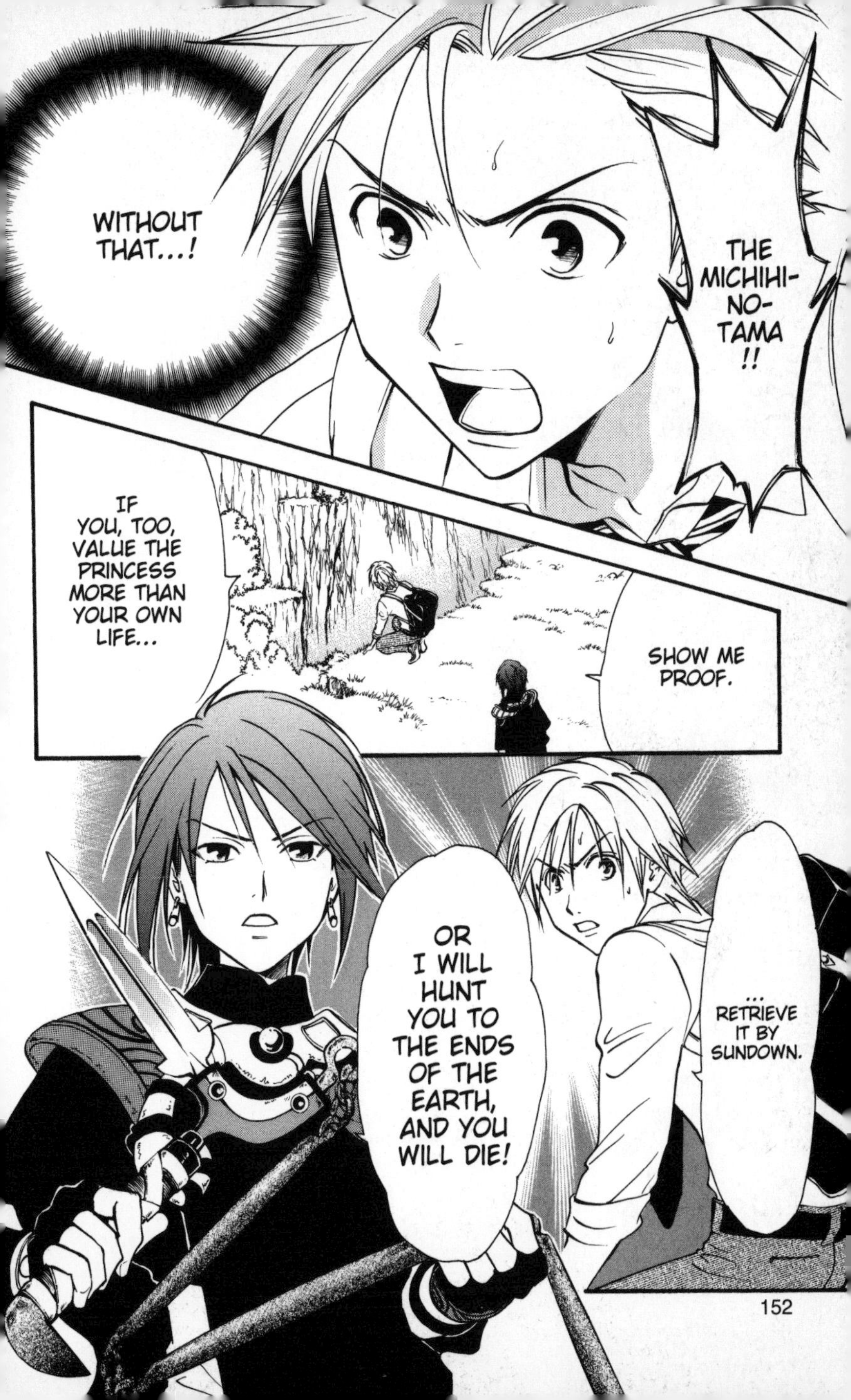
THE MICHIHI-NO-TAMA!!
WITHOUT THAT...!
SHOW ME PROOF.
IF YOU, TOO, VALUE THE PRINCESS MORE THAN YOUR OWN LIFE...
...RETRIEVE IT BY SUNDOWN.
OR I WILL HUNT YOU TO THE ENDS OF THE EARTH, AND YOU WILL DIE!

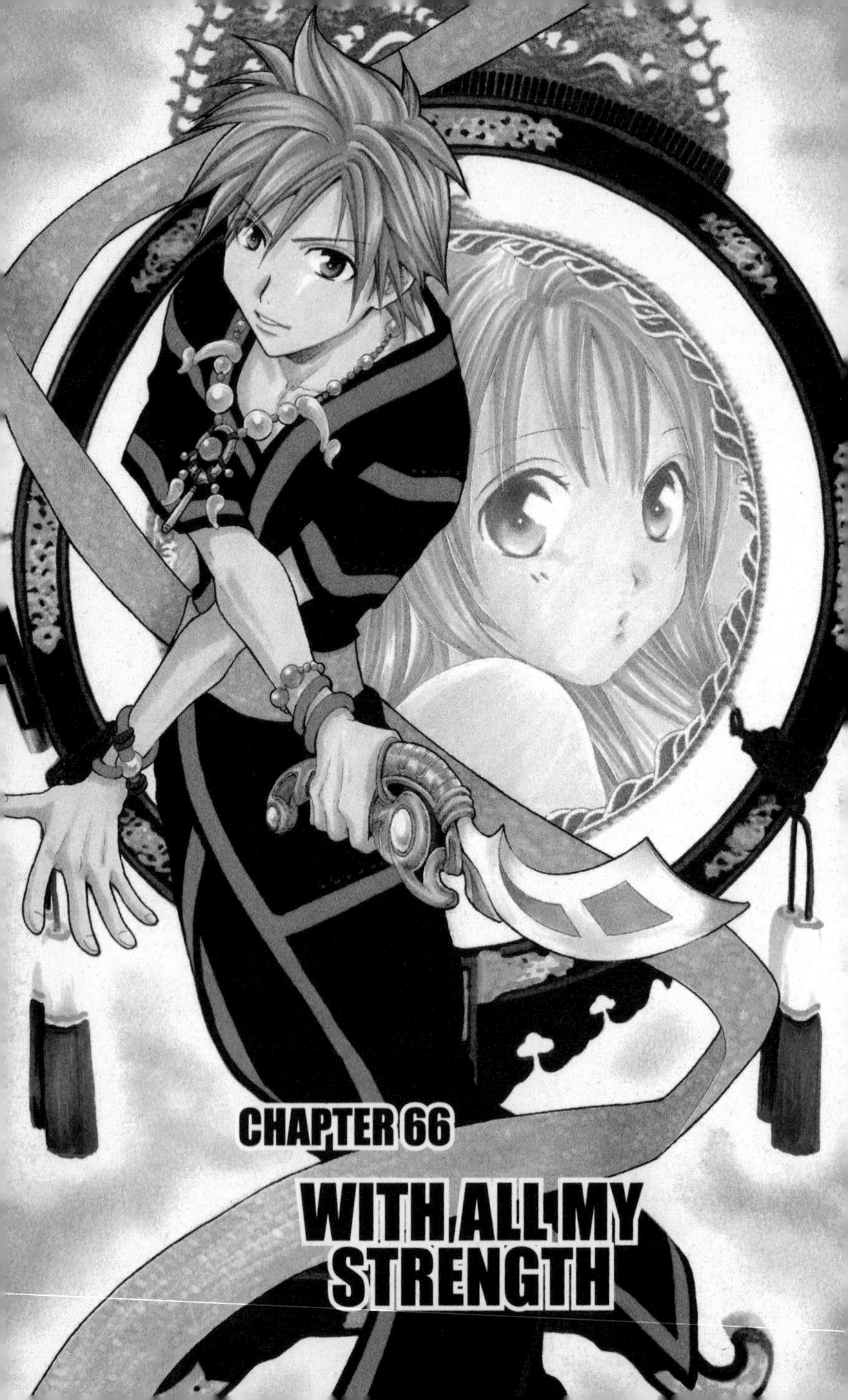
CHAPTER 66
WITH ALL MY STRENGTH

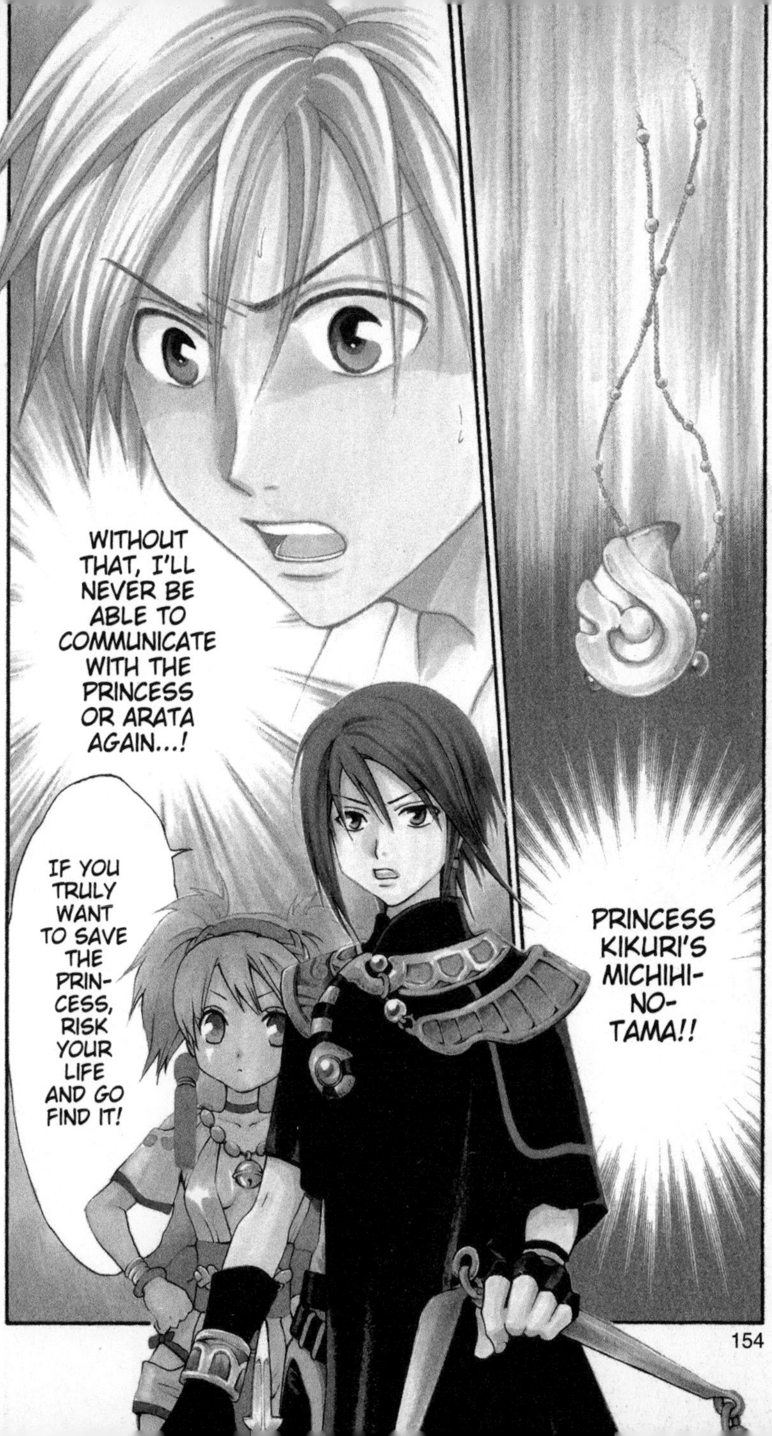

PRINCESS KIKURI'S MICHIHI-NO-TAMA!!
WITHOUT THAT, I'LL NEVER BE ABLE TO COMMUNICATE WITH THE PRINCESS OR ARATA AGAIN...!
IF YOU TRULY WANT TO SAVE THE PRIN-CESS, RISK YOUR LIFE AND GO FIND IT!

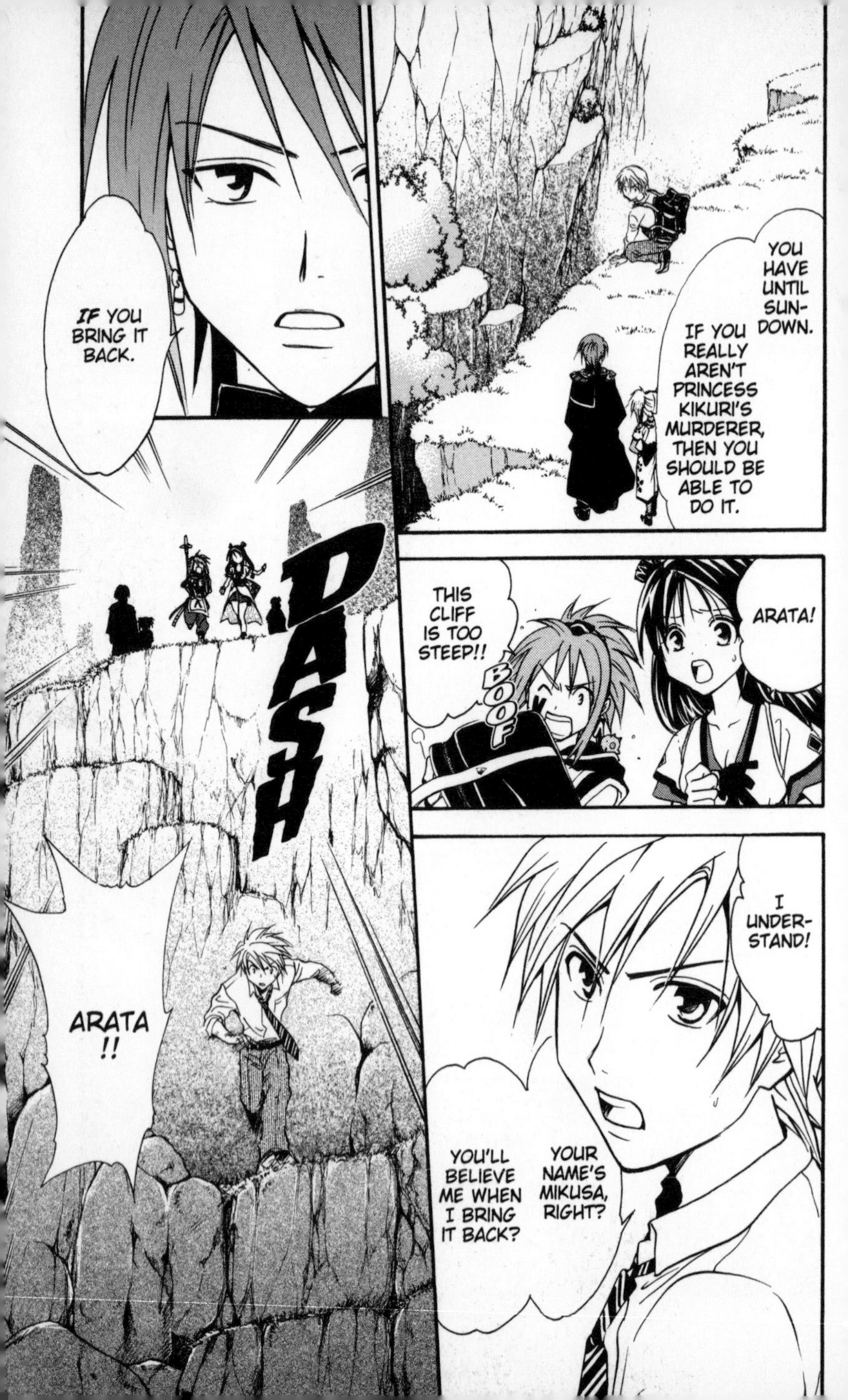
YOU HAVE UNTIL SUN-DOWN.
IF YOU REALLY AREN'T PRINCESS KIKURI'S MURDERER, THEN YOU SHOULD BE ABLE TO DO IT.
IF YOU BRING IT BACK.
ARATA!
THIS CLIFF IS TOO STEEP!!
BOOF
I UNDER-STAND!
YOUR NAME'S MIKUSA, RIGHT?
YOU'LL BELIEVE ME WHEN I BRING IT BACK?
DASH
ARATA!!

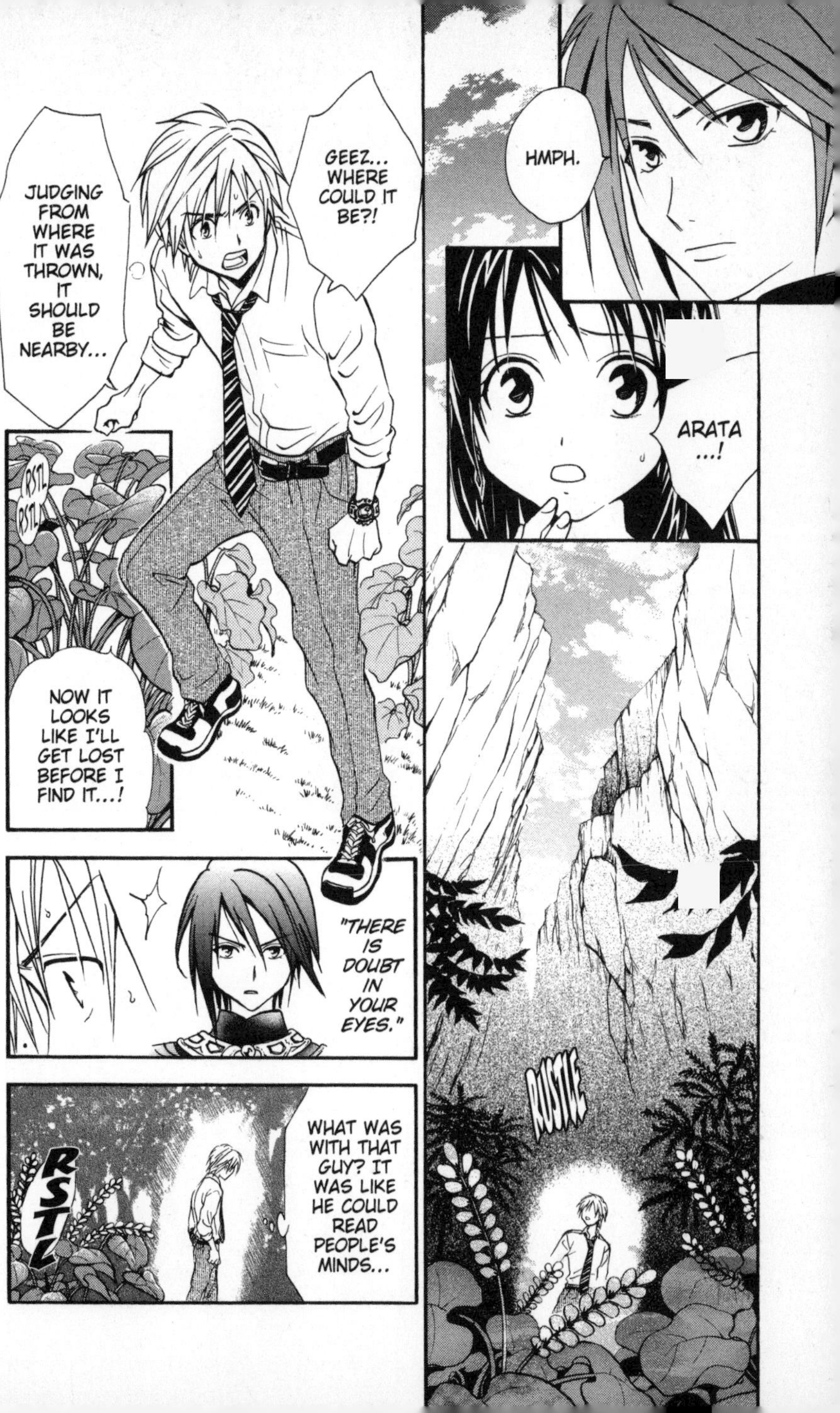
HMPH.
ARATA ...!
RUSTLE
GEEZ... WHERE COULD IT BE?!
JUDGING FROM WHERE IT WAS THROWN, IT SHOULD BE NEARBY...
RSTL RSTL
NOW IT LOOKS LIKE I'LL GET LOST BEFORE I FIND IT...!
"THERE IS DOUBT IN YOUR EYES."
RSTL
WHAT WAS WITH THAT GUY? IT WAS LIKE HE COULD READ PEOPLE'S MINDS...

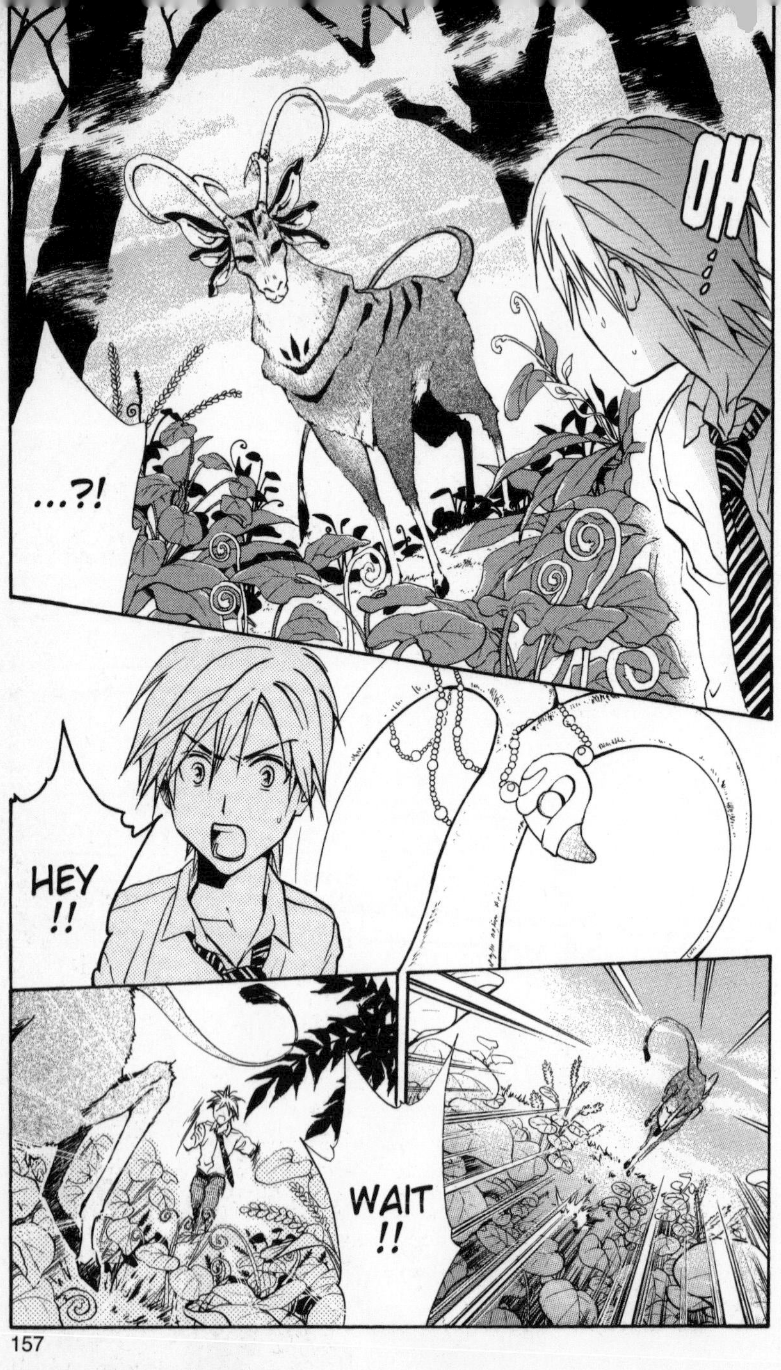
OH
...?!
HEY !!
WAIT !!

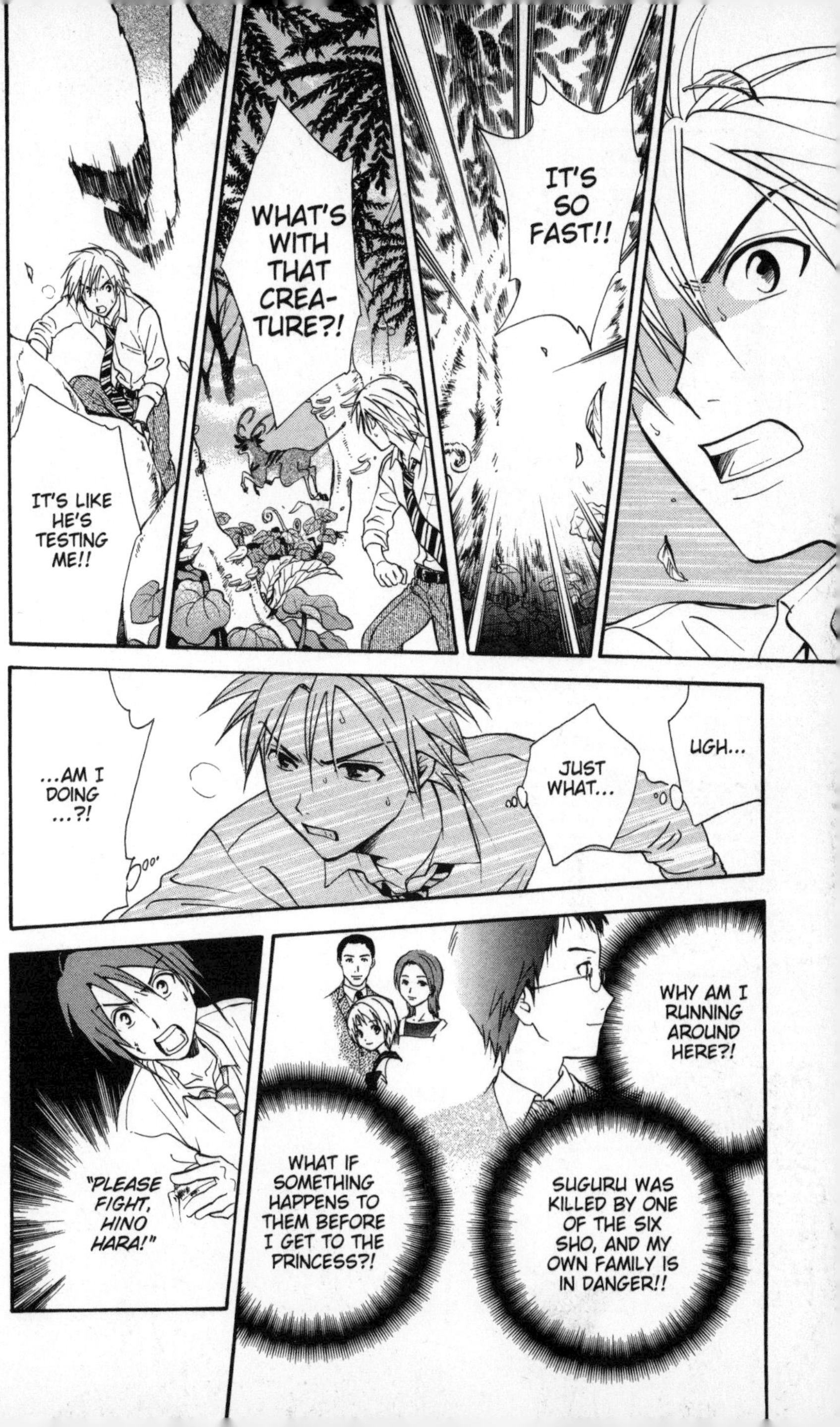
IT'S SO FAST!!
WHAT'S WITH THAT CREA-TURE?!
IT'S LIKE HE'S TESTING ME!!
UGH...
JUST WHAT...
...AM I DOING ...?!
WHY AM I RUNNING AROUND HERE?!
SUGURU WAS KILLED BY ONE OF THE SIX SHO, AND MY OWN FAMILY IS IN DANGER!!
WHAT IF SOMETHING HAPPENS TO THEM BEFORE I GET TO THE PRINCESS?!
"PLEASE FIGHT, HINO HARA!"

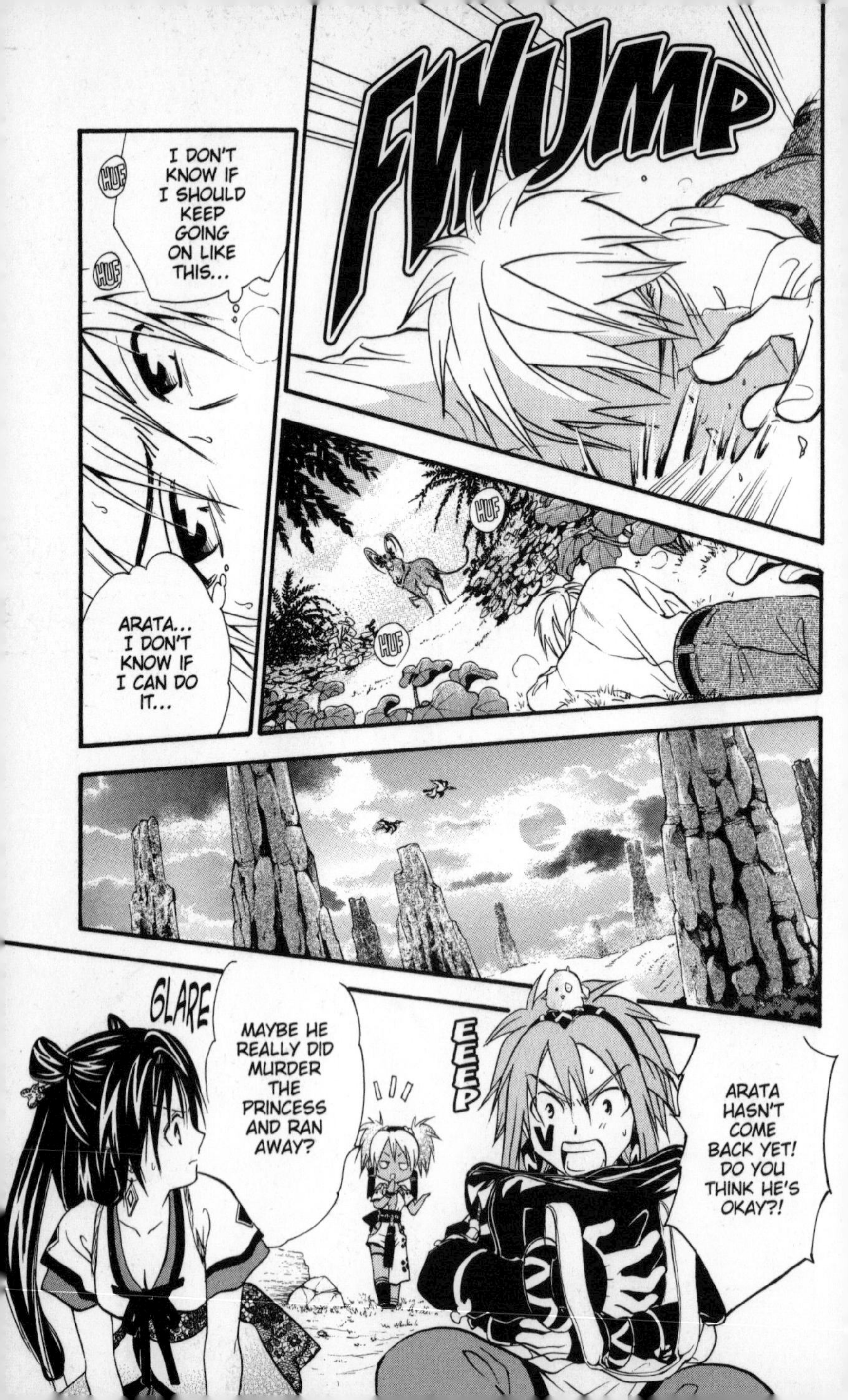
FWUMP
HUF
HUF
I DON'T KNOW IF I SHOULD KEEP GOING ON LIKE THIS...
HUF
HUF
ARATA... I DON'T KNOW IF I CAN DO IT...
ARATA HASN'T COME BACK YET! DO YOU THINK HE'S OKAY?!
EEEP
MAYBE HE REALLY DID MURDER THE PRINCESS AND RAN AWAY?
GLARE

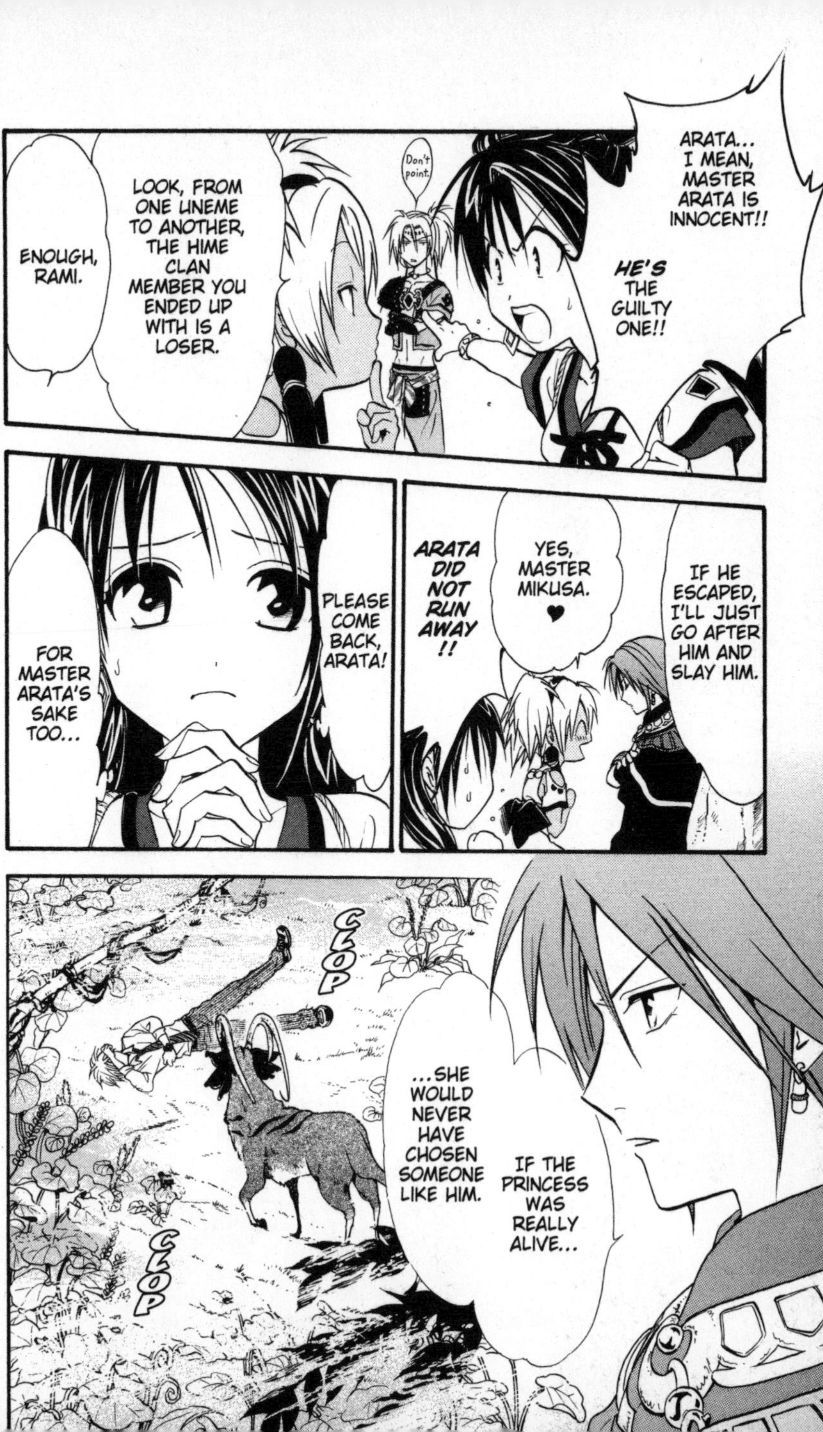
ARATA... I MEAN, MASTER ARATA IS INNOCENT!!
HE'S THE GUILTY ONE!!
Don't point.
LOOK, FROM ONE UNEME TO ANOTHER, THE HIME CLAN MEMBER YOU ENDED UP WITH IS A LOSER.
ENOUGH, RAMI.
IF HE ESCAPED, I'LL JUST GO AFTER HIM AND SLAY HIM.
YES, MASTER MIKUSA. ♥
ARATA DID NOT RUN AWAY!!
PLEASE COME BACK, ARATA!
FOR MASTER ARATA'S SAKE TOO...
IF THE PRINCESS WAS REALLY ALIVE...
...SHE WOULD NEVER HAVE CHOSEN SOMEONE LIKE HIM.
CLOP
CLOP

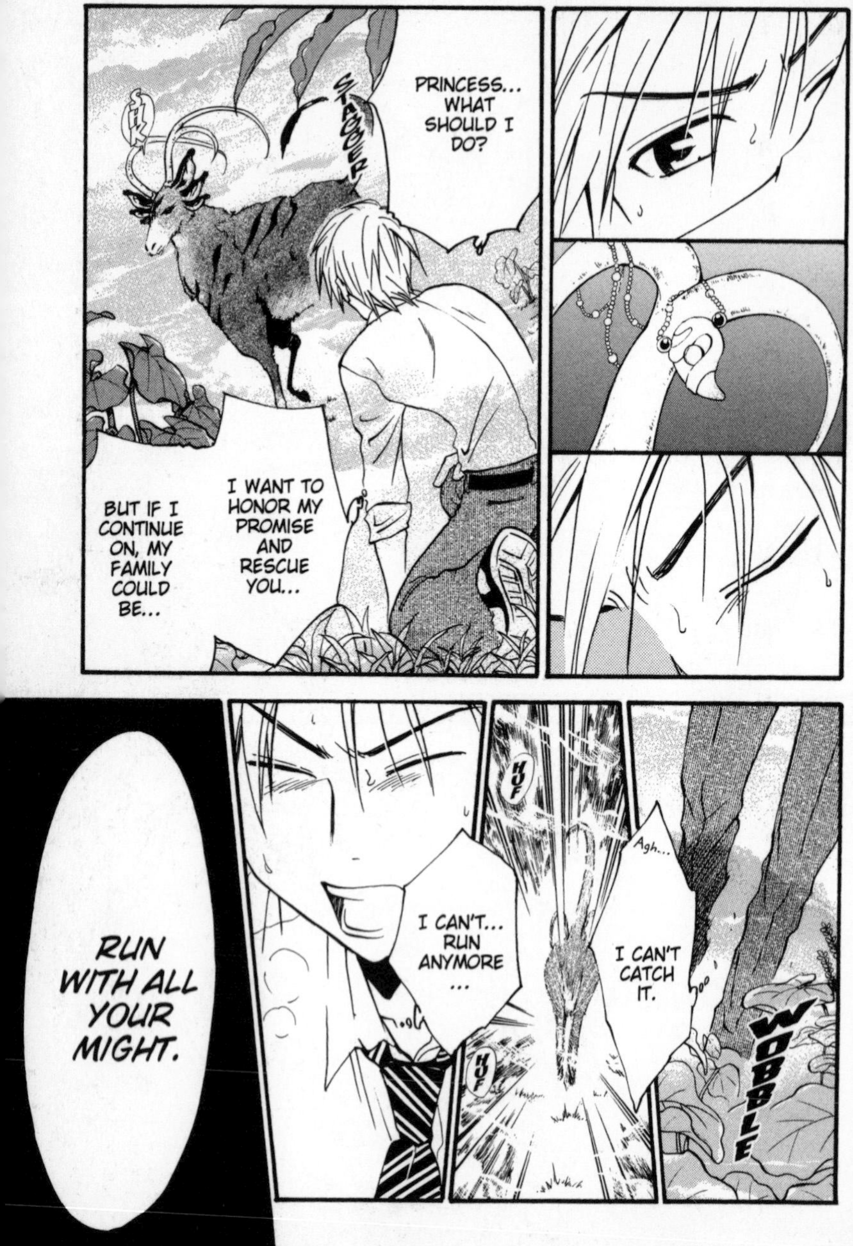
PRINCESS... WHAT SHOULD I DO?
STAGGER
SHK
I WANT TO HONOR MY PROMISE AND RESCUE YOU...
BUT IF I CONTINUE ON, MY FAMILY COULD BE...
Agh...
I CAN'T CATCH IT.
WOBBLE
HUF
HUF
I CAN'T... RUN ANYMORE ...
RUN WITH ALL YOUR MIGHT.

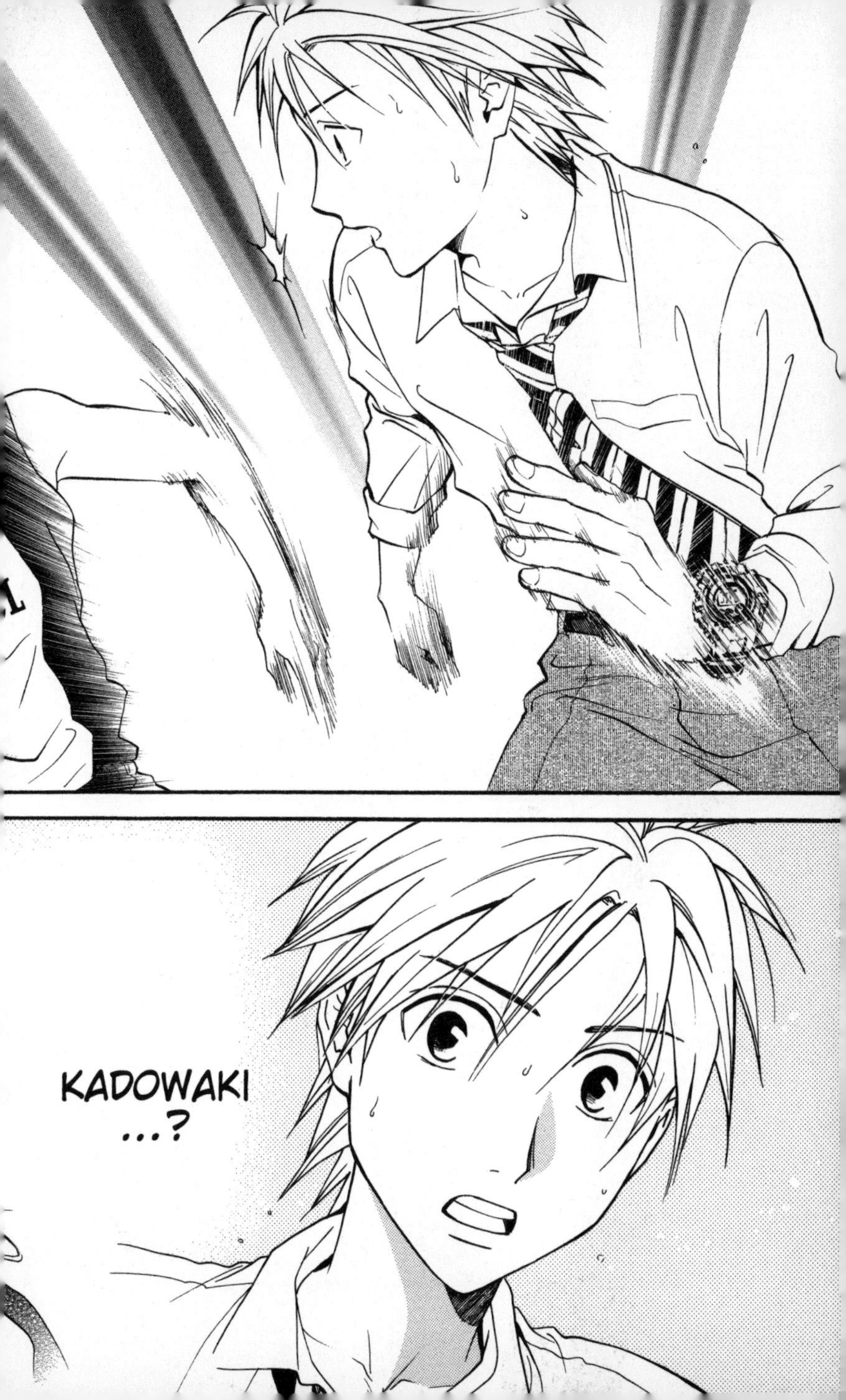
KADOWAKI ...?

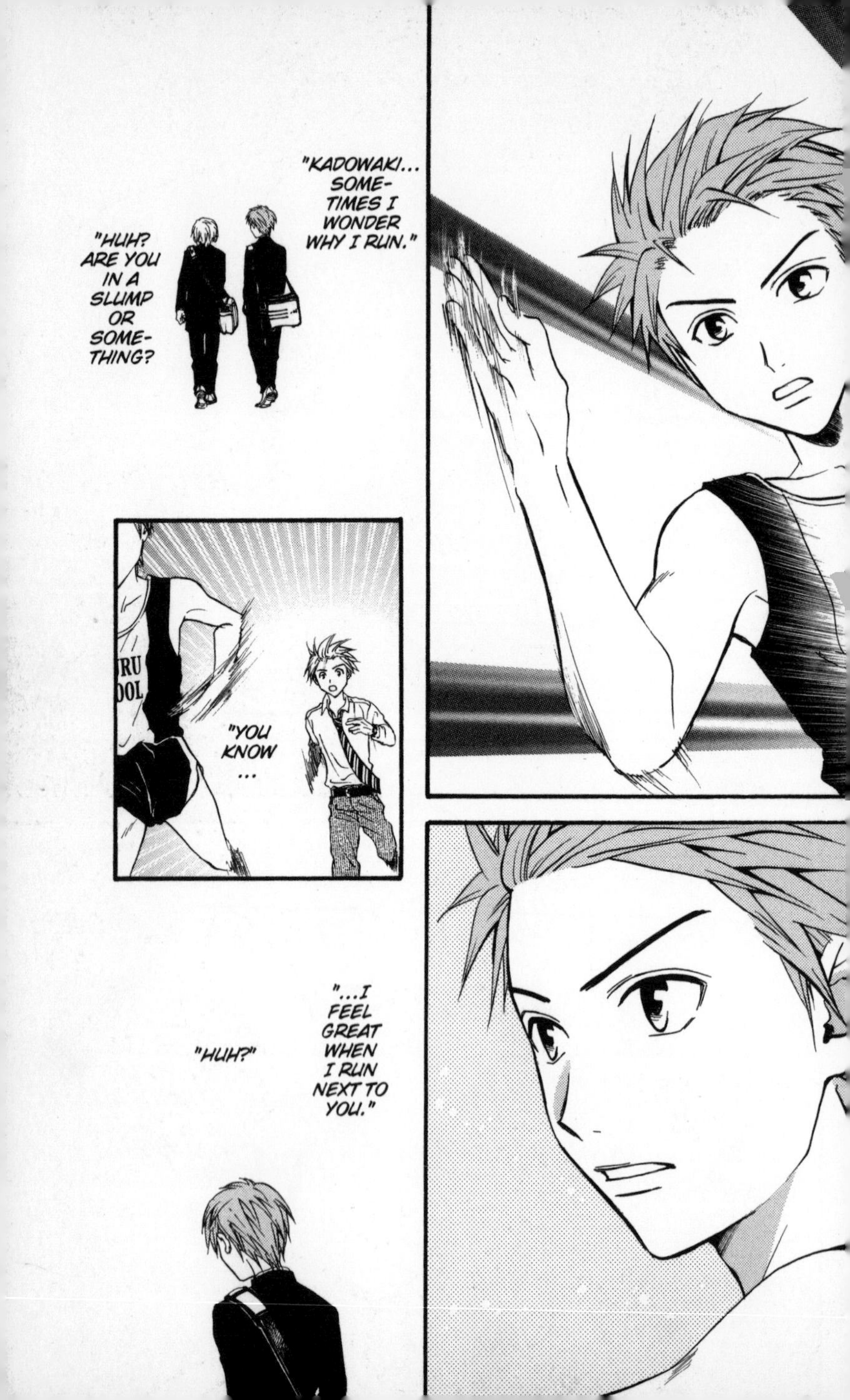
"KADOWAKI... SOMETIMES I WONDER WHY I RUN."
"HUH? ARE YOU IN A SLUMP OR SOMETHING?"
"YOU KNOW ..."
"...I FEEL GREAT WHEN I RUN NEXT TO YOU."
"HUH?"

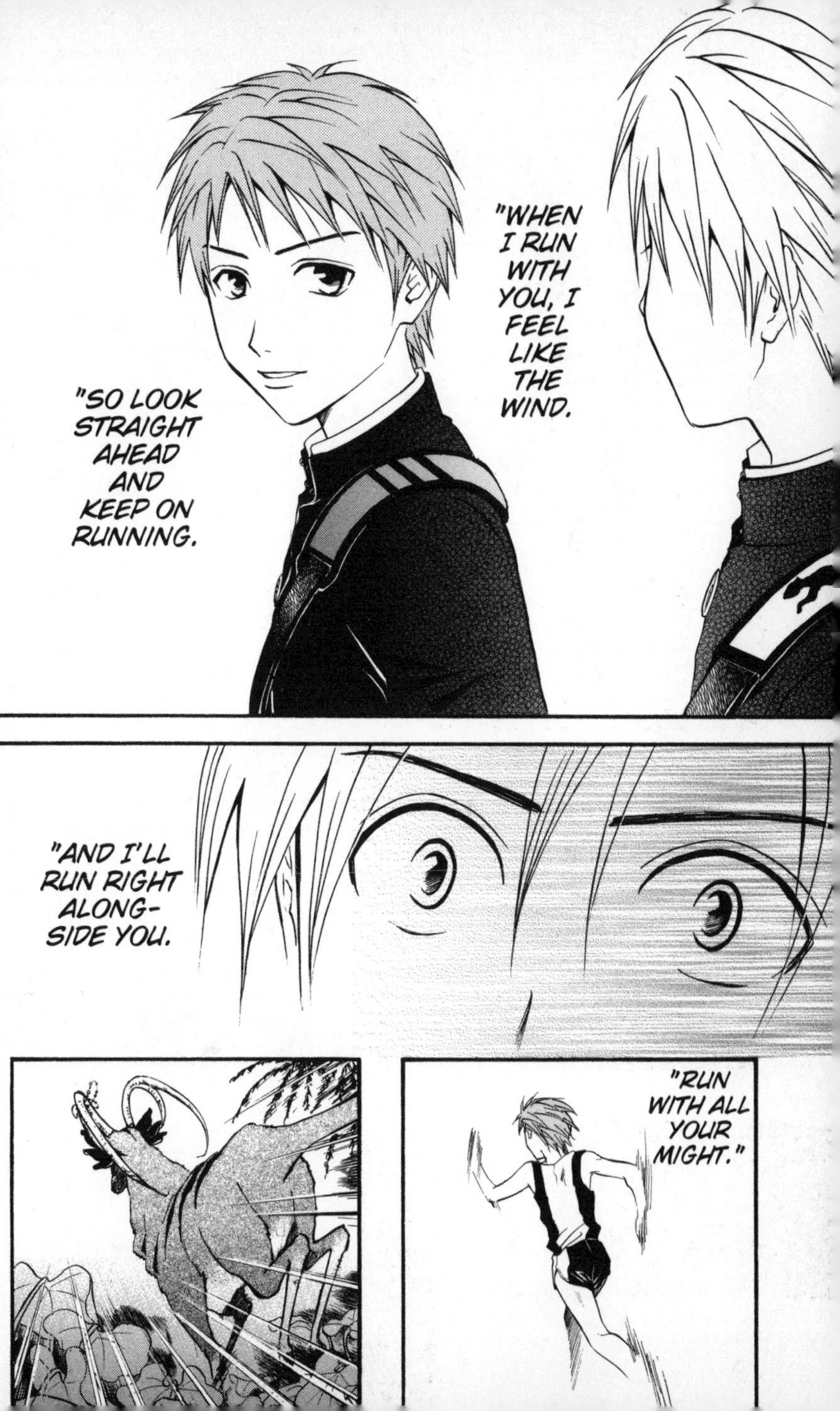
"WHEN I RUN WITH YOU, I FEEL LIKE THE WIND.
"SO LOOK STRAIGHT AHEAD AND KEEP ON RUNNING.
"AND I'LL RUN RIGHT ALONG-SIDE YOU.
"RUN WITH ALL YOUR MIGHT."

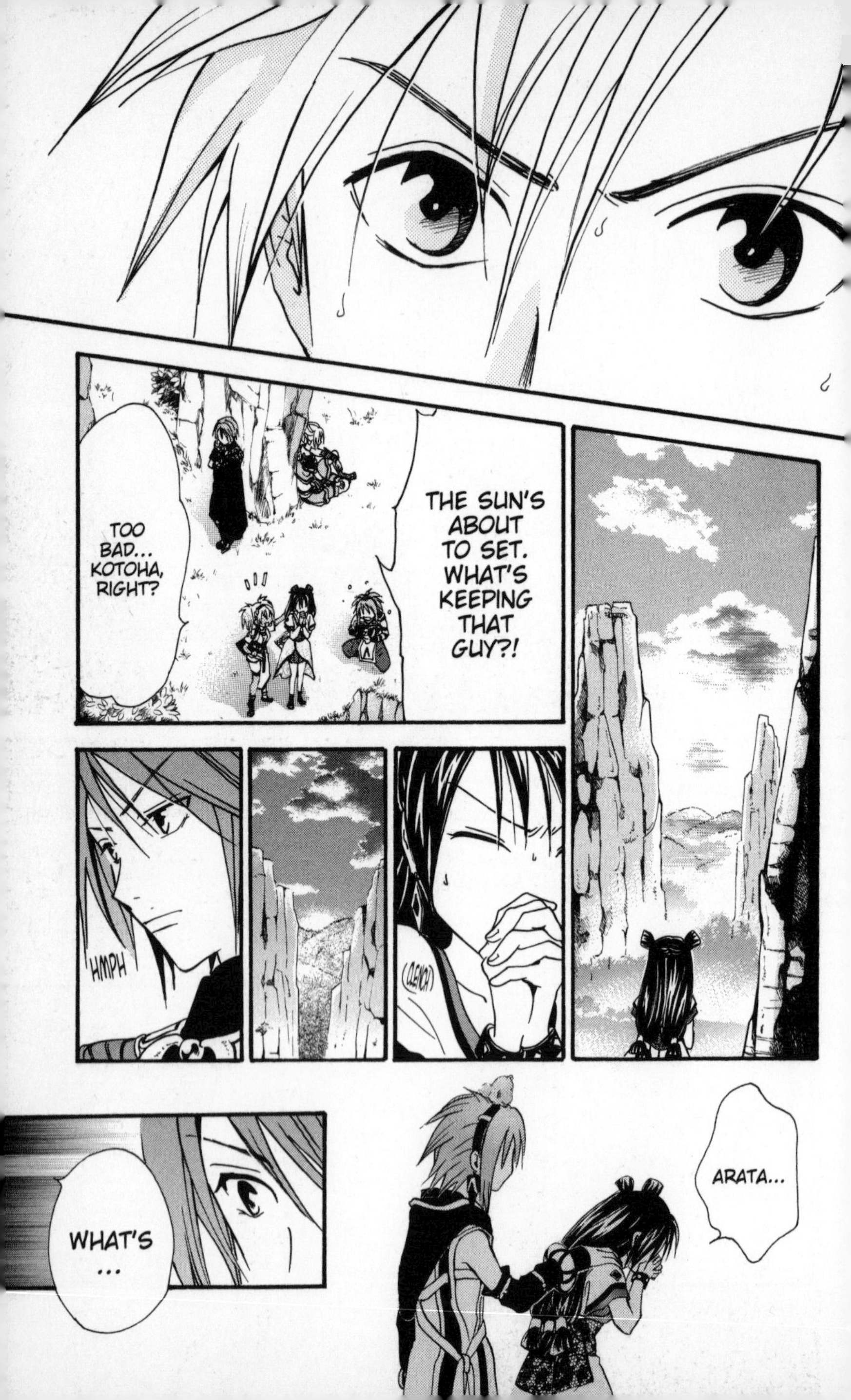
THE SUN'S ABOUT TO SET. WHAT'S KEEPING THAT GUY?!
TOO BAD... KOTOHA, RIGHT?
(CLENCH)
HMPH
ARATA...
WHAT'S ...

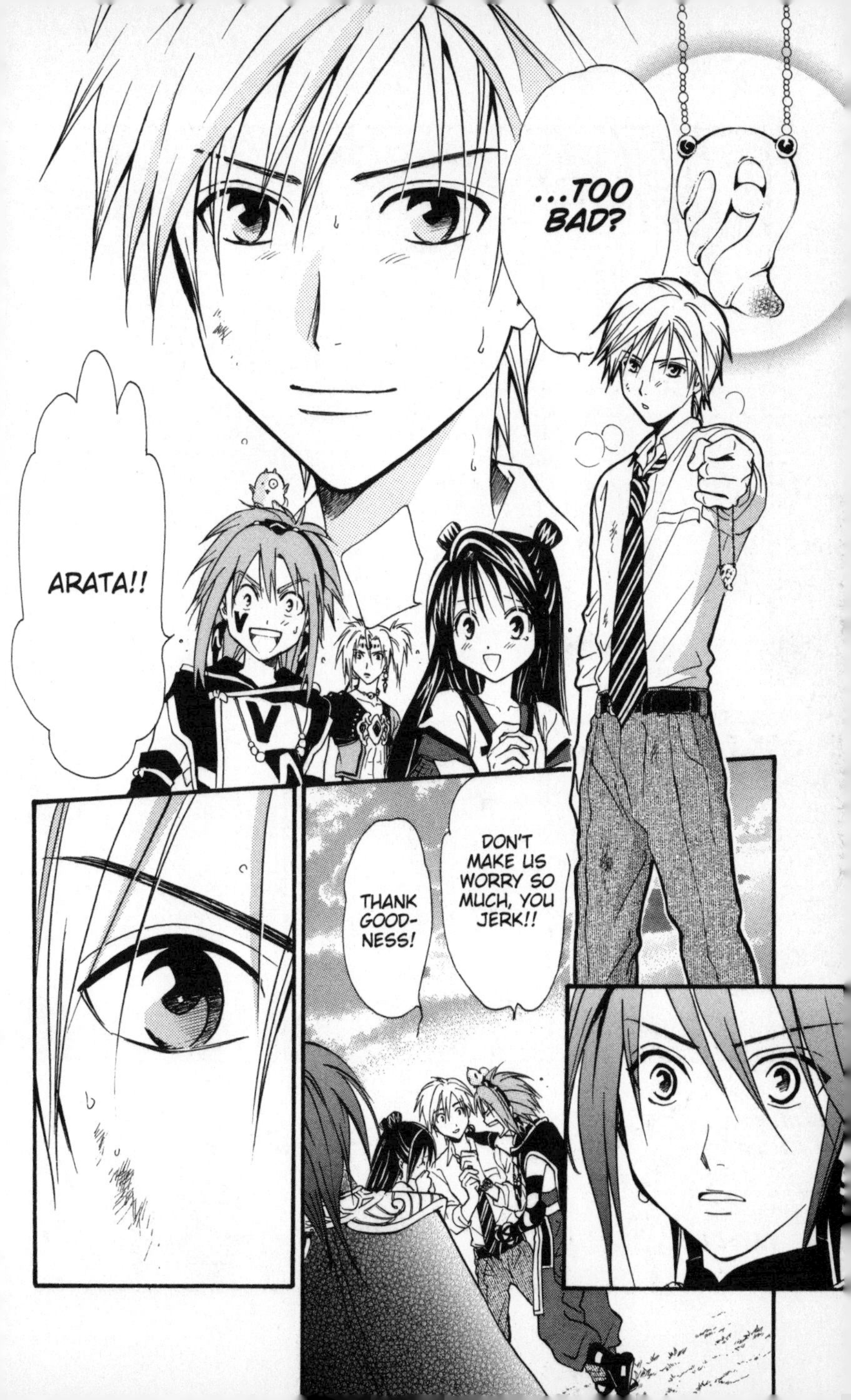
...TOO BAD?
ARATA!!
DON'T MAKE US WORRY SO MUCH, YOU JERK!!
THANK GOODNESS!

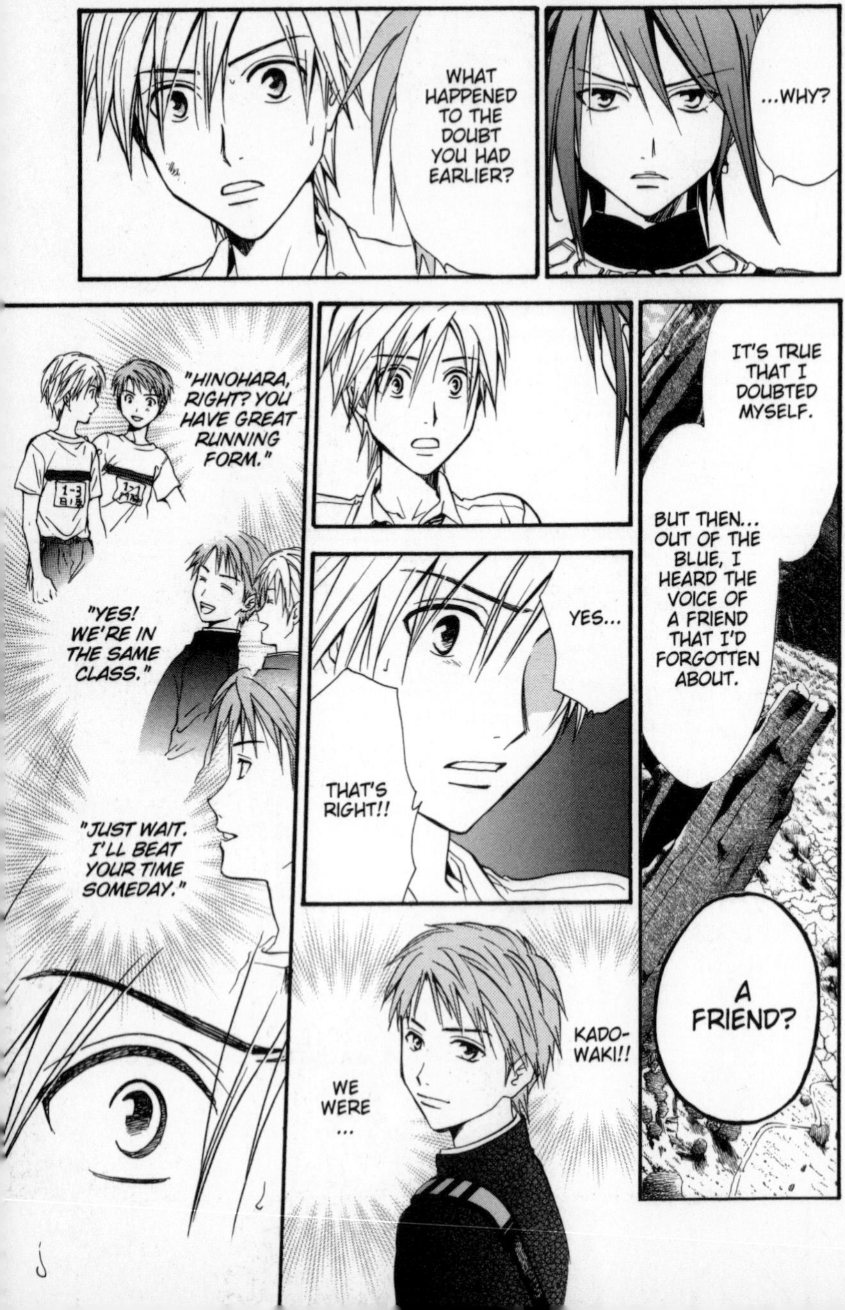
...WHY?
WHAT HAPPENED TO THE DOUBT YOU HAD EARLIER?
IT'S TRUE THAT I DOUBTED MYSELF.
BUT THEN... OUT OF THE BLUE, I HEARD THE VOICE OF A FRIEND THAT I'D FORGOTTEN ABOUT.
A FRIEND?
YES...
THAT'S RIGHT!!
KADO-WAKI!!
WE WERE ...
"HINOHARA, RIGHT? YOU HAVE GREAT RUNNING FORM."
"YES! WE'RE IN THE SAME CLASS."
"JUST WAIT. I'LL BEAT YOUR TIME SOMEDAY."

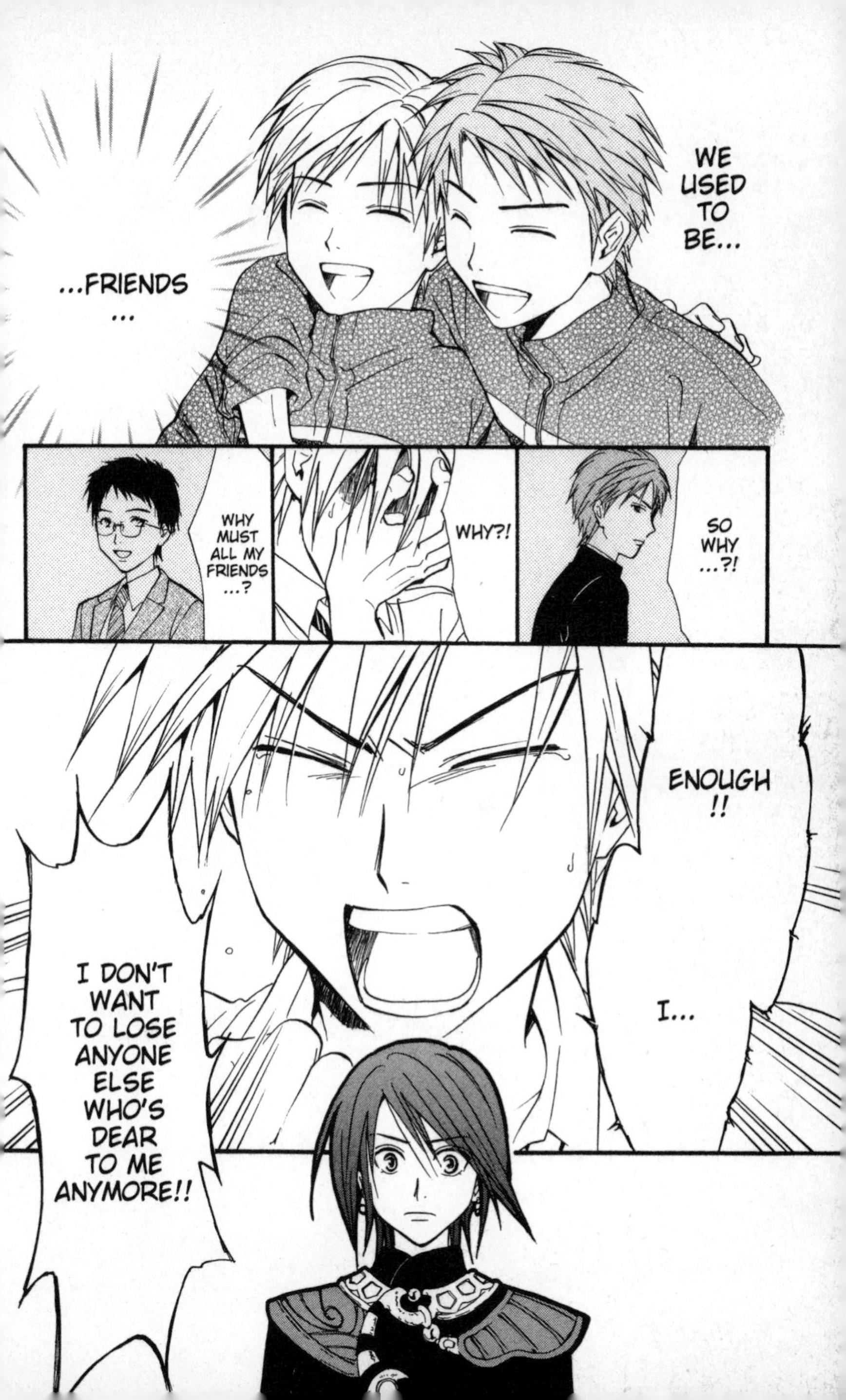
WE USED TO BE...
...FRIENDS ...
SO WHY ...?!
WHY?!
WHY MUST ALL MY FRIENDS ...?
ENOUGH !!
I...
I DON'T WANT TO LOSE ANYONE ELSE WHO'S DEAR TO ME ANYMORE!!

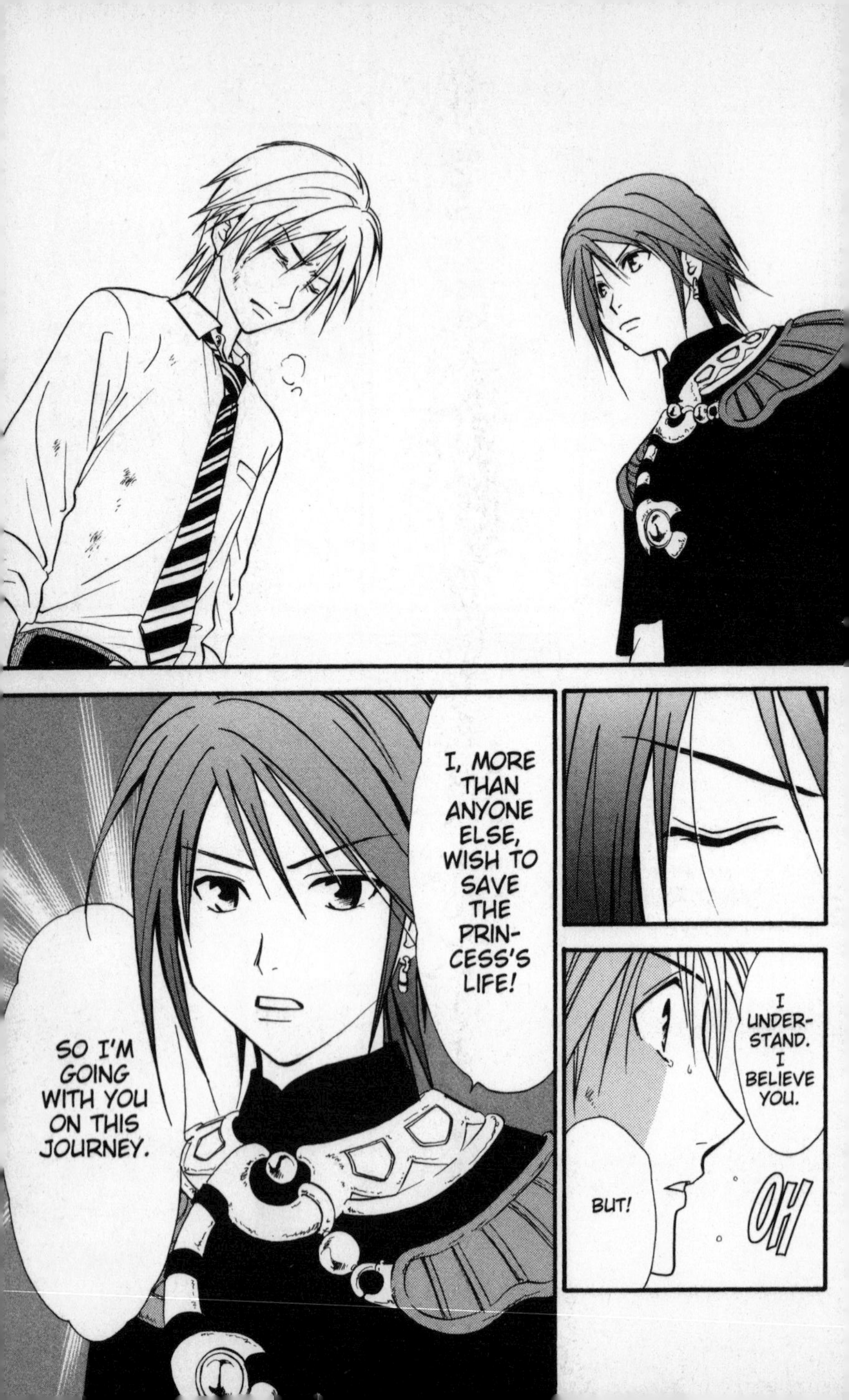
I UNDERSTAND. I BELIEVE YOU.
OH
BUT!
I, MORE THAN ANYONE ELSE, WISH TO SAVE THE PRINCESS'S LIFE!
SO I'M GOING WITH YOU ON THIS JOURNEY.

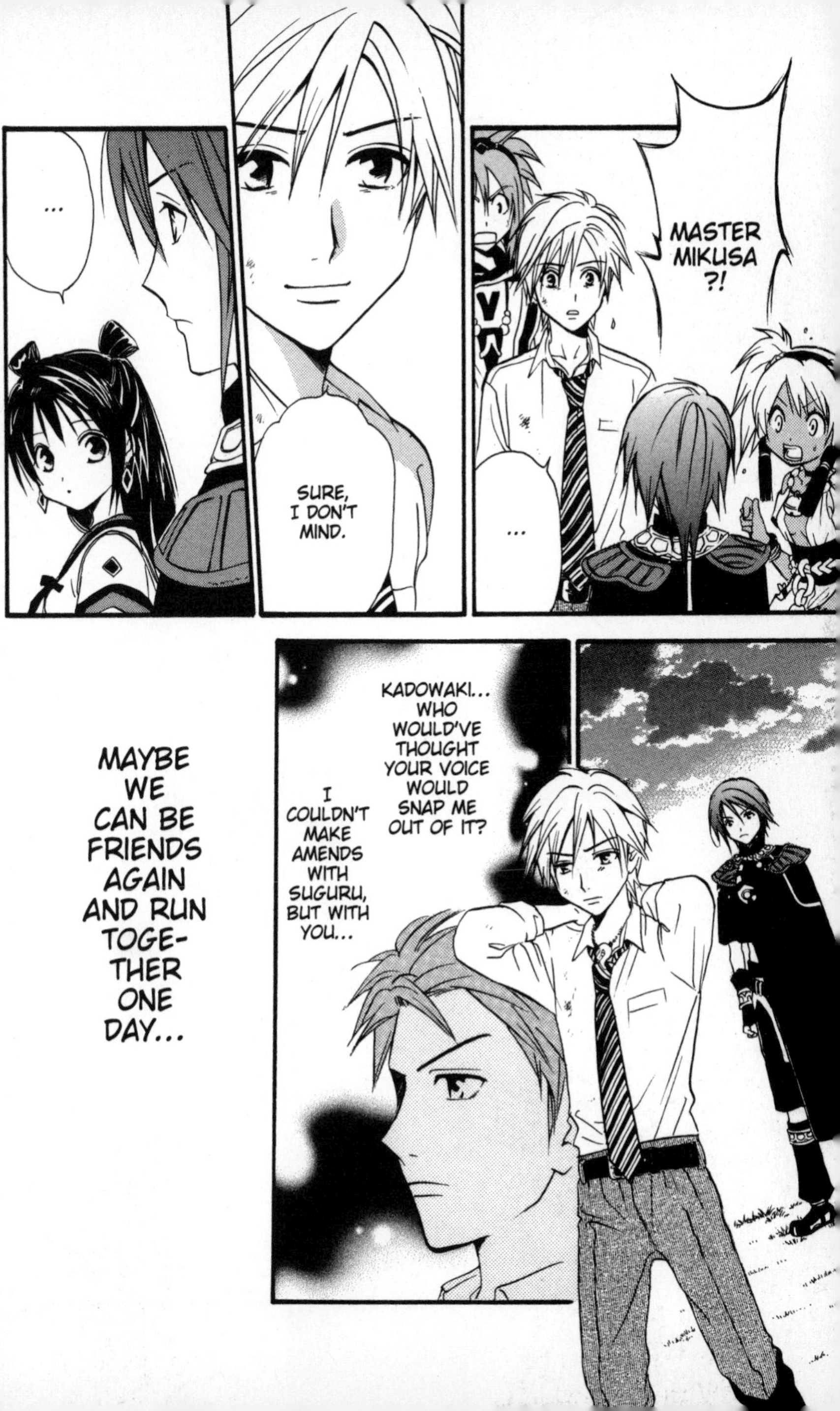
MASTER MIKUSA ?!
...
SURE, I DON'T MIND.
...
KADOWAKI... WHO WOULD'VE THOUGHT YOUR VOICE WOULD SNAP ME OUT OF IT?
I COULDN'T MAKE AMENDS WITH SUGURU, BUT WITH YOU...
MAYBE WE CAN BE FRIENDS AGAIN AND RUN TOGE-THER ONE DAY...

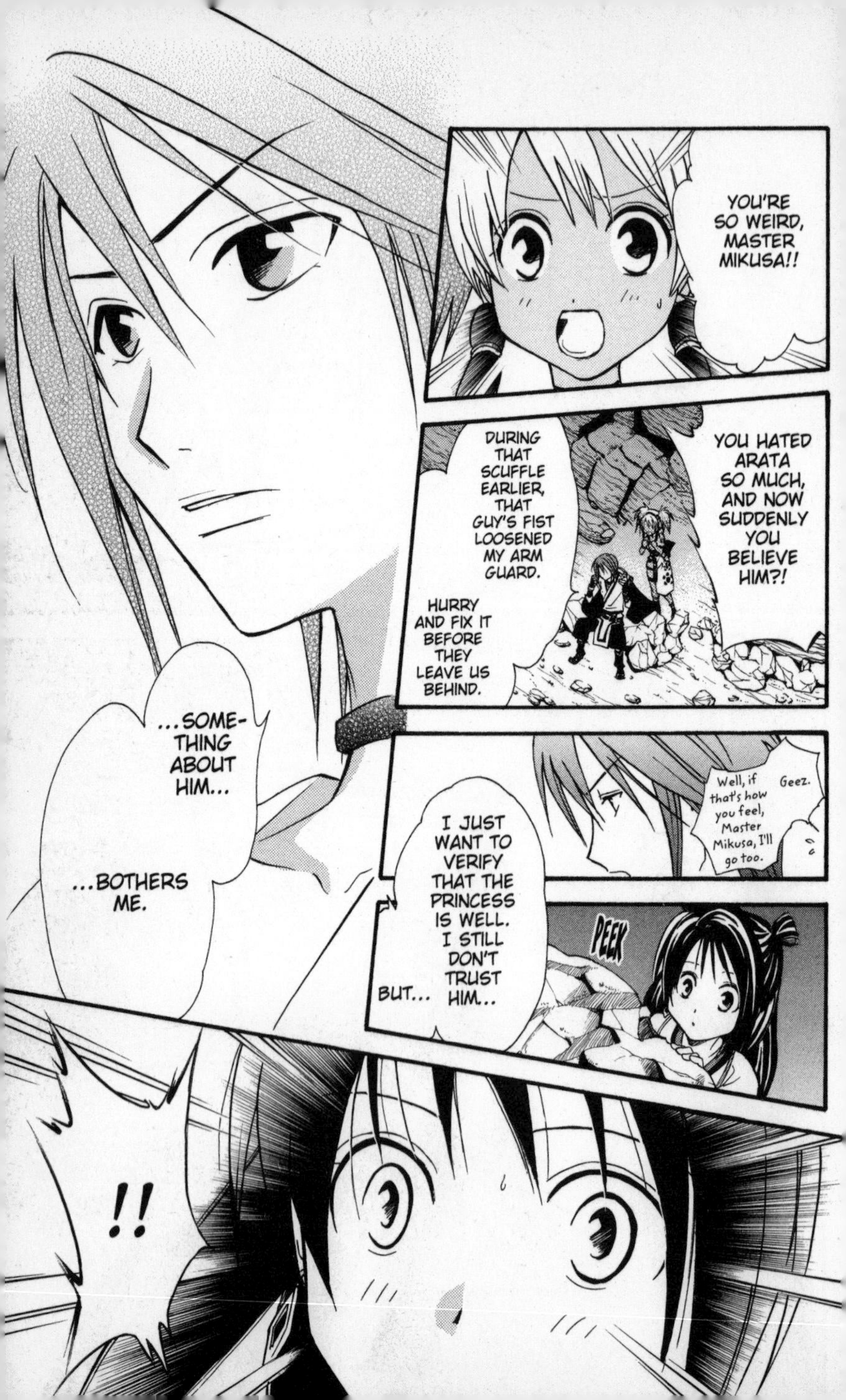
YOU'RE SO WEIRD, MASTER MIKUSA!!
YOU HATED ARATA SO MUCH, AND NOW SUDDENLY YOU BELIEVE HIM?!
DURING THAT SCUFFLE EARLIER, THAT GUY'S FIST LOOSENED MY ARM GUARD.
HURRY AND FIX IT BEFORE THEY LEAVE US BEHIND.
I JUST WANT TO VERIFY THAT THE PRINCESS IS WELL. I STILL DON'T TRUST HIM...
BUT...
...SOME-THING ABOUT HIM...
...BOTHERS ME.
Geez.
Well, if that's how you feel, Master Mikusa, I'll go too.
PEEK
!!

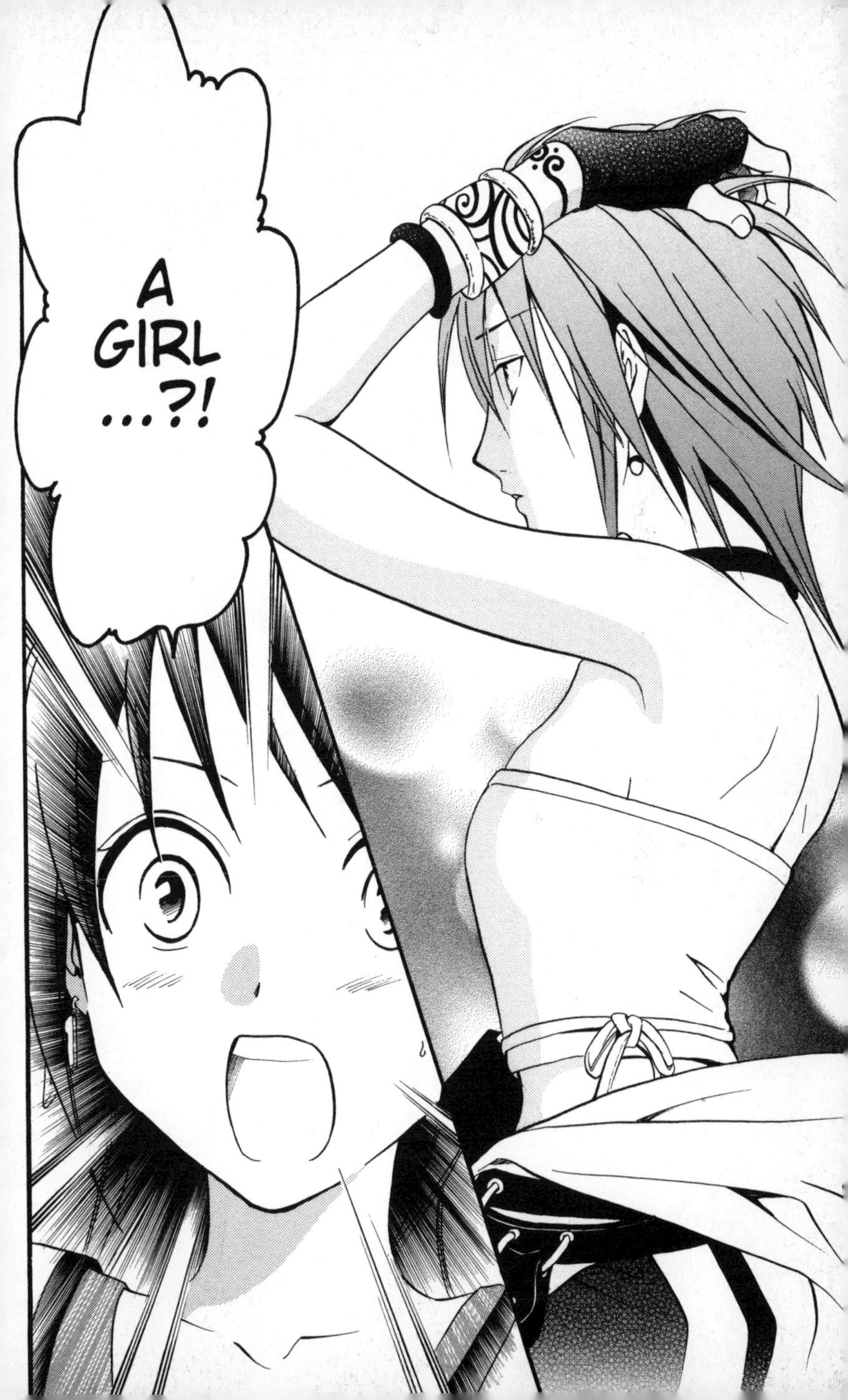
A GIRL ...?!

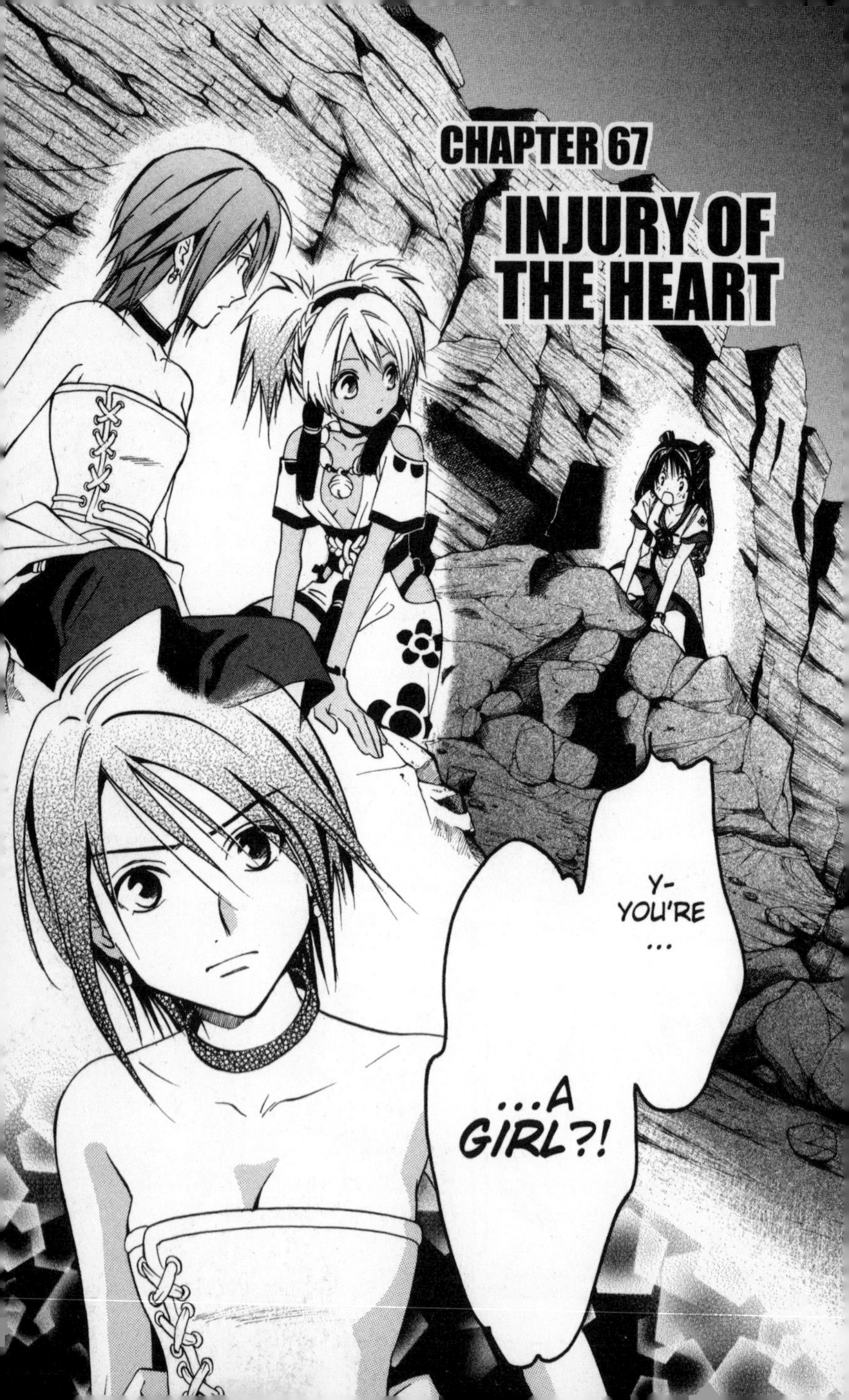
CHAPTER 67
INJURY OF THE HEART
Y-YOU'RE ...
...A GIRL?!

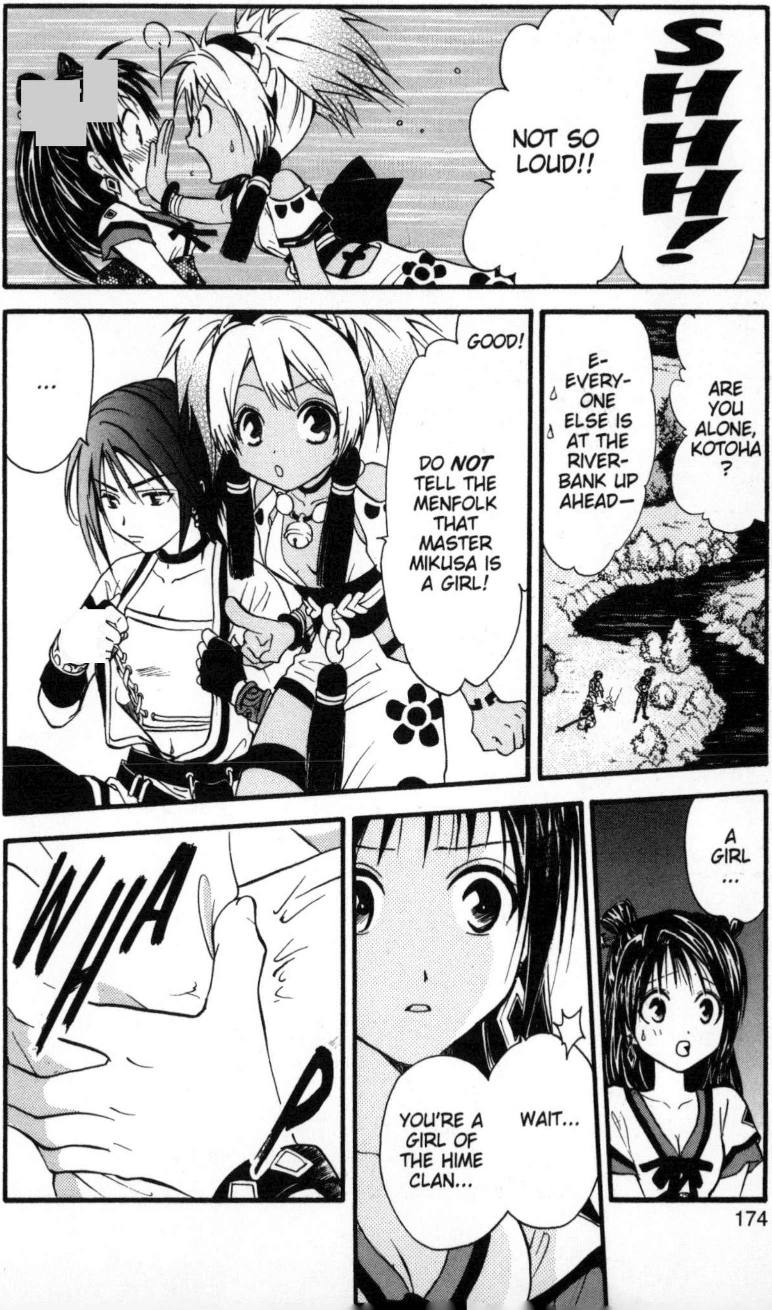
SHHH!
NOT SO LOUD!!
ARE YOU ALONE, KOTOHA?
E- EVERYONE ELSE IS AT THE RIVERBANK UP AHEAD—
GOOD!
DO **NOT** TELL THE MENFOLK THAT MASTER MIKUSA IS A GIRL!
...
A GIRL ...
WAIT...
YOU'RE A GIRL OF THE HIME CLAN...
WHAP

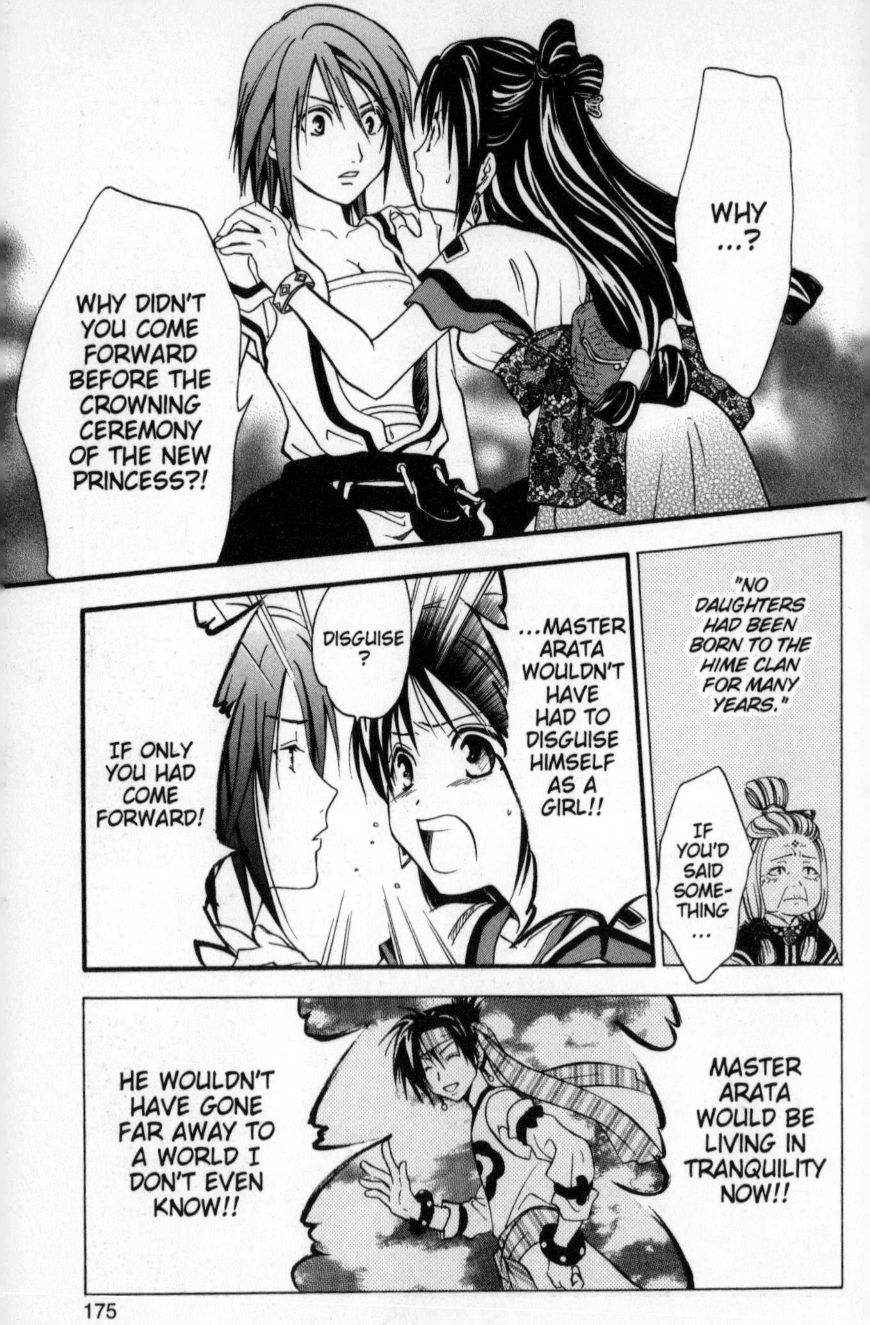
WHY ...?
WHY DIDN'T YOU COME FORWARD BEFORE THE CROWNING CEREMONY OF THE NEW PRINCESS?!
"NO DAUGHTERS HAD BEEN BORN TO THE HIME CLAN FOR MANY YEARS."
IF YOU'D SAID SOME-THING ...
...MASTER ARATA WOULDN'T HAVE HAD TO DISGUISE HIMSELF AS A GIRL!!
DISGUISE?
IF ONLY YOU HAD COME FORWARD!
MASTER ARATA WOULD BE LIVING IN TRANQUILITY NOW!!
HE WOULDN'T HAVE GONE FAR AWAY TO A WORLD I DON'T EVEN KNOW!!

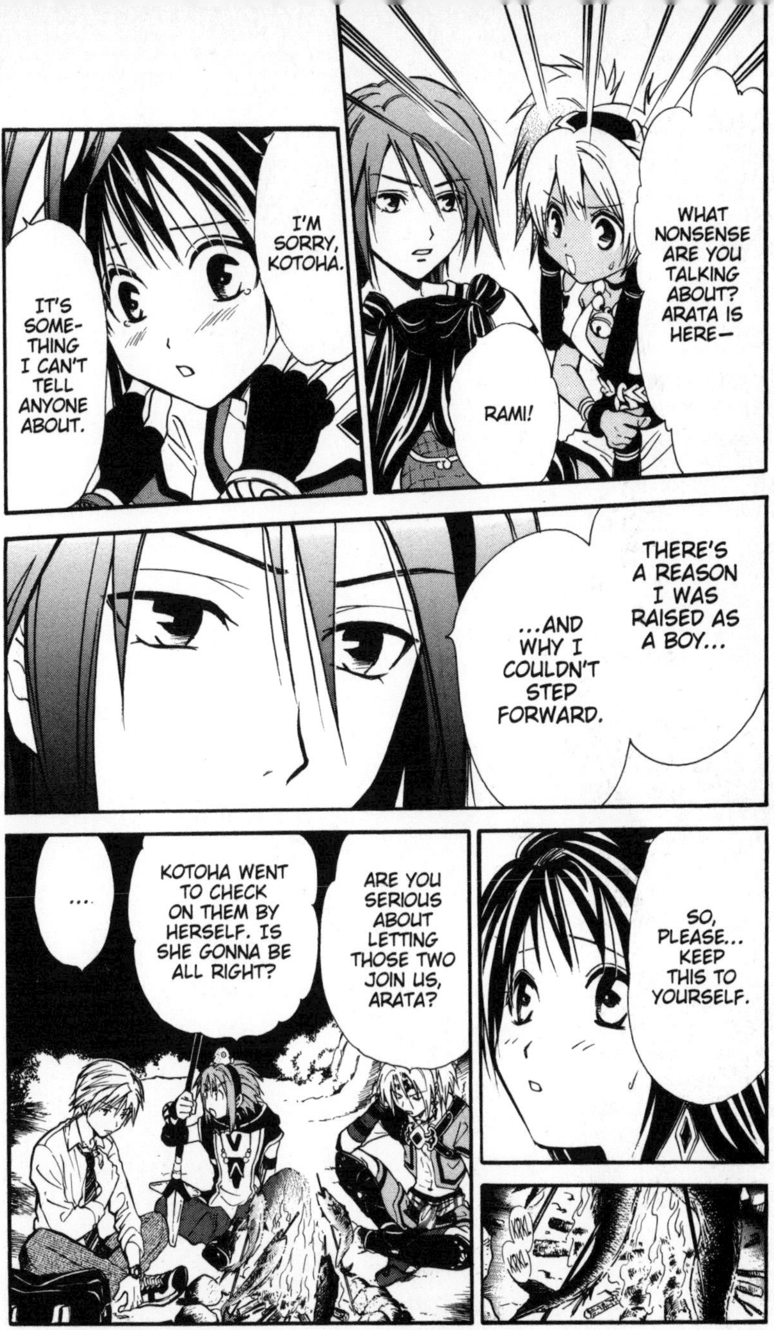
WHAT NONSENSE ARE YOU TALKING ABOUT? ARATA IS HERE—
RAMI!
I'M SORRY, KOTOHA.
IT'S SOMETHING I CAN'T TELL ANYONE ABOUT.
THERE'S A REASON I WAS RAISED AS A BOY...
...AND WHY I COULDN'T STEP FORWARD.
SO, PLEASE... KEEP THIS TO YOURSELF.
KRKL
KRKL
ARE YOU SERIOUS ABOUT LETTING THOSE TWO JOIN US, ARATA?
KOTOHA WENT TO CHECK ON THEM BY HERSELF. IS SHE GONNA BE ALL RIGHT?
...

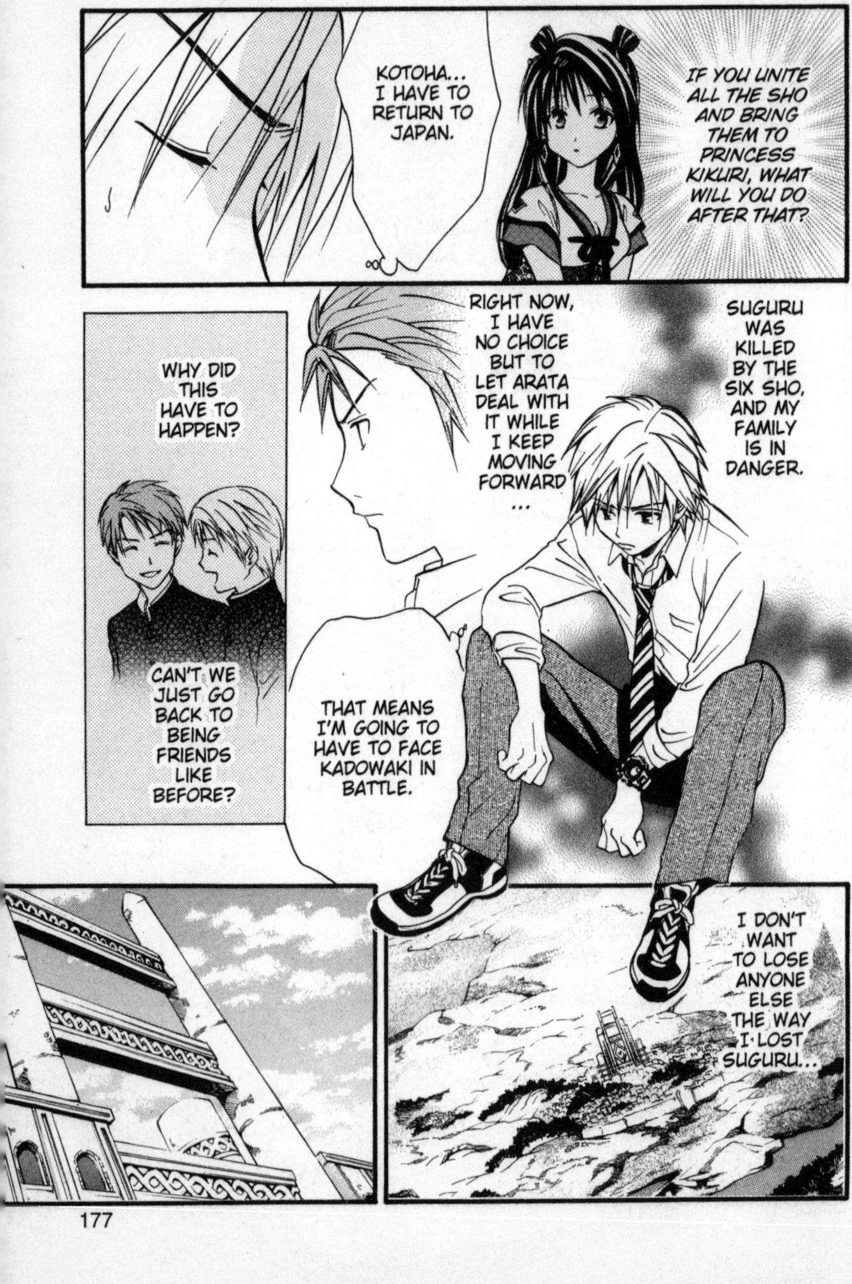
IF YOU UNITE ALL THE SHO AND BRING THEM TO PRINCESS KIKURI, WHAT WILL YOU DO AFTER THAT?
KOTOHA... I HAVE TO RETURN TO JAPAN.
SUGURU WAS KILLED BY THE SIX SHO, AND MY FAMILY IS IN DANGER.
RIGHT NOW, I HAVE NO CHOICE BUT TO LET ARATA DEAL WITH IT WHILE I KEEP MOVING FORWARD...
THAT MEANS I'M GOING TO HAVE TO FACE KADOWAKI IN BATTLE.
WHY DID THIS HAVE TO HAPPEN?
CAN'T WE JUST GO BACK TO BEING FRIENDS LIKE BEFORE?
I DON'T WANT TO LOSE ANYONE ELSE THE WAY I LOST SUGURU...

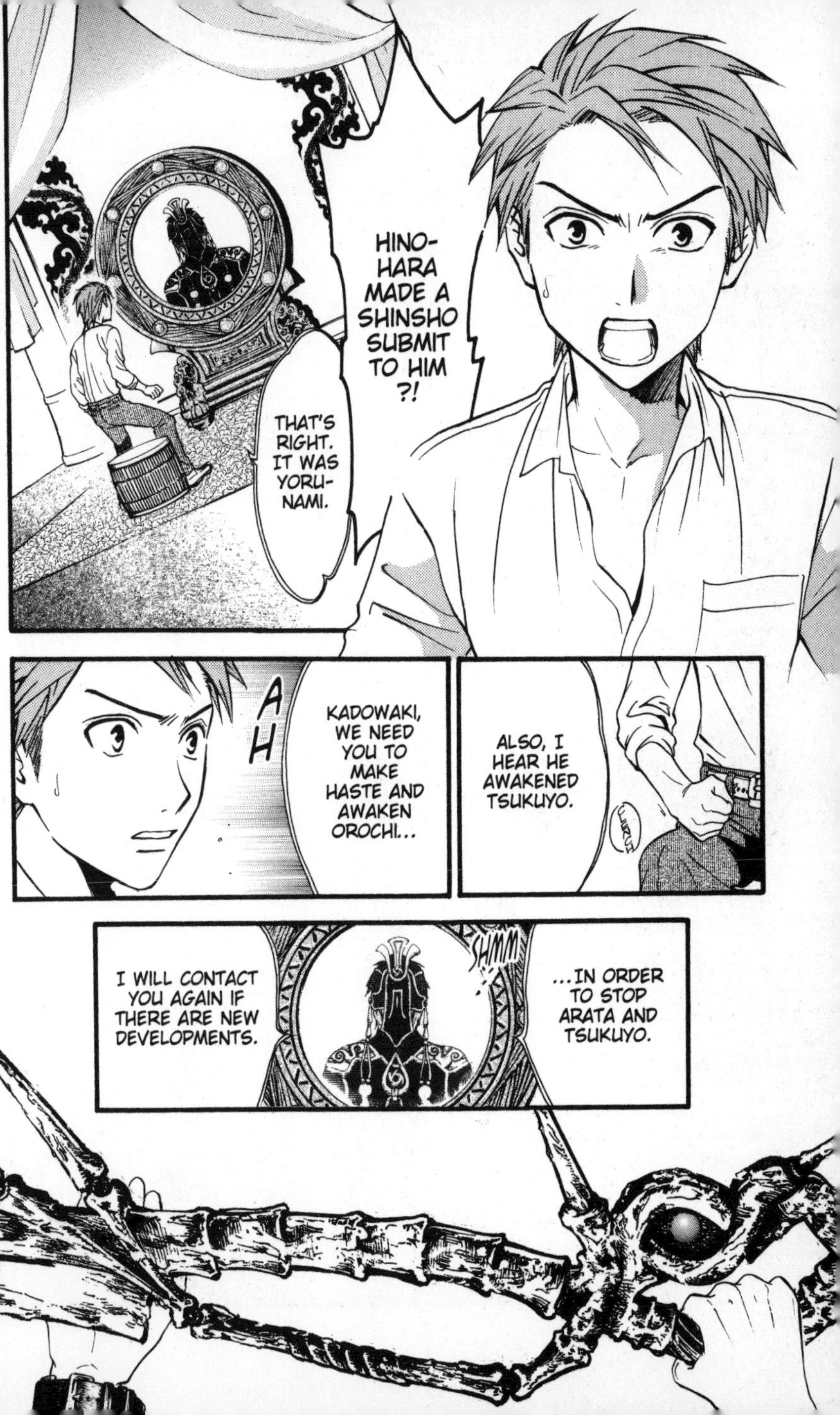
HINO-HARA MADE A SHINSHO SUBMIT TO HIM ?!
THAT'S RIGHT. IT WAS YORU-NAMI.
ALSO, I HEAR HE AWAKENED TSUKUYO.
KADOWAKI, WE NEED YOU TO MAKE HASTE AND AWAKEN OROCHI...
AH
...IN ORDER TO STOP ARATA AND TSUKUYO.
SHMM
I WILL CONTACT YOU AGAIN IF THERE ARE NEW DEVELOPMENTS.

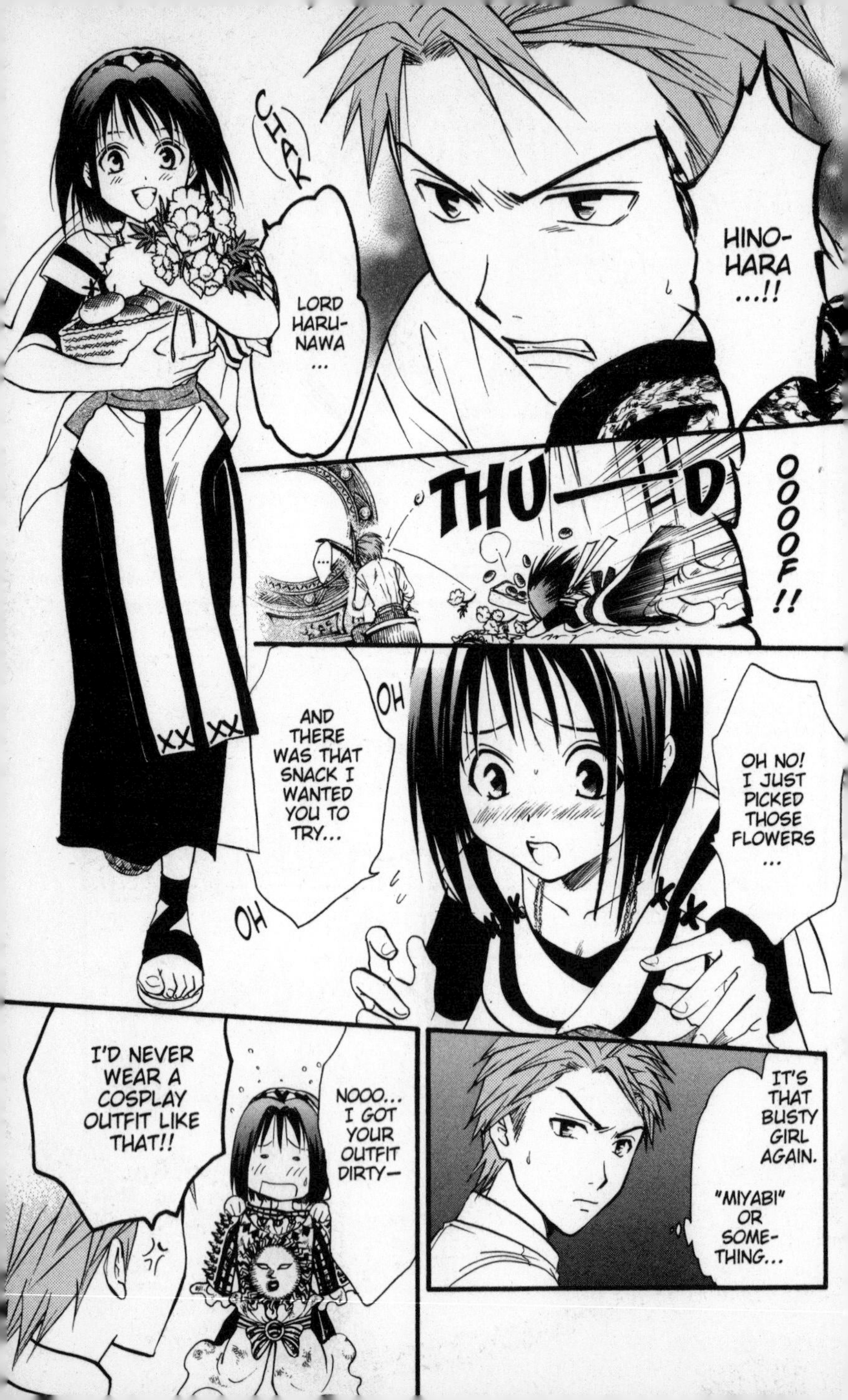
HINO-HARA ...!!
CHAK
LORD HARU-NAWA ...
OOOOF!!
THU—D
...
OH NO! I JUST PICKED THOSE FLOWERS ...
OH
AND THERE WAS THAT SNACK I WANTED YOU TO TRY...
OH
IT'S THAT BUSTY GIRL AGAIN.
"MIYABI" OR SOME-THING...
NOOO... I GOT YOUR OUTFIT DIRTY—
I'D NEVER WEAR A COSPLAY OUTFIT LIKE THAT!!

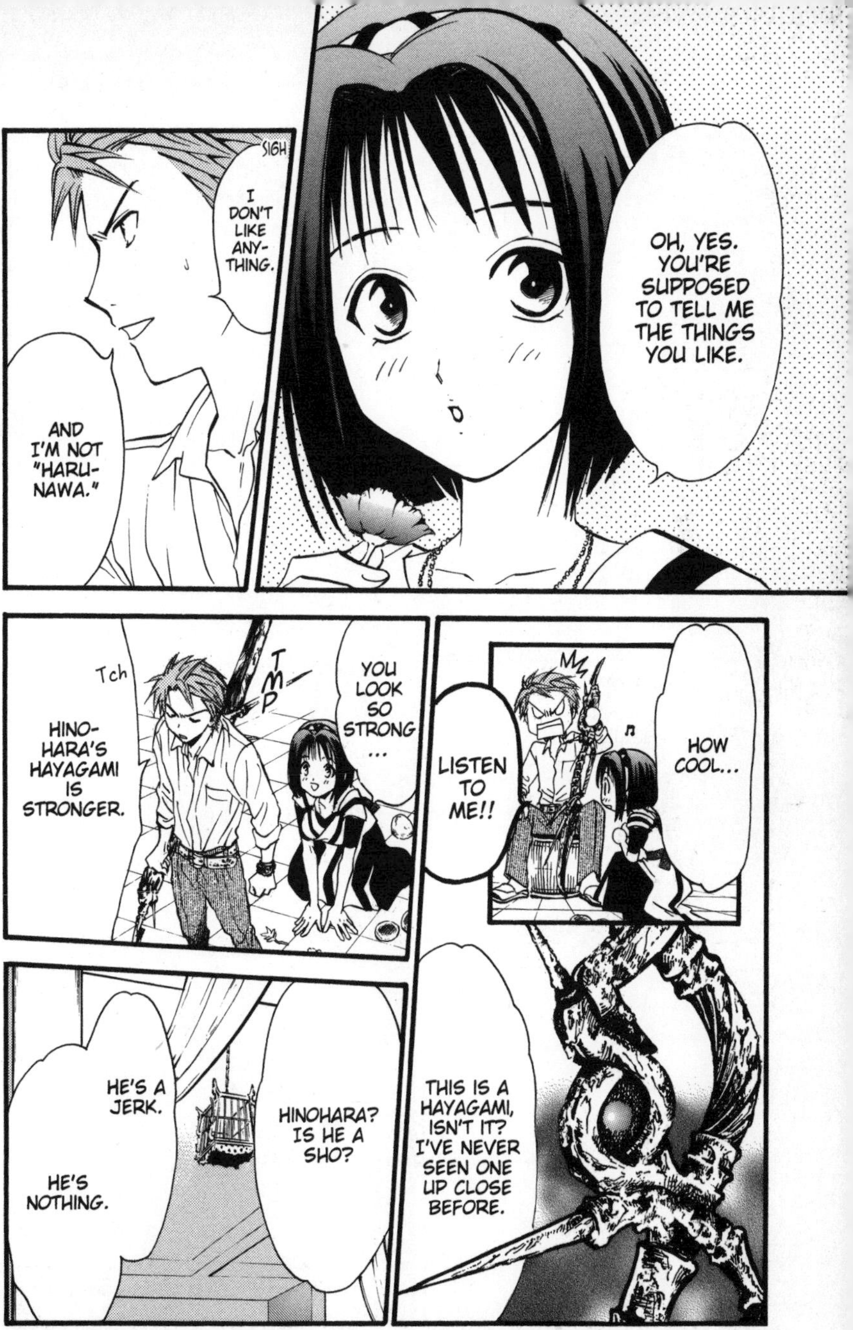

OH, YES. YOU'RE SUPPOSED TO TELL ME THE THINGS YOU LIKE.
SIGH
I DON'T LIKE ANYTHING.
AND I'M NOT "HARUNAWA."
HOW COOL...
LISTEN TO ME!!
THIS IS A HAYAGAMI, ISN'T IT? I'VE NEVER SEEN ONE UP CLOSE BEFORE.
YOU LOOK SO STRONG...
TMP
Tch
HINOHARA'S HAYAGAMI IS STRONGER.
HINOHARA? IS HE A SHO?
HE'S A JERK.
HE'S NOTHING.

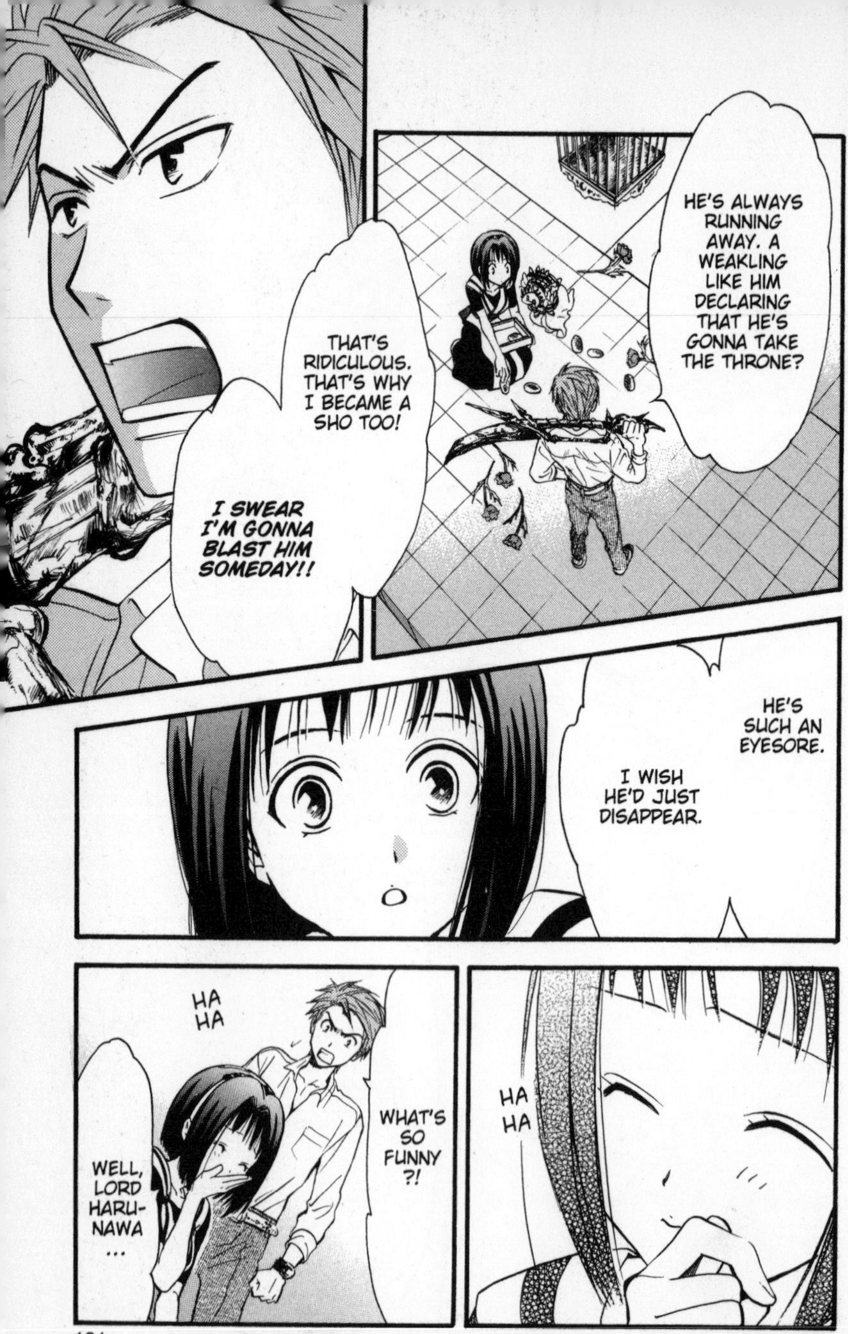
HE'S ALWAYS RUNNING AWAY. A WEAKLING LIKE HIM DECLARING THAT HE'S GONNA TAKE THE THRONE?
THAT'S RIDICULOUS. THAT'S WHY I BECAME A SHO TOO!
I SWEAR I'M GONNA BLAST HIM SOMEDAY!!
HE'S SUCH AN EYESORE.
I WISH HE'D JUST DISAPPEAR.
HA HA
HA HA
WHAT'S SO FUNNY ?!
WELL, LORD HARU-NAWA ...

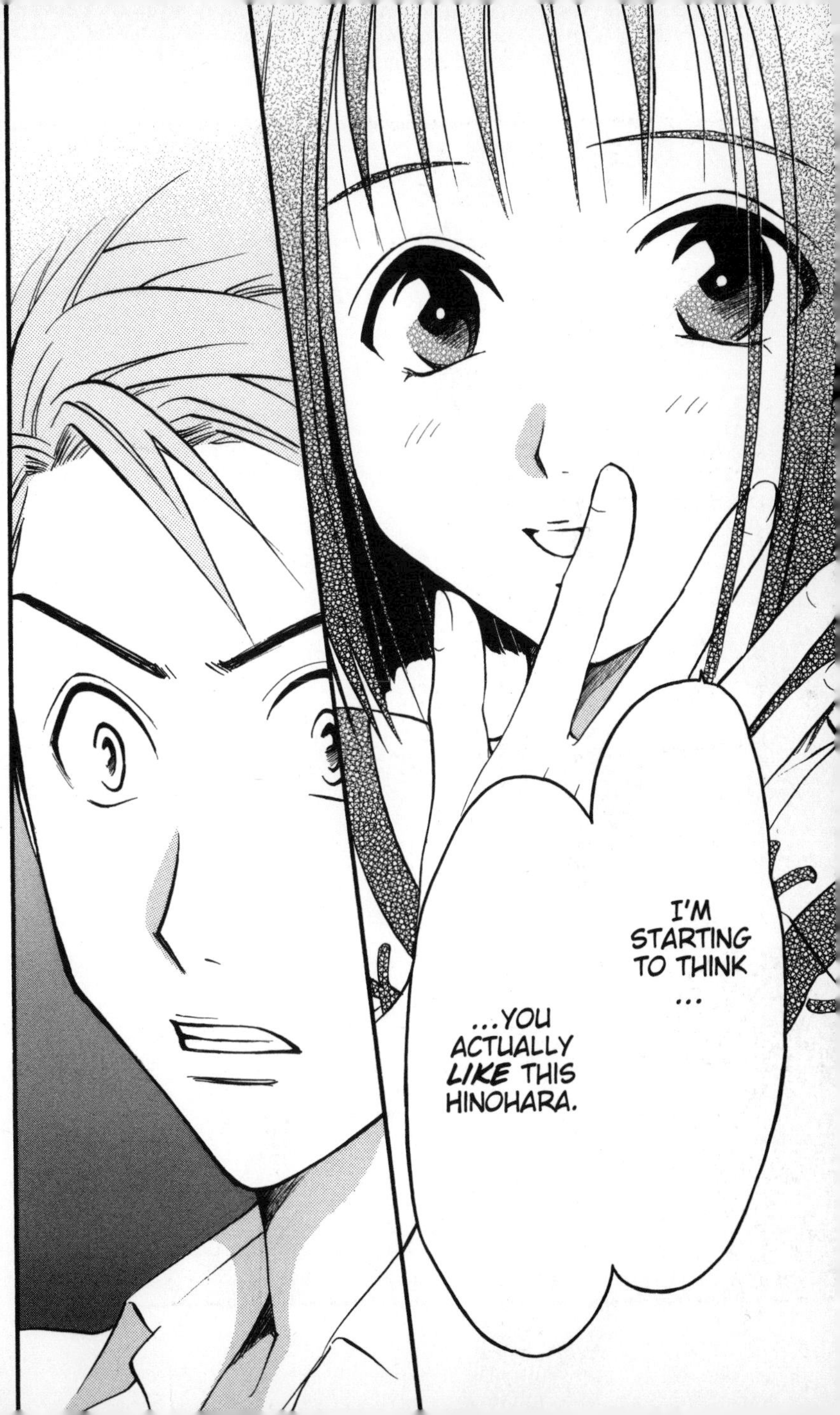
I'M STARTING TO THINK ...
...YOU ACTUALLY *LIKE* THIS HINOHARA.

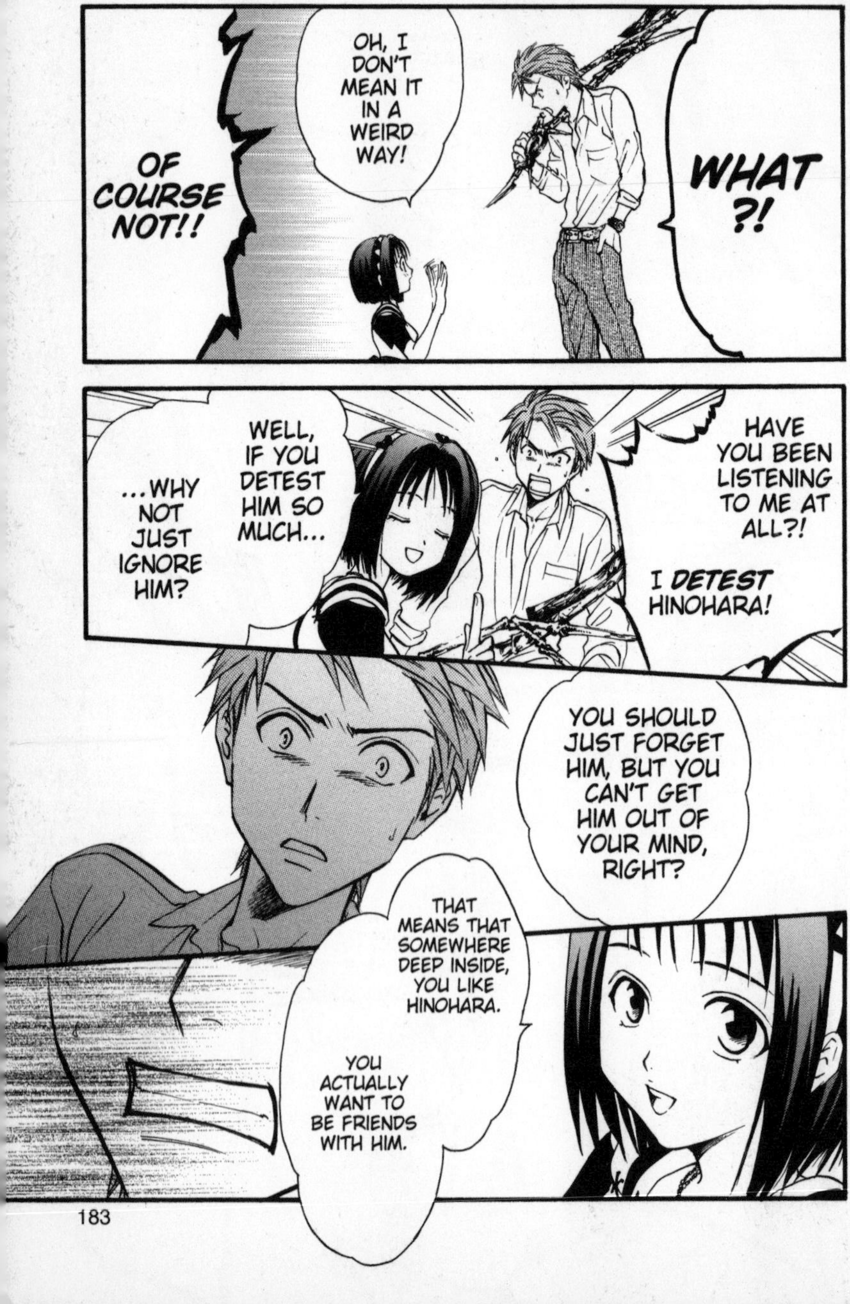
WHAT?!
OH, I DON'T MEAN IT IN A WEIRD WAY!
OF COURSE NOT!!
HAVE YOU BEEN LISTENING TO ME AT ALL?!
I DETEST HINOHARA!
WELL, IF YOU DETEST HIM SO MUCH...
...WHY NOT JUST IGNORE HIM?
YOU SHOULD JUST FORGET HIM, BUT YOU CAN'T GET HIM OUT OF YOUR MIND, RIGHT?
THAT MEANS THAT SOMEWHERE DEEP INSIDE, YOU LIKE HINOHARA.
YOU ACTUALLY WANT TO BE FRIENDS WITH HIM.

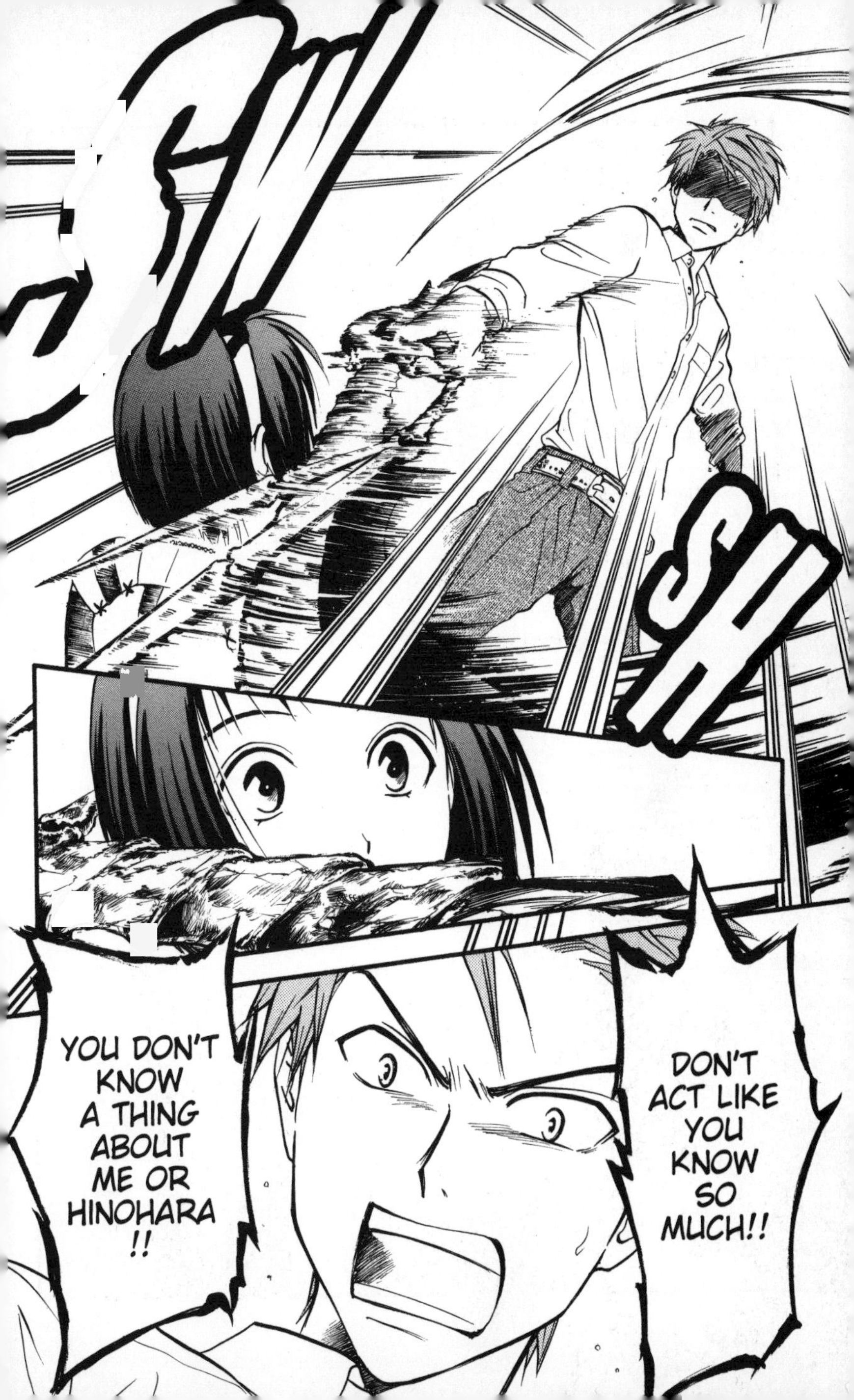
SH
DON'T ACT LIKE YOU KNOW SO MUCH!!
YOU DON'T KNOW A THING ABOUT ME OR HINOHARA!!

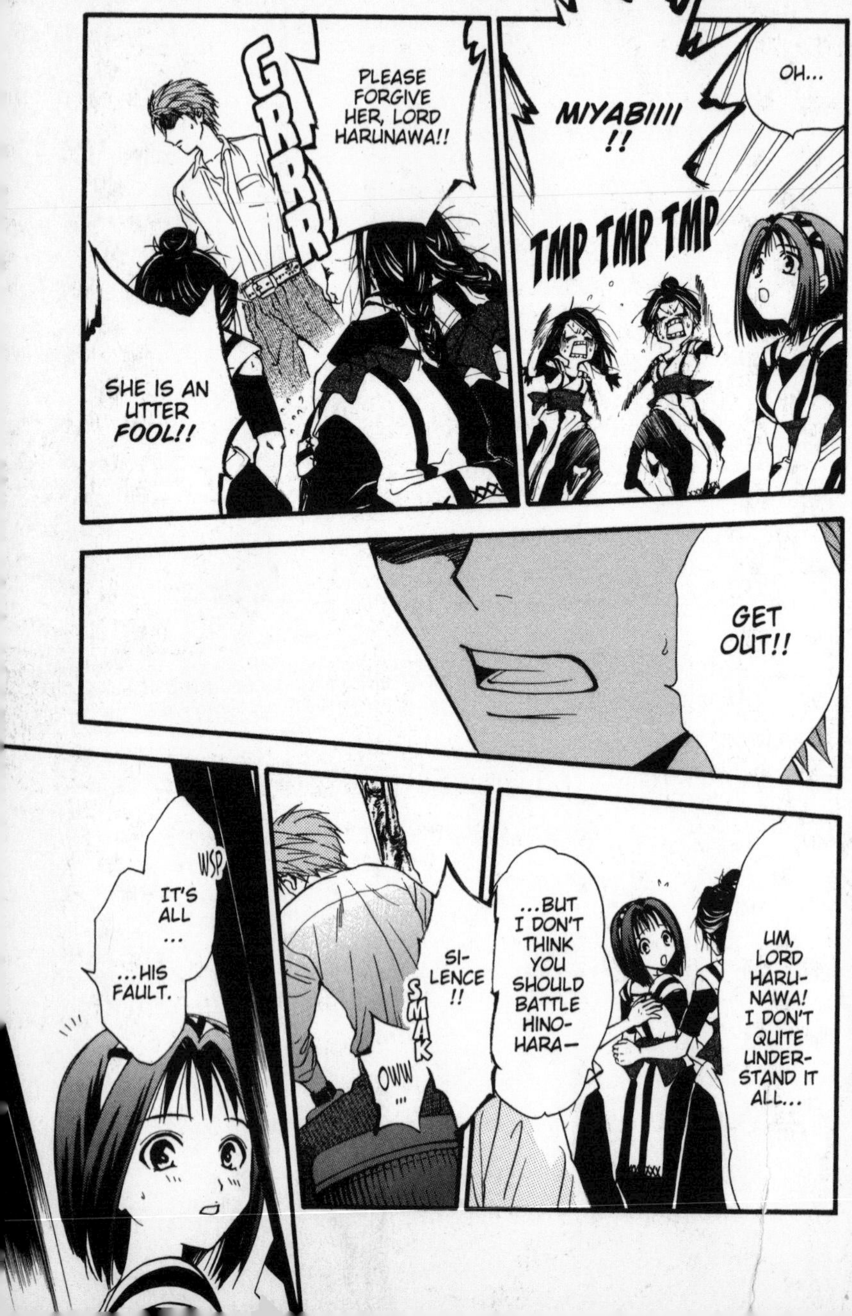
OH...
MIYABI!!!!
!!
TMP TMP TMP
PLEASE FORGIVE HER, LORD HARUNAWA!!
GRRR
SHE IS AN UTTER *FOOL!!*
GET OUT!!
UM, LORD HARU-NAWA! I DON'T QUITE UNDER-STAND IT ALL...
...BUT I DON'T THINK YOU SHOULD BATTLE HINO-HARA—
SI-LENCE!!
SMAK
OWW...
WSP
IT'S ALL...
...HIS FAULT.

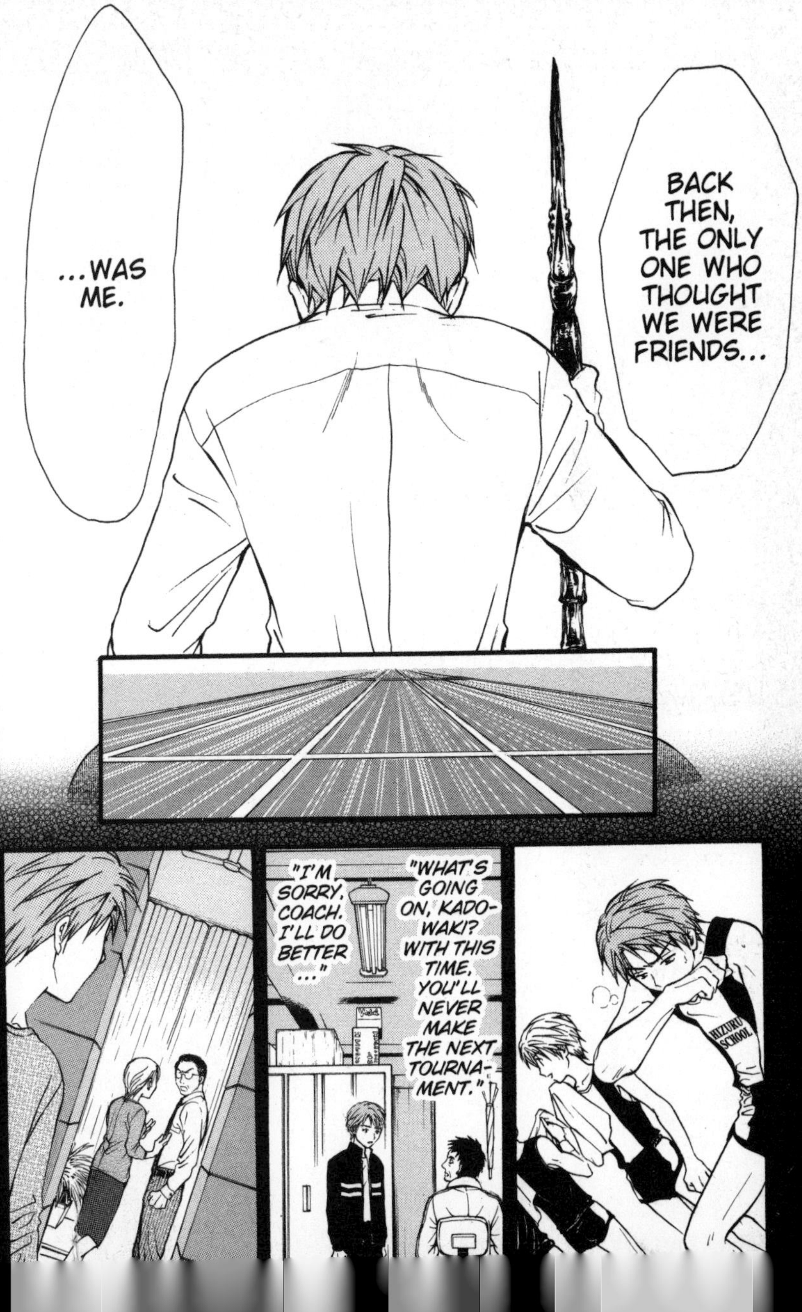
BACK THEN, THE ONLY ONE WHO THOUGHT WE WERE FRIENDS...
...WAS ME.
HIZURU SCHOOL
"WHAT'S GOING ON, KADO-WAKI? WITH THIS TIME, YOU'LL NEVER MAKE THE NEXT TOURNA-MENT."
"I'M SORRY, COACH. I'LL DO BETTER..."

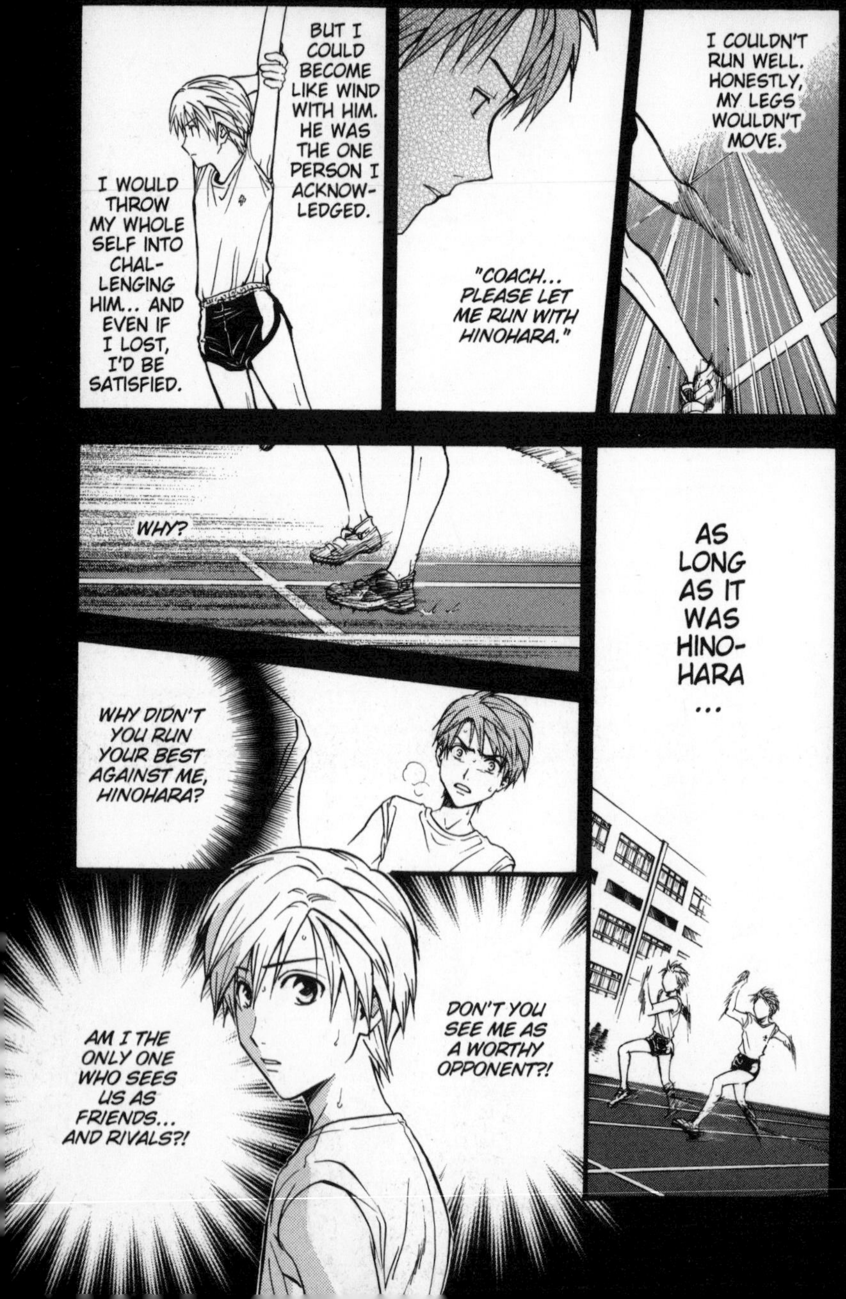
I COULDN'T RUN WELL. HONESTLY, MY LEGS WOULDN'T MOVE.
"COACH... PLEASE LET ME RUN WITH HINOHARA."
BUT I COULD BECOME LIKE WIND WITH HIM. HE WAS THE ONE PERSON I ACKNOWLEDGED.
I WOULD THROW MY WHOLE SELF INTO CHALLENGING HIM... AND EVEN IF I LOST, I'D BE SATISFIED.
AS LONG AS IT WAS HINOHARA...
WHY?
WHY DIDN'T YOU RUN YOUR BEST AGAINST ME, HINOHARA?
DON'T YOU SEE ME AS A WORTHY OPPONENT?!
AM I THE ONLY ONE WHO SEES US AS FRIENDS... AND RIVALS?!

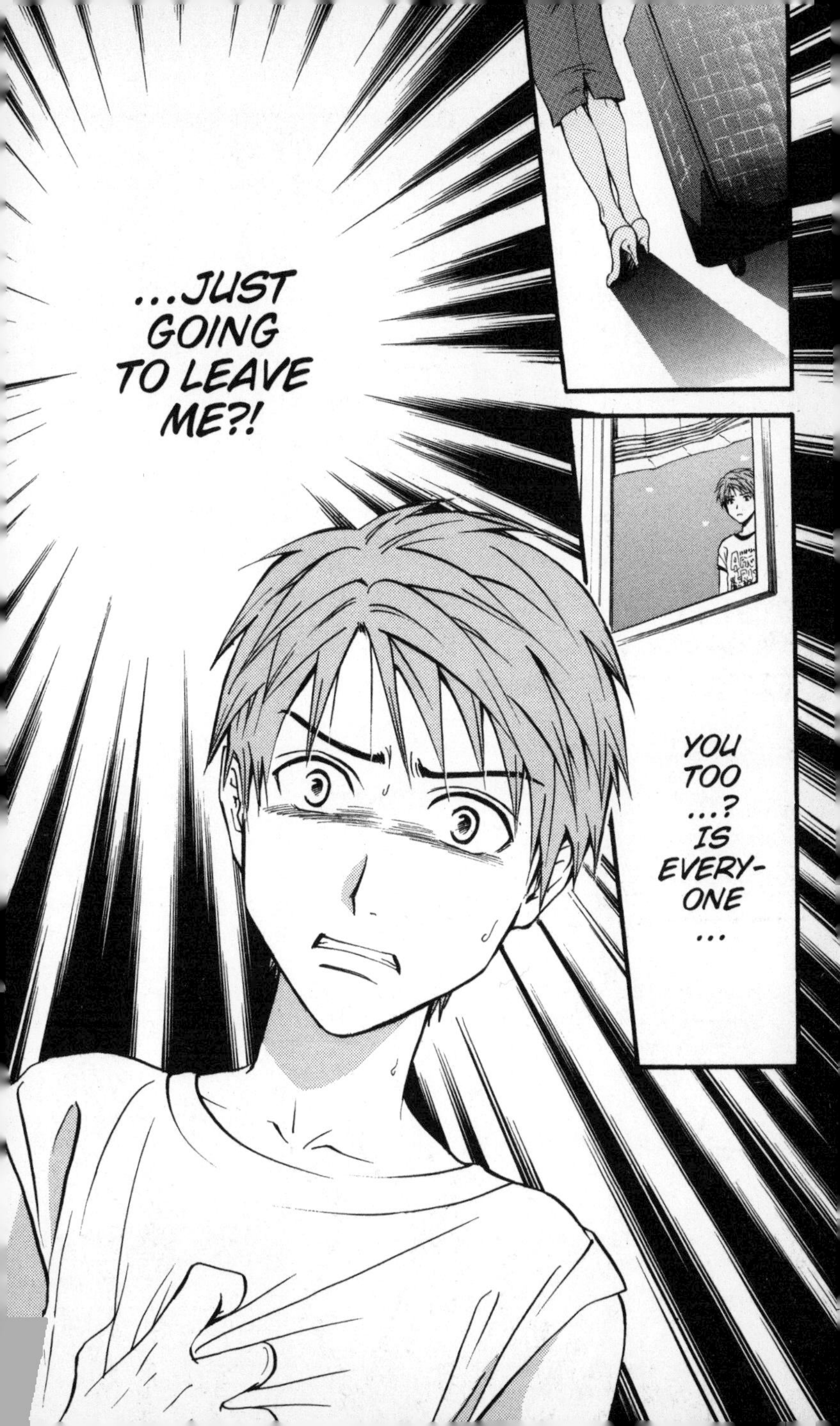
YOU TOO ...? IS EVERY-ONE ...
...JUST GOING TO LEAVE ME?!

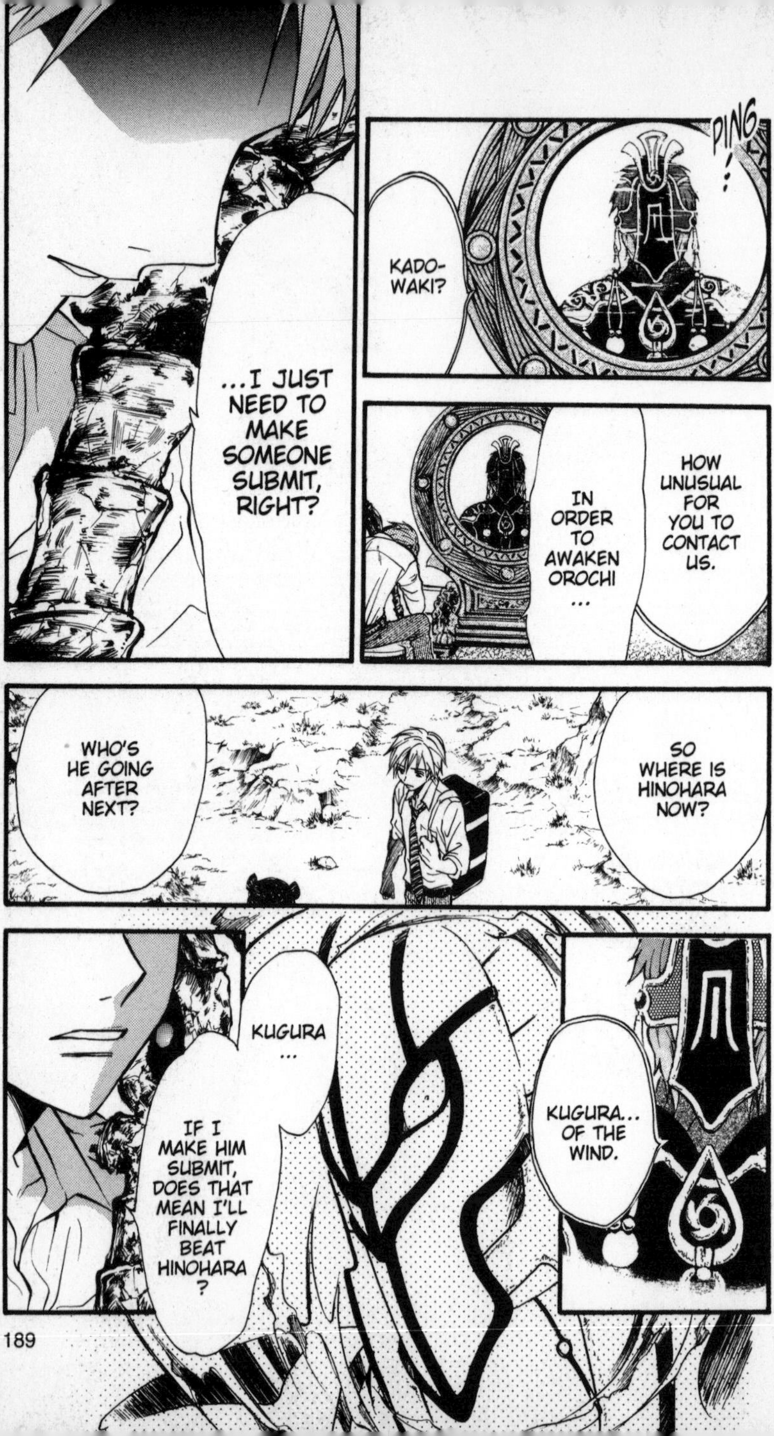
PING
KADO-WAKI?
HOW UNUSUAL FOR YOU TO CONTACT US.
IN ORDER TO AWAKEN OROCHI...
...I JUST NEED TO MAKE SOMEONE SUBMIT, RIGHT?
SO WHERE IS HINOHARA NOW?
WHO'S HE GOING AFTER NEXT?
KUGURA... OF THE WIND.
KUGURA...
IF I MAKE HIM SUBMIT, DOES THAT MEAN I'LL FINALLY BEAT HINOHARA?

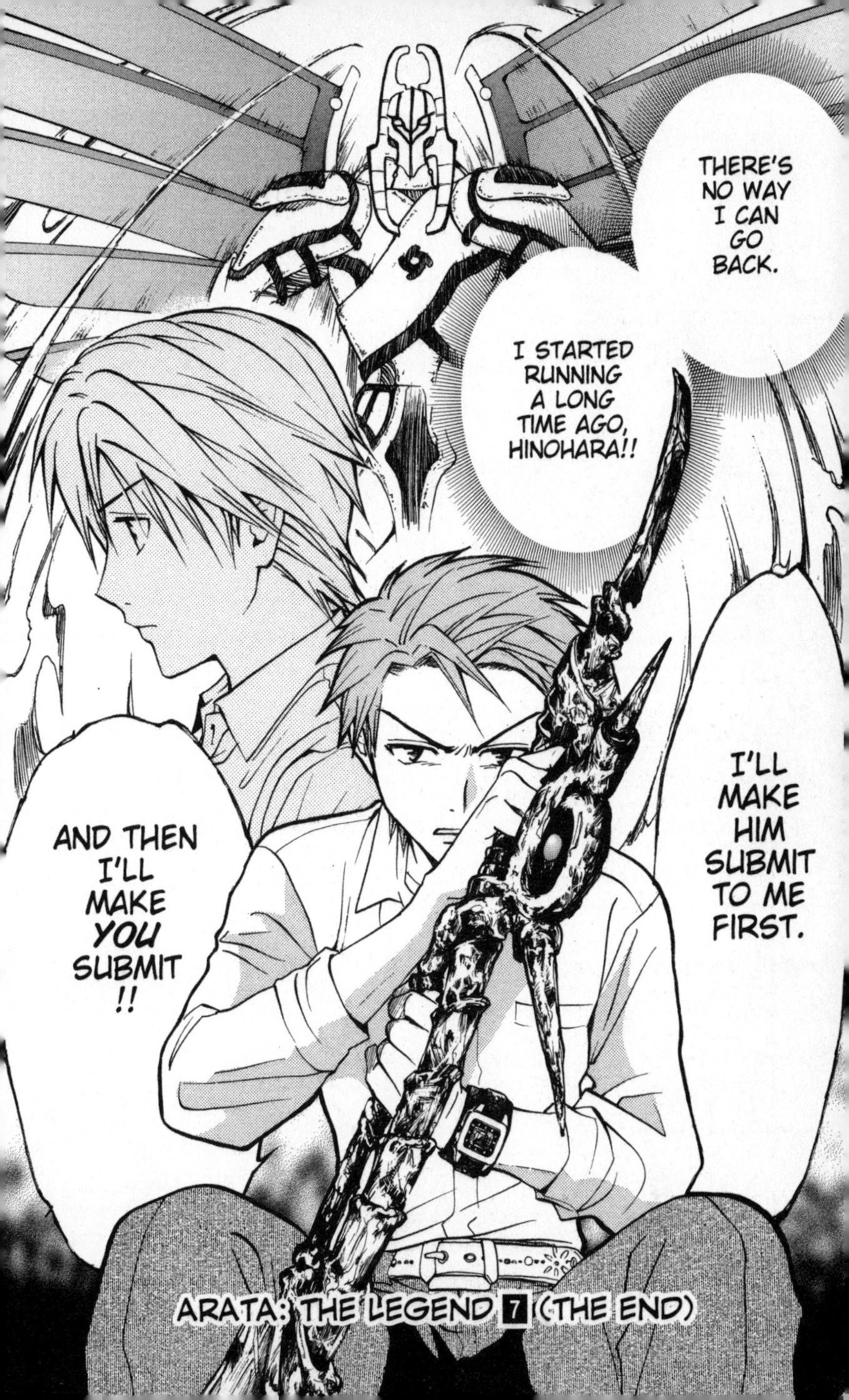
THERE'S NO WAY I CAN GO BACK.
I STARTED RUNNING A LONG TIME AGO, HINOHARA!!
I'LL MAKE HIM SUBMIT TO ME FIRST.
AND THEN I'LL MAKE *YOU* SUBMIT!!
ARATA: THE LEGEND 7 (THE END)

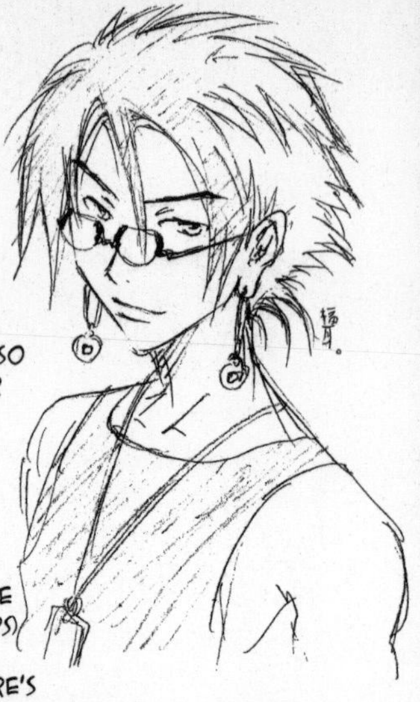

- WE'RE ALREADY AT VOLUME 7 OF *ARATA!*
HOW QUICKLY TIME FLIES.
ABOUT HIRUKO WHO DEBUTED IN THE PREVIOUS VOLUME... HE'S... WELL, HE'S LIKE "EBBESSAN" [EBISU, THE GOD OF PROSPERITY]. YOU KNOW, IT'S LIKE THE SAYING, "BUSINESS IS BOOMING, SO BRING YOUR BAMBOO LEAVES."♪ (THOUGH I WONDER WHY IT'S BAMBOO LEAVES...)
ANYWAY, THE SHINSHO AND THEIR ZOKUSHO DISPLAY THEIR CRESTS (MARKS) UNPRETENTIOUSLY ON THEIR PERSON.
HIRUKO'S IS THIS: AND YORUNAMI'S IS THIS:
ALSO UNPRETENTIOUS IS YORUNAMI'S CREST ON THE BACK OF HIRUKO'S OUTER COAT. (ACTUALLY, IT'S QUITE PRETENTIOUS.) SUCH A LOYAL GESTURE, ISN'T IT? (TEARS) OTHER ZOKUSHO WHO WISH TO DISPLAY THEIRS DO SO TOO. IT'S SIMILAR TO A CANINE SOCIETY... IF THERE'S AN ALPHA DOG, THEY'RE QUITE LOYAL TO HIM. HOW THEY MUST SUFFER IF THEIR BOSS IS CRUEL! I WAS RELUCTANT TO MAKE YORUNAMI SUBMIT. BUT HE'S STILL IN ARATA'S HAYAGAMI, SO MAYBE, JUST MAYBE, HE'LL REAPPEAR. (WHICH IS IT?)

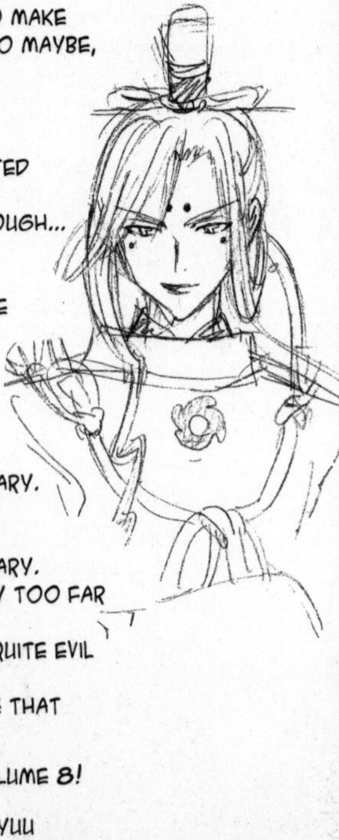

- PUTTING THE MEN'S SOCIETY OF SHO ASIDE... IN THIS VOLUME, TWO NEW FEMALE CHARACTERS DEBUTED.
KOTOHA HAS BEEN A LONE FEMALE REGULAR, AND I WANTED TO ADD A BIT MORE PIZZAZZ.
ONE OF THE NEW CHARACTERS LOOKS PRETTY BOYISH THOUGH... WELL, LOOK OUT, MEN! (LOOKS CAN BE DECEIVING.)
ANYWAY, IN THE NEXT VOLUME (ASSUMPTIONS CAN BE DANGEROUS TOO), PLEASE LOOK FORWARD TO SEEING THE "KUGURA" STORY ARC RISE TO A WHOLE NEW LEVEL.

- AND WHO COULD FORGET SUGURU! HE WASN'T SUCH A BAD GUY.
HARUNAWA *IS* A BAD GUY THOUGH—NOT TO MENTION SCARY. BUT WHEN I'M WORKING ON HIM AT WORK, MY ASSISTANT ALWAYS EXCLAIMS, "DAMN, HE'S GOOD-LOOKING!"
COME TO THINK OF IT, BEING GOOD-LOOKING CAN BE SCARY. (AND DECEIVING. AND DANGEROUS.) BUT IS HIS SOUL REALLY TOO FAR GONE, I WONDER?
AND FINALLY, THERE'S THE SOMEWHAT WARPED BUT NOT QUITE EVIL KADOWAKI. WILL HE EVER RETURN TO HIS OLD SELF?
SINCE BOTH HE AND ARATA ARE SHO NOW, IS IT INEVITABLE THAT ONE OF THEM WILL SUBMIT TO THE OTHER?

PLEASE CONTINUE TO SUPPORT ME. (^O^) SEE YOU IN VOLUME 8!

-YUU
MAY 2010

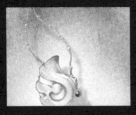

I always have trouble with color illustrations.

When an image comes to mind, it seems great at first. Then the composition and colors come into play, and I can't decide which is best. I can spend a lot of time on the basic rough sketch, but luckily with *Arata: The Legend*, we just feature the main characters of each volume, so that makes it easier...

Still, positioning them is difficult. (So it is hard after all.)

For this volume, I shaded Yorunami mostly in blue to feature the other two characters more prominently. Of course, if he actually were blue, his face would look far too sickly... (*Laugh*)

–YUU WATASE

AUTHOR BIO

Born March 5 in Osaka, Yuu Watase debuted in the *Shôjo Comic* manga anthology in 1989. She won the 43rd Shogakukan Manga Award with *Ceres: Celestial Legend*. One of her most famous works is *Fushigi Yûgi*, a series that has inspired the prequel *Fushigi Yûgi: Genbu Kaiden*. In 2008, *Arata: The Legend* started serialization in *Shonen Sunday*.

ARATA: THE LEGEND

Volume 7
Shonen Sunday Edition

Story and Art by YUU WATASE

© 2009 Yuu WATASE/Shogakukan
All rights reserved.
Original Japanese edition "ARATAKANGATARI"
published by SHOGAKUKAN Inc.

English Adaptation: Carol Fox
Translation: JN Productions
Touch-up Art & Lettering: Rina Mapa
Design: Ronnie Casson
Editor: Amy Yu

The rights of the author(s) of the work(s) in this publication
to be so identified have been asserted in accordance with the
Copyright, Designs and Patents Act 1988. A CIP catalogue
record for this book is available from the British Library.

Printed in the U.S.A.

Published by VIZ Media, LLC
P.O. Box 77010
San Francisco, CA 94107

10 9 8 7 6 5 4 3 2 1
First printing, September 2011

www.viz.com

MANGA STARTS ON SUNDAY
WWW.SHONENSUNDAY.COM

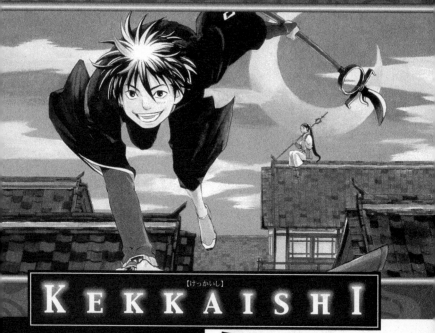
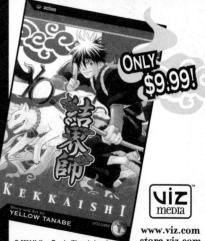

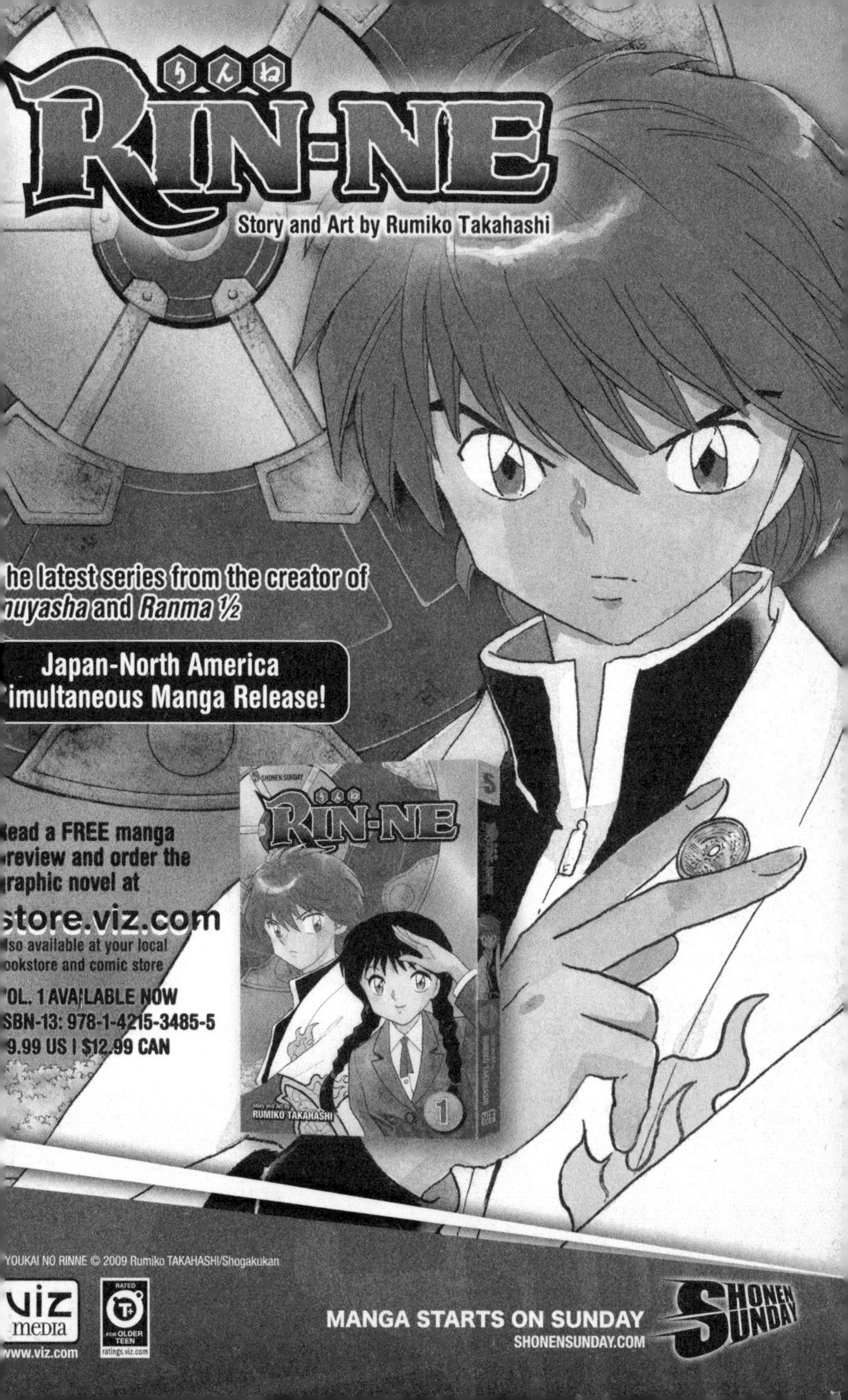
RIN-NE
Story and Art by Rumiko Takahashi
he latest series from the creator of
nuyasha and Ranma ½
Japan-North America
imultaneous Manga Release!
ead a FREE manga
review and order the
raphic novel at
store.viz.com
lso available at your local
ookstore and comic store
OL. 1 AVAILABLE NOW
SBN-13: 978-1-4215-3485-5
9.99 US | $12.99 CAN
SHONEN SUNDAY
RIN-NE
Story and Art by
RUMIKO TAKAHASHI
1
YOUKAI NO RINNE © 2009 Rumiko TAKAHASHI/Shogakukan
viz media
www.viz.com
RATED T+ FOR OLDER TEEN
ratings.viz.com
MANGA STARTS ON SUNDAY
SHONENSUNDAY.COM
SHONEN SUNDAY

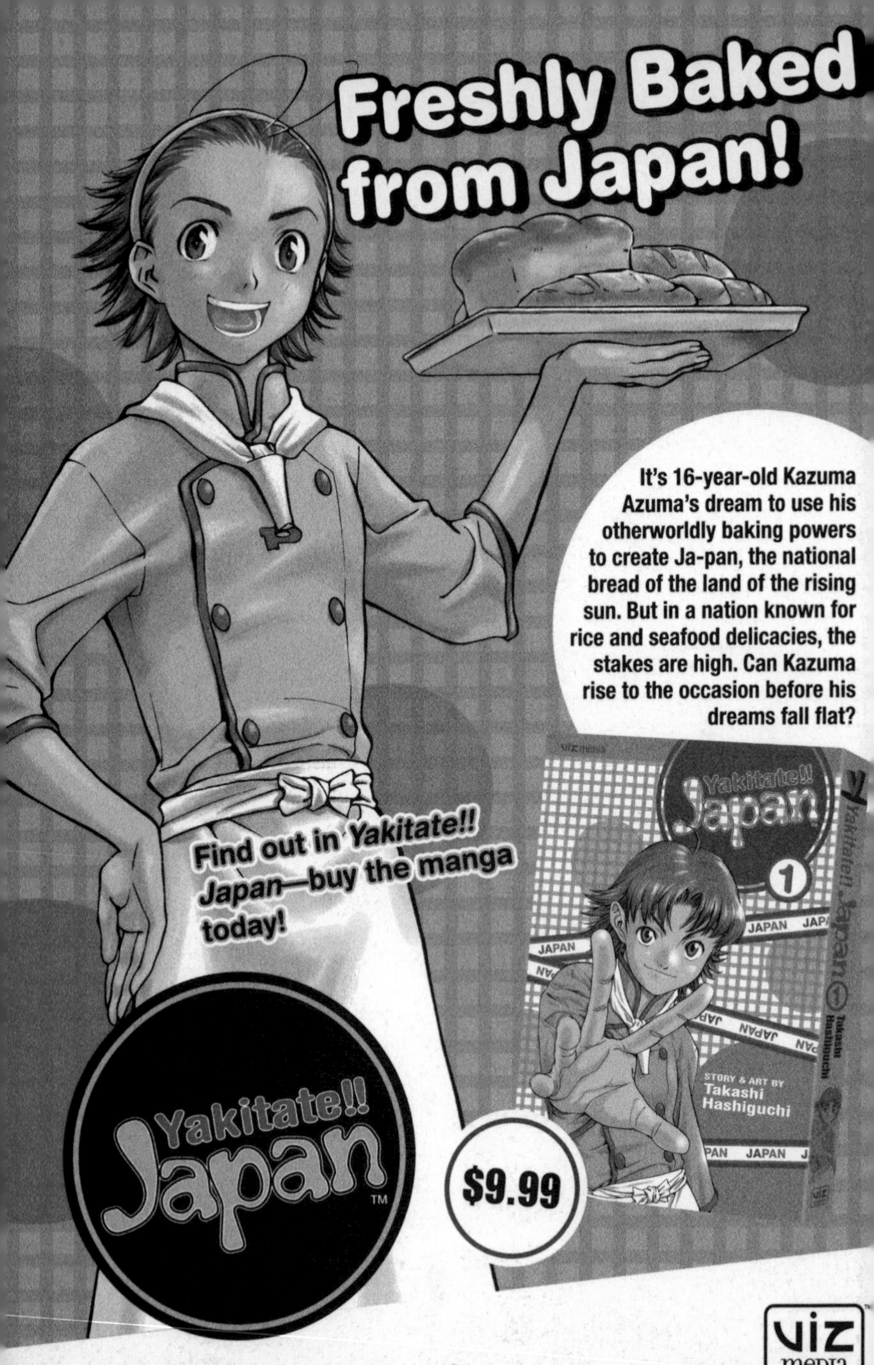
Freshly Baked from Japan!
It's 16-year-old Kazuma Azuma's dream to use his otherworldly baking powers to create Ja-pan, the national bread of the land of the rising sun. But in a nation known for rice and seafood delicacies, the stakes are high. Can Kazuma rise to the occasion before his dreams fall flat?
Find out in Yakitate!! Japan—buy the manga today!
Yakitate!! Japan™
$9.99
Yakitate!! Japan 1
STORY & ART BY Takashi Hashiguchi
viz media
www.viz.com

TV SERIES & MOVIES ON DVD!

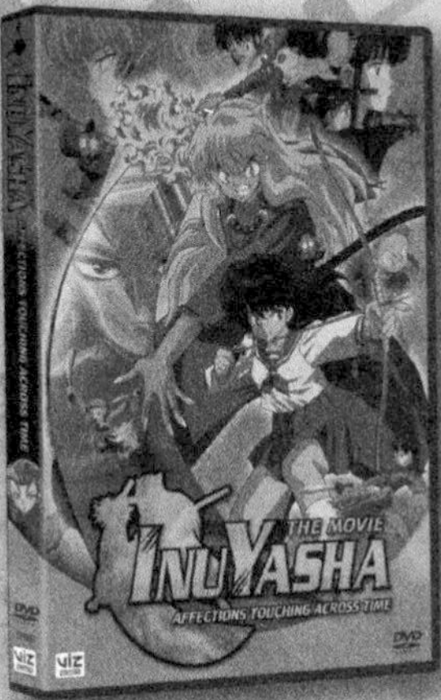
THE MOVIE
INUYASHA
AFFECTIONS TOUCHING ACROSS TIME

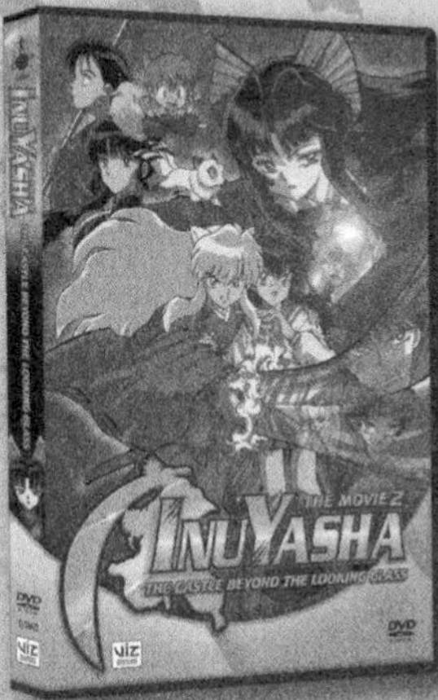
THE MOVIE 2
INUYASHA
THE CASTLE BEYOND THE LOOKING GLASS

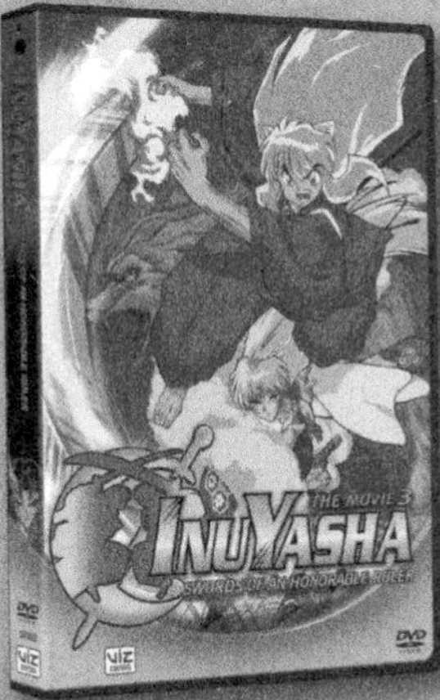
THE MOVIE 3
INUYASHA

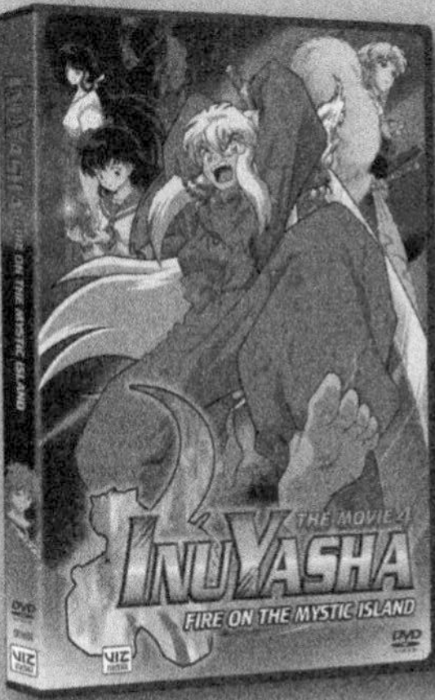
THE MOVIE 4
INUYASHA
FIRE ON THE MYSTIC ISLAND

See more of the action in *Inuyasha* full-length movies

RATED T FOR TEEN
ratings.viz.com

viz media

www.viz.com
inuyasha.viz.com

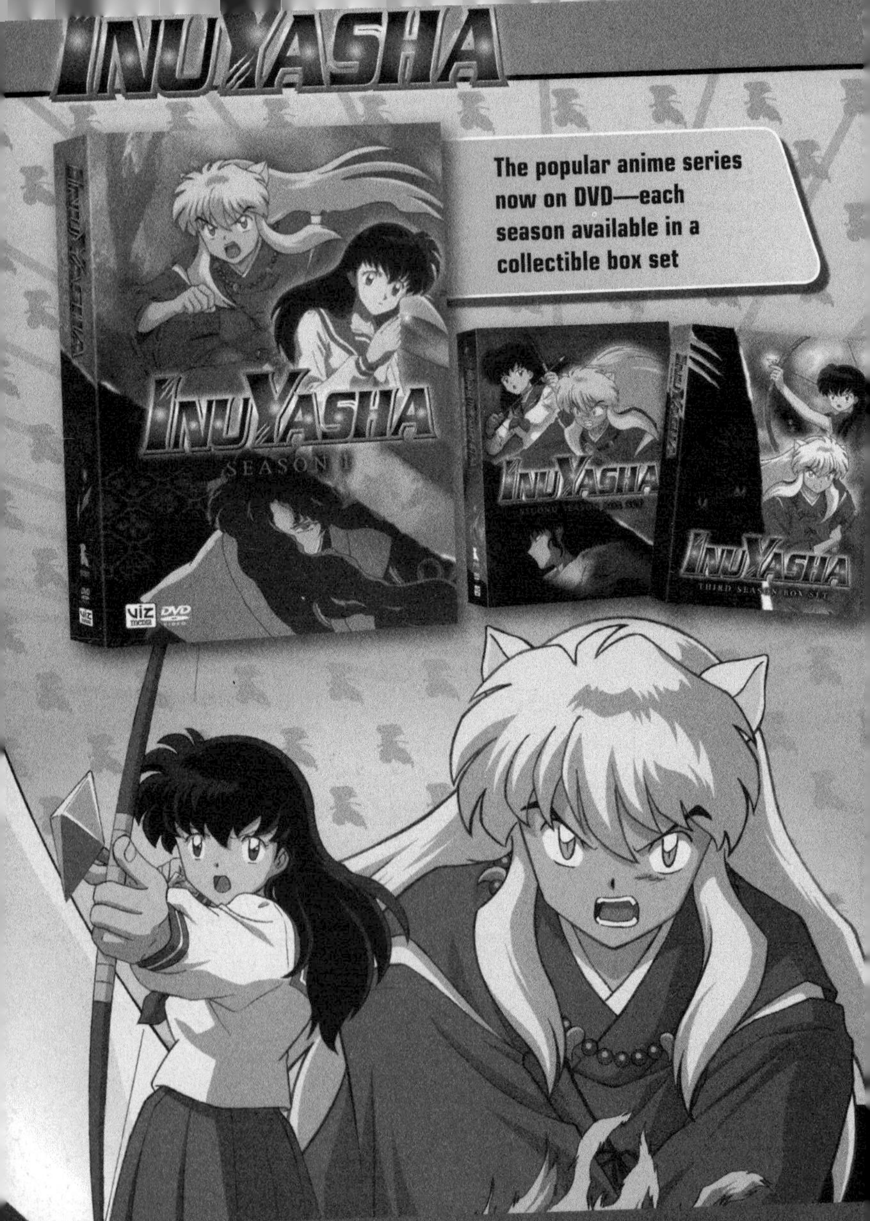
INUYASHA
The popular anime series now on DVD—each season available in a collectible box set
INUYASHA
SEASON 1
INUYASHA
INUYASHA
THIRD SEASON BOX SET

At Your Indentured Service

Hayate's parents are bad with money, so they se[...] this org[...]
Hayate doesn't like this plan, so he comes up w[...]
a girl from a wealthy family. Solid plan… so ho[...]

Find out in *Hayate the Combat Butler*—
buy the manga at store.viz.com!

Hayate the Combat Butler™

Kenjiro Hata

viz MEDIA

www.viz.com
store.viz.com